THE STILLMEADOW ROAD

OTHER BOOKS BY GLADYS TABER

Another Path

The Best of Stillmeadow: A Treasury of Country Living

The Book of Stillmeadow

My Own Cape Cod

Still Cove Journal

(EDITED AND WITH AN INTRODUCTION BY CONSTANCE TABER COLBY)

The Stillmeadow Road

By GLADYS TABER

ILLUSTRATED BY EDWARD SHENTON

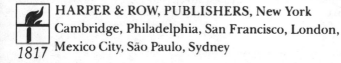
HARPER & ROW, PUBLISHERS, New York
Cambridge, Philadelphia, San Francisco, London,
Mexico City, São Paulo, Sydney

1817

This is a 1984 reissue of a book first published by J. B. Lippincott in 1962.

A portion of the material in this book first appeared in *Everywoman's Family Circle*, in the monthly feature, "Butternut Wisdom." My thanks go to *Everywoman's Family Circle* and to the editor, Mr. Robert Jones, for graciously giving permission to use it here.

G.B.T.

The lines from "The Treasure," by Rupert Brooke, appearing on page 188 are reprinted by permission of Dodd, Mead & Company and McClelland and Stewart Limited, from *The Collected Poems of Rupert Brooke*. Copyright 1915 by Dodd, Mead & Company, Inc. Copyright 1945 by Edward Marsh.

ISBN: 0-06-015241-9
LIBRARY OF CONGRESS CATALOG CARD NUMBER: 83-48388

84   85   86   87   88   10   9   8   7   6   5   4   3   2   1

FOR
STEVE AND OLIVE
"FRIENDSHIP IS A SHELTERING TREE"

Contents

Foreword

1

AND so we bought Stillmeadow.

Although Jill always said Stillmeadow bought us.

We lived in New York City. I was raising my daughter in a sixth-floor apartment about the size of a station wagon. It had what I called a sometime elevator for it did run sometimes. The windows looked out on a well and people kept throwing milk bottles from adjacent apartments. They all, I thought, lived on cabbage. I didn't smell it so much in my own kitchen because the gas stove leaked and I smelled gas. I seemed to spend a lot of time urging a small, beautiful child buried in a snow suit to go up or down the stairs. (She hadn't wanted to go outdoors anyway.)

Then, since life was insupportable for me without a dog, I had Dark Star, a small, temperamental black cocker. She had to be "taken out" four times a day and she was terrified of traffic, policemen, and all the dogs in the neighborhood. She also hated elevators and would never put paw on the stairs but expected to be carried. I also had two wild kittens who were born free at the animal shelter and kept swooping through the air.

Jill had no cat. She lived around the corner on a nice wide avenue jammed with trucks and buses. I considered she lived in the traditional lap of luxury for she had daylight in her apartment all day. She had a small son and a daughter and two black-and-white cockers. Sister was all a cocker should be, gay and loving and adorable, but she had a minor fault. When left alone, she ate pieces of the kitchen linoleum and the arms of the best dining room chairs. In those days of our innocence, we had bought her a lovely wicker dog bed, which she also ate. Blue Waters Ripplemark was almost too good to be real. He was, at four months, already a gentleman and stuffed with virtue.

We both worked, or thought we did, although there were times later on when we felt the old life was sheer idleness.

I almost hate to admit that during this era, we went to a dog show, just to see what a dog show was like. So we bought another parti-colored cocker because she insisted on it.

"After all, four dogs are as easy as three," said Jill.

The kittens had been turned over to someone else because I had to have the windows open now and then and flying cats are no help. So it wasn't very crowded. The main problem was that Star never did get leash-trained and wound me up like a Maypole when we went out, leaving Sweet Clover off at an angle where people kept running into her.

On Saturdays we used to take the children and cockers to City Island, then a lonely dirty piece of shore lapped by doubtful water. Jill acted as a sheep dog herding the flock while I sat on a rock.

"What we need," said Jill one day as we breasted the traffic back to the brawling, roaring, fume-ridden city, "what we need is a place in the country. Fresh air," she added, coughing as a truck ground past. "We could put up tents and spend lovely summer week ends."

"And the children could play in the brook," I said. "And think of all the money we would save."

This was a remarkable statement to which we referred often in subsequent times.

"I could raise fresh vegetables and fruit," said Jill, avoiding one of those freight cars on wheels that abound in the city.

We felt very sensible at the moment. All we needed was a small piece of land with apple trees and a brook. It was as good as done, I thought, lugging Star up the stairs and hoisting Connie while Clover toiled along behind. "Tenting on the old camp ground," I hummed.

We were on our way.

But after weeks we discovered that land cost more money than we dreamed of ever having. And the price of tents and camping equipment seemed to put them in the class for millionaires, who wouldn't need them anyway. We also figured out, belatedly, that we would have to have water and some sanitation even while tenting. We must dig a well, have a septic tank.

The children were what I must call unenthusiastic. Connie was allergic to wasps and bugs. Dorothy was scared of snakes. Don was too small to do anything except get tired out driving around all day. The more we talked of the wonders of country life, the less they thought of it.

"We'll have to go farther out," said Jill, "and look for an old beat-up house, an abandoned farm. Or just a barn. I could do it over, week ends."

I consulted all the magazines and found out that for ten thousand dollars we could do over a barn and make a charming home of it. All we would have to do would be add plumbing, floors, windows, a new roof, fireplace, etc. etc. etc. And dig a well. Put in septic tank. Afterwards you furnished such a home with priceless antiques from your aunt's attic. We had neither aunts with attics nor any attics at all.

At this point, when sensible women would have given the whole thing up, we started hunting for an old house. We looked at houses in which you had to be wary or you fell into the cellar. Houses with plaster falling in chunks. A house with a dead pig on the parlor sofa. It had no front steps so you went in through the woodshed bothering the rats no end.

Also at houses which were very cheap at $30,000 or at $40,000.

I gave up. But Jill never stopped cutting out ads from the Sunday paper for more places to look at. There was very little of New Jersey and Connecticut we did not traverse. We got to know a country road meant a teeth-knocking challenge. And Jill developed an aversion to hard-boiled eggs and sandwiches which she never fully overcame.

I saw that we would be aging in subways forever, and the children would grow up with never a breath of cool country air. A museum full of dead things or a zoo full of caged animals, I said morosely, was their destiny.

It was February, I think, after we had hunted hopelessly for over two years that we decided to take Rip to the Eastern States dog show.

"May as well see how good he is," observed Mr. Rees, that father of cockerdom.

We drove off in a blizzard in the worn-out car with no heater. We had Rip tucked up in blankets and with a hot-water bottle. We just got numb.

"We're early," said Jill, "let's stop and look at this place listed in last Sunday's *Times*." She added, "We can warm up at the agent's house."

The agent had not expected anyone so foolhardy as to look at houses in such weather. In fact, he got stuck and spent his time shoveling out while we waded through snow and ice to see the house. We had no key so we crawled up from the cellar.

"Well," said Stillmeadow, "I've been waiting for you. What took you so long?"

There it stood, half-buried in snow. Built in 1690 or a bit earlier, it had withstood the years. It even had plumbing, and how were we to know it was all cracked? It had floors pegged with square hand-cut nails. It had fireplaces. Twelve-by-eight windows, some with the old bubbly glass panes. It had what must be maple shade as giant sugar maples overhung the roof. (Planted too close, said Jill.)

It had some furniture, tables with broken legs, chests that sagged sadly, an old iron cookstove. It had, also, a wellhouse. And a frozen brook. And forty acres of land.

So we came home. We paid a deposit that made our bank balances sigh into oblivion.

We hardly noticed the sleet storm as we drove home that day. Rip had not won, he was too carsick to show well, but we bore his defeat better than we bore some in later years at later dog shows. Everything is relative, I notice.

The windshield wiper gave out and Jill hopped in and out scraping the sleet from the windshield. The hot water bottle was cold and Rip just melted slightly down my neck as I snuggled him. But we were so busy wallpapering the house (won't take any time at all, said Jill) that we hardly noticed we were the only car on the road. We were in a tranced state, no doubt of it.

For the house was a wonderful bargain. It was not only on a dead-end road (which never got ploughed in winter for years) but had to be sold to settle an estate. The previous owner had shot his wife and killed himself, and murder and suicide do not add to the superficial value of a house.

"Think of Christmas in the country," I said. "Yule log burning in the great fireplace, cutting our own tree, the children sliding downhill in clean fresh snow. We can have winter week ends as long as there is a furnace."

The furnace was broken but we didn't know it. It had kind of rusted away, we were told afterward.

We also did not know how hard it is to manage a Yule log with a dull axe. In fact, there were many things we did not know. Even if we had, I think we would have gone ahead just as recklessly.

Because we heard the house say, "I've been waiting for you. What took you so long?"

2

Our basic equipment for this venture consisted of a staggering fortitude and no common sense. But we didn't know it then. We came out the next week end and paid some more money. By then most of the furniture had vanished, except three carders and five spinning wheels, and one rope bed which had been too big for moving out quickly.

High-hearted, we advanced. We bought tons of wallpaper, and it turned out to be tons, since we had never papered before. For years we gave away wallpaper. I sent for some furniture stored in Virginia and some weeks later a disturbed Kentucky race horse arrived while the furniture rode along to some race track. It takes time to swap a horse for your furniture. But by then we had discovered the fatal truth about every sink, toilet, and tub in the house. "Well, one could not expect a man to drain the pipes before shooting his wife," said Jill. "He didn't think of it."

We had to borrow money. But once we got in shape, we said, we would really save money. This day has yet to come, but it might.

We took ten days of vacation, so-called, in which we cleaned and scoured and got a back door built, and wallpapered and found a mason to repair the chimney and a neighbor who would help scrub the woodwork. The previous owners had just heaved things at it, we felt.

The front bedroom leaked. The pump didn't pump water. Just air.

We found wallpapering was quite a job for women who had no manual skills. Wallpaper has a fiendish way of falling on you and winding you up in paste. The paint did not dry on the upstairs hall either.

But at the end of ten days of twelve or more hours' hard labor we had accomplished a good deal. Also gone in debt more to get the pump pumping and the furnace going. We put a pan under the leak in the front bedroom. And went in to bring the children out to the dream house. Also the four cockers and some more furnishings. It was, we felt, a triumphal tour.

And the fact that it was still winter we hardly noticed. Most people, we afterward learned, buy country houses when the lilacs are in bloom and not when they are up to their knees in snow.

The children were bored stiff. They did not like the frozen outdoors. That they had no feeling for making snowmen was predictable. Who makes snowmen in the city? They did not like to flounder around collecting fallen branches for the fire. They just huddled. And they did not care whether the wallpaper was on or not. Even the cockers were nervous about plunging into the snow in the yard and what, Ma, no leash?

That was a highly unsuccessful week end. There were not enough blankets and the stove kept going out. However, Jill and I were undaunted. This was a house in the country and never mind if we scraped snow from the window sills every morning.

We had brought out plenty of food and although Don sat on the cake and somebody squashed the butter, it seemed a minor affair. There we were in the country, under our own roof, though leaking. And the furnace was working. Jill went down every hour to throw on more coal. It was very warm in the middle of the house, but around the edges it was pretty chilly.

After the children had gone to bed, we sat by the fire and had one of the few moments of relaxation we were to know for years.

"Isn't it wonderful?" Jill poked the fire.

"You are sure the furnace won't blow up in the night," I said.

"No, it won't," she said.

"And once we pay the mason and the furnace man and the man who is going to fix the roof," I said, "we can really begin to save money."

"I'm going to put in a garden in May," Jill said.

"Do you know anything about growing vegetables?"

"I can learn," said Jill.

So this was the way it began.

This much has been told to friends as we sat by the fire popping corn and eating wine-sweet apples. But every now and then, one of the children says, "Tell how we got Stillmeadow."

And I do.

3

When we finally moved to the country for good, we brought my Siamese cat, Esmé, plus a litter of cockers, plus four adult cockers, plus the three children. It is amazing how much and how many you can get into a small sedan, even when you tie a lot of things on top.

We had an antique bureau, picked up for what is called a song. It was roped to the top of the car, but it slipped every few miles and Jill spent a lot of time hopping out and lashing it back. The inside of the car was jammed, but Jill finally got two rope ends through the windows and instructed the children to hang on to them. This upset Esmé, the Siamese, so she screamed during the rest of the journey. It was a memorable trip.

But I suspect if Jill and I had crossed the country in a covered wagon, we would have whistled (Jill) and hummed (me). We visualized the children growing rosy and healthy, cockers and cat happy in the fresh air and a subsistence farm supporting everything. Jill had a whole carton of pamphlets from Washington, catalogs, books. I had a carton of manuscript paper, for in the peace and quiet of the country, I would write books all day long.

As Jill got back in the car after a struggle with the bureau, she said, "I wonder if we should get a cow? A nice sweet Jersey."

"No," I said, "no cow." I did not add that I was deathly afraid of cows.

When we finally got to Stillmeadow that day, I would have settled for a nice restaurant dinner in town. But we had to unpack and get a meal and make beds and try to persuade Esmé to come down from the top of the curtains.

"Well, here we are," said Jill as we had a last cup of coffee. "Now we can look forward to a quiet life in the country."

"There's all that lawn to mow," I said doubtfully.

It wasn't a lawn, it was a hayfield growing up to the front steps and back as far as the swamp.

"There's a bulletin on sheep," Jill remarked dreamily. "They mow lawns."

"And where would the cockers be while sheep were mowing?"

"We'd have to work it out," said Jill calmly.

Instead of sheep we bought a lawn mower. It wouldn't have to be sheared and dipped and it would not produce baby lawn mowers. But when I think of my psychic remark about mowing the lawn, I wonder. For the natural area of the yard was about the size of a college green. And Connecticut soil is passionate about growing grass. By the time we got around one side of the house, it was time to mow the other. And aside from hay, it consisted of dandelions. The first few springs we ate dandelion greens until the children went on strike.

Jill felt sad, because dandelions were for free. And it turned out not much else was. Our financial situation could only be called precarious, we lived from mortgage payment to mortgage payment. Our main assets were fortitude and Jill's Scotch stubbornness. This was before the do-it-yourself era when, according to the magazines, young couples run up houses on week ends. But maybe Jill was a do-it-yourself pioneer.

Neither of us had any manual skills. We never had any kind of practical training at college but Jill said any intelligent woman could figure things out. She did, but I never could master carpentry, or the art of patching plaster, or how to make storm windows fit. My contribution was to stand and admire and hand tools. (They also serve who only stand and wait.)

But we had the house, not a tent. We had forty acres of land, woods, brooks, swamp. And we had a handsome, wonderful barn which Jill made into a kennel so we could raise cockers. We always raised them in the house, but when we had a nervous mother, we retired the other adult cockers briefly to the kennel. The house is the slant-roofed pre-Colonial type, built to hand down for generations. The white clapboards were hand-cut. The center chimney made three fireplaces possible downstairs. Originally there was at least one upstairs but this had been plastered over before our day. The heart of the house is the big central fireplace which Don used to be able to stand up in. The sides and hearth are of hand-hewn stone, probably dug up from what became our garden. Side panels and mantel of mellow pine frame it. The original swinging crane is there and many a pot roast has been hung from it.

Downstairs there were five rooms and a summer kitchen. We had to use that for the big iron range. The regular kitchen was the old milk room with a sink in it. Upstairs were three bedrooms, one for each child. Two closets were bathrooms, and there was of course a secret room which couldn't have done much good ever as you had to lie down to get in it and stay lying down until you crawled out. But we loved having it.

The small borning room, just off the main fireplace room, became Jill's bedroom. Every very early house had a borning room off the warmest room in the house. Presumably enough heat would percolate to keep young mothers and babies from freezing to death, although since there was no cellar underneath, Jill often felt in January that it would take a sturdy baby to survive a night in there with no heat. For even with the furnace going full blast, her radiator barely warmed up.

My bedroom must have been a second parlor. It has always been also my workroom, the gathering place of everybody in the house, the one place expectant cocker mothers decided to have their babies. Also, having four windows, it has been light enough to be the center of bandaging cuts, tending to bruises, examining rashes and so on. It also had one wall of bookcases so, although we have books in every room in the house except the back kitchen, it is more of the library. I sometimes wonder, when I think there are three hundred books in this room, why Connie could wander in and say, "Mama, haven't you ANYTHING to read?"

The stairs give off from the family room and they are so steep we put in a ship's rope to help people get up them. At the foot of the stairs is the coffin door which visitors always admire. In early times, people died in their beds, and if upstairs, it was a problem. But our forefathers solved it by cutting a chunk out of the house wall at the foot of the stairs and putting in a door. We found it helpful when we tried to get beds upstairs.

There are four outside doors to Stillmeadow. But nobody ever uses any but what we call the back-back door.

The true front door opens on a tiny hall to the right of my bedroom. I use the hall as a dressing room and any unwary visitor who decides this is the way to come in, faces the butternut blanket chest with heart-shaped wrought-iron drawer pulls. Usually while they say "Ah—ah—" I am able to stuff my shoes, slippers, etc., behind the closet door. Normally the front door is used only by the dogs. They like it better than the other doors, and I am not going to figure that out. Life is complicated enough as it is.

The old house accepted us casually. It gave us a few days to settle in. Jill and I were in a blessed state, if you believe the old saying that ignorance is bliss. But as far as the children were concerned, we found out right away that the country bored them. I am sorry to admit it but children do not naturally rush into the delights of playing in brooks, gathering wildflowers, and helping mow the lawn.

Our children were not peculiar, they were just used to city life.

Don was a thin, leggy boy, looking like Christopher Robin. He had two cowlicks, an aversion to washing, and a wide slow disarming grin. And he had a genius for not being around to gather fallen branches for kindling. The girls complained justifiably that he did not help at all. But it took more energy to get him to do a chore than to do it ourselves.

My daughter did not see why we did not sit around reading good books more. "You just work all the time," she said accusingly.

None of this bothered Jill. She was planting the garden and I sometimes felt she didn't even notice what she ate (cooked by me). But after a day of heaving boulders from what was to be a famous vegetable garden, she came in bent like a fishhook and ate whatever there was. In the evening, crouched over a garden book, she might say absently, "Have we had supper?"

Sometimes I made a remark, sometimes my better nature prevailed.

4

The well went dry the first of August. Jill hung head down with a flashlight and reported that yes, there was no water there. All she could observe was two tin cans left by a former tenant. So we had to get the well cleaned out and then lug water from the spring at a neighbor's. It bothered me a lot as I like a daily bath. Jill said in early days people took sponge baths. She also said, somewhat tartly, that all of New York didn't need to week-end with us and take baths all the time.

As soon as the well filled up, the rains came and the roof leaked alarmingly. Jill said it was good for the garden. There were times when I hated her incurable optimism. But I had known her since we were fourteen, and the only time I had seen her discouraged was when she went on a camping trip with me and my family and Papa pitched the tent over a den of snakes. She did not, as Mama said, cotton to snakes. Jill and I slept in the car crouched respectively in the front seat and the back seat. But we were fifteen then.

I had forgotten all about it but the day Jill came screaming to the house saying a blacksnake was right in the radish row, I remembered. I got the rake and killed the snake. And decided my only virtue was in being a snake-killer.

But it gave me stature. For we had a good many snakes the first years, and I could always rise from the typewriter and grab the rake and fare forth. Snake-killing involves being very fast, and bringing the rake down just behind the head and then shutting your eyes. And snakes are very good people, by and large, but who wants them in the cellar or in the kennel with a lot of maniac cockers?

And it is disturbing to bring a carton in from the barn and find a very long snake coiled in it. A snake in the house is a nervous-making affair. For if you lose him, he may turn up in bed with you. And if you feel about snakes as Jill felt, even a small garter snake looks like the Loch Ness monster.

But Jill was the spider-killer, so it balanced out. A large black many-legged spider threw me into a panic. We had a lot of spiders too, at first, since the old house had been uninhabited for quite a time. We had wasps in the attic, rats in the cellar, and bats in the back kitchen.

And we were happy, a fact difficult to explain to our friends snugged down in the city. We used to take our breakfast trays to the terrace (now repaired) and look at our land and watch the cockers digging holes in the lawn and hear the children's voices as they decided for or against poached eggs. Don wanted his fried. Birds winged in the summer air.

Jill sat on the wooden bench (which needed repairing). She looked like something out of a covered wagon indeed, her sea-blue eyes framed in a weathered face, her dark hair like a flat cap. Her long rangy figure was not what you would call relaxed, for she was ready to leap into the day's work. She wore, then, a sweat shirt and blue jeans and it was easy to trace what she had last been painting by the color of the jeans. Her moccasins always had garden dirt clinging to them.

I, alas, resembled a rabbit. A pink rabbit, for I never got coppery as she did, I just got redder. Country living did not thin me. It only made streaks in my hair as the sun got to work. But the harder I worked the hungrier I got and the more I dreamed up lovely things to eat, all with sauces.

"I don't see why you bother about it," said Jill, "you look all right to me."

And then she handed me her tray and picked up the hoe and headed for the garden.

I may say there was never a time when we were not thankful that Stillmeadow had decided we belonged. We were very proud when experts began to call and crawl around in the attic and discover the hand-cut lath and crept into the cellar to announce we had dry-laid foundation walls. This was not to our credit at all. We just fell in love with the house and the house fell in love with us.

It was a surprise to us when we discovered we had a treasure. People came to look at it. To take pictures. What was just an old house that wanted us to belong to it, suddenly took on a life of its own. And I found out I could not have a bay window for my African violets even when I could afford it because it was not in the period. We could not put a dining room wing on, it would spoil the house.

We had to live up to the house and not CHANGE things. So we went on opening the windows with screwdrivers and propping them up with sticks. We nailed on the storm windows because the house had not been built for storm windows but we were weak enough not to like living in a freezer when it was below zero. The storm windows never have really fitted but they help.

Nobody could call Stillmeadow modern, even when we acquired an oil burner. We also retired the clothes washer in time, which "is froze," the repairman said. And we added some electric outlets which took some doing, drilling through chestnut beams.

"I'd as soon cut through cement," said the electrician.

I began making a record of our adventures in country living almost as soon as we moved in. Every day seemed so exciting and every day so different that I had to put down what was happening as a letter to my friends. After all, I had a typewriter.

Now, herewith, my latest journal of life at Stillmeadow, which I would wish to share with my neighbors all over the world.

WINTER

January

Now in our New England valley we begin the year with the big snow. We have an appointment with winter, and we are ready. The woodshed is stacked with seasoned applewood and maple, the snow shovel leans at the back door, the shelves are jammed with supplies. When the first innocent flakes drift down, we put out more suet and fill the bird feeders. (The grocer says he can't keep enough suet for everyone simply snatches it.)

When the snow begins to come in all directions at once and the wind takes on a peculiar lonely cry, we pile more wood on the fire, and hang the old iron soup kettle over it, browning the pot roast in diced salt pork and onions. As the blizzard increases, the old house seems to steady herself like a ship against a gale wind. She has weathered too many winter storms to bother about a new one! Snow piles up against the windowpanes, sifts in under the ancient sills, makes heaps of powdered pearl on the ancient oak floors. But the house is snug in the twilight of the snow and we sit by the fire and toast our toes feeling there is much to be said for winter after all.

"Now we can read all those good books," says Jill, "those we were going to read last summer."

"And I'll do the jigsaw that nice man sent me, the really impossible one."

Jigsaws bore Jill. My partner in the sport is Faith Baldwin and when she comes to visit we work for hours at a peculiarly sadistic one. But as suppertime approaches, Jill drifts by, picks up a piece and fits it in a critical hole. This can be maddening after we have hunted an hour for the right piece, but it expedites supper. It is also frustrating when Holly, the Irish, puts her paws in the middle of the table and breathes away a whole section.

I used to dream of a game corner with one of those elegant game tables set up with ivory chessmen the way they are in magazines. But Jill said we couldn't play chess anyway and where would we find a corner?

Stillmeadow is full of corners but they are already full. The only free one is behind the kitchen door and this is because the door hits the wall whenever you open it. The only possible place would be the one occupied by the very early corner cupboard which houses the milk glass collection. So a card table is the only solution, set plumb in the middle of the front-room floor. As the cockers and Holly fly past, we grab the legs of the table and hope for the best.

For a time I cut out glamorous pictures of rumpus rooms from the magazines. Made from cellars. Our cellar, however, had no idea of being a rumpus room. Jill had already fixed the fruit closet into a darkroom, but she had to sit down to work in it. If she stood up she cracked her head on a beam. In the main part of the cellar the ceiling was six feet, and even higher where the furnace panted away. But anyone trying to play games there would acquire a permanent crouch. Besides, the fourteen-foot-square chimney took up a lot of room, so did the well pump, the hot water heater, and the hotel-size freezer. Also we began piling logs and kindling under the stairs when we found out how fast the woodshed emptied.

And when Jill's garden began to pay off, the rest of the cellar was full of root vegetables, a sand barrel rich with endive, and a screen contraption for storing bulbs. The only thing we did not have in the cellar was drying laundry, we have always hung that in the upstairs hall.

"Moisture good for the furniture up there," said Jill.

It worked very well if you avoided meeting a wet sheet at the top of the stairs. And we were always careful to take down the web of clotheslines before company came. Or almost always. One time Jill flew up to wind the line around the fire extinguisher and absently hung her glasses on one of the hand-wrought hooks in the hall. We found them two years later.

Two years ago, we bought a washer-dryer combination. It is one thing to hang out in the sweet sun and wind, but comes January if you venture outside, you may have to chop the sheets from the line. And when the children were at home, the upstairs lines were a bother.

"And we are no longer five," Jill pointed out, "we add up to twelve when they are at home."

Children grow up, get married, and have babies. You enter a world of diapers before you realize it! So we got the washer-dryer and Ed Koch fitted it in the back kitchen by knocking out part of the sink counter. We took it pretty lightly for we had Erma, our neighbor, to run it for us. Mechanical equipment is a challenge to Erma, and she figured out the new machine in no time. For her, it purred.

But came the week end that Connie and Curt, her husband, and Muffin, a lively one-and-a-half-year-old, arrived with more than the usual caravan-load of luggage. Connie had brought a lot of washing.

"The dryer fluffs things up so beautifully," she observed.

"Nothing like it," I agreed, "but mechanics is not my field and Jill isn't here and Erma has gone to Bridgeport."

"Have you got a book?" asked Curt. As an editor, he believes stoutly in the written word.

While I hunted for the book, he and Connie read all the labels on the switches, of which there are many. After the usual frenzied search I found the book in with the cookbooks. Why not? It was tucked in with *The Gentleman's Companion* and *Magic with Herbs*.

Curt read the book. "It's foolproof," he said.

So we tossed the wash in and recklessly pushed a button. Like magic, the machine began to stir into life and whizz along. So we went in and removed the light cord from Muffin who was chewing it. We removed Muffin's pink rabbit from Holly. Teddy had eaten the teething biscuit. Jonquil was giving Muffin nice warm licks. All was serene. We sat around the fire disagreeing about politics while the washer washed. And washed. And washed. And washed. Finally we wondered about it.

"Better turn on the dryer," said Curt, "I think it's washed enough."

So he manipulated a button or so with casual grace while Connie and I stood admiring his masculine efficiency. The machine took on a new lease of life and started filling with water again.

"Oh, Curt," said Connie, "it's beginning all over. And we've got to leave for New York in a little while."

So Curt pushed the off buttons and fished the sodden laundry out, dripping.

"Everything is blue," said Connie with surprise.

"My non-run socks," said Curt grimly.

One of Curt's admirable qualities is calmness in times of stress. He wrung out the laundry, loaded the washbasket and went out to the line. He felt it would dry faster outdoors than upstairs.

He was just pinning the last diaper up when it began to snow.

"Oh, Mama," wailed Connie, "we ought to start right back to town!"

I then offered my first and perhaps my last advice to my child.

"Give him ten minutes to sit down," I suggested, "before you ask him to take it all in."

So they carried a soaking wash back with them and Connie borrowed a friend's washing machine and did it all over again. She did not think Muffin should wear blue diapers.

I broke the news gently to Erma the next day. What I said was, "I have bad news. We better call Ed Koch. The washing machine is out of order."

"It worked fine Thursday," said Erma with surprise.

She tossed in a load, pushed buttons, and brought me a pile of warm fluffy towels a short time later.

"But it might have lint in the drain," she said, and got half inside the machine and found a ball of lint. "Now just let me show you," she said, "it really is foolproof."

But I was thinking what a complex world we live in.

Making New Year's resolutions used to be serious business when I was growing up. I used to make a list of mine, and tack it over my dresser. If I had faithfully followed all of it, no doubt I should have died young. But by February I went right back to reading in the bathtub (forbidden), writing verse in church under the cover of the hymnal, and turned the clocks back an hour before I went out on a date.

Nowadays I seldom hear people discussing New Year's resolutions. It may be that with the world as it is, a year seems too long a span to consider. Or it may be that time moves so fast that aside from the emotion of New Year's Eve, we just find one year no different than another. Every year is a crisis in the world situation. Space buzzes with missiles and rockets and there is an air of desperation about most governments. Even the moon has become something to hit.

I no longer make lists of my resolutions. What I do is take stock of the past year, going over my failures and mistakes and hoping to avoid them in the coming year. There is no use brooding over them, for after all, they are past as the leaf on the calendar is turned. The only purpose in remembering them now is to learn from them. And then it is time to go ahead with a steadfast hope.

A blizzard is a beautiful thing. As the drifts pile up topping the picket fence, I can see from my window the meadow brimmed with silver. The pines in the back yard stand black-green in the veiling snow. The sugar maples seem to reach the pewter sky. Inside, the Christmas greens still make the house festive, the bayberry candles are ready to burn to the socket and the house is spicy with pine. The cranberry-glazed ham and all the fixings are ready, and the

problem is whether the snow will be too deep for the neighbors to get down the road.

There is something comfortable about a ham, for it will not spoil if a few guests have to stop and shovel out the cars. Stillmeadow is on a narrow country road that dips down a hill. Where the brook crosses it, there is a ditch on each side. If the snow is bad, the village plough does not get around until the main roads are ploughed. And few sounds in the world are more wonderful than the sound of a snowplough coming swoosh-swoosh down the road.

There is considerable controversy in our valley as to the best way to beat the snow. Some of us believe in what are known as "snow treads." Some crackle around with chains. Some use both, which the rest of us think does no good at all. But most of us carry shovels in the car trunk. The truth is we all get stuck now and again.

I have a doubtful distinction of getting stuck at the filling station in Seymour, which was what we call "a glass of ice." This led me to reflect, as men kept coming around, that in America a filling station is a sort of men's club. This is one reason it is often difficult to get to the gas pumps. But it is a nice custom, nevertheless. It gives the men a chance to discuss the new models of cars, the political situation, and taxes. And it also means the filling-station owner has plenty of volunteer help.

I knew this, but still I was surprised as man after man emerged from the inner sanctum and applied a willing shoulder to my spinning car. I also was confused by the advice. "Turn her this way." "Put her in low." "Put her in reverse." "Ease her over this way." "Take it easy."

Trying to obey all the advice I had, I advanced murderously toward the gas pump and used my own intuition to put her in neutral before I bashed my car up. After which I slid to the highway with a bevy of well-wishers waving me on.

"You're O.K.," they called.

Yes, I was, but I went weaving around a sand truck with some misgivings. And I was glad to get home.

January is a bitter month for the birds. There is a mystery about birds which I have never understood. A bird is a delicate creature. I have occasionally held a damaged bird in my hand and was always reminded of Shakespeare's "Oh, so light a foot, can ne'er wear out the everlasting flint." You feel as if you are holding air when you hold a chickadee. The delicate feet seem too small to support anything. Under the softness of feathers, the body is too small.

So how in our below-zero January weather can these small birds fly? And sing? And why don't their feet freeze on the branch? My friend Hal Borland says a few birds have feathered feet, such as the snowy owl. But the small winter birds that eat all day long at our feeders have no insulation. There they are, juncoes, towhees, evening grosbeaks, bluejays and chickadees. And the small sparrows, always so busy. They sleep in the pines for in early morning the branches quiver as they come out to eat.

I think it is a miracle when I see these small people hopping over ice and through snow. I also was amazed the first time I saw a chickadee and a fox sparrow sitting down in the window feeder. The way they did it was to disappear those delicate legs and stick their tail feathers out flat behind them. And then they whacked away at the suet, SITTING DOWN.

This I never read in a book. I saw it. And although the chickadee is no bigger than a butternut, the sound of pecking was tremendous. I have spent a good deal of time at the window by my desk watching the hammering of tiny beaks at frozen suet. This energy harnessed by man would undoubtedly run a lot of power stations.

One of my favorites is the nuthatch, which doesn't look spectacular at a distance. He is a rather timid bird and hard to know. The name, I am told, comes from his habit of thrusting a seed in a crevice in the bark of a handy tree and then hammering with the point of his bill until the shell breaks. In the first place it is not a nut he stashes away and he does not hatch it, but this is as sensible as most bird experts are. In any case, he runs head down on the sugar maples and it makes me dizzy. And in the window feeder he has trouble because he cannot eat upside down, it is a flat feeder. Seen close to, while he figures how to eat right side up, I notice he is beautiful, with shiny dark eyes, polished grey upper body, jet-black crown and nape of neck. He has an air of competence, possibly because he spends so much time head down and manages not to get dizzy.

When we came to the country neither Jill nor I knew any birds except robins. And the best bird books present the same problem as dictionaries. To look things up you have to know what you are looking up, in a general sort of way. Otherwise you read madly from least bitterns right through to the index and you get absolutely nowhere.

"It's not in the illustrations," Jill said often, "it has to be an accidental."

I think we had more accidental birds than anyone ever had. But when we did find out an accidental was an evening grosbeak, triumph intoxicated us. And this week when I tracked down the strange and lovely birds at the feeder, birds I had never seen, I hopped up and down with excitement.

"Meadow larks, meadow larks." And I shut the book and remarked, "Why are they here now? What are they doing?" In over twenty years we had never seen a meadow lark. We heard them in the meadow, loud, clear, beautiful, but we never saw them. So here they were, at the ground feeder with the regular members of the gang.

We have a number of bird books, but the small compact Hausman and Peterson are the favorites. We pencil in the date and location of new birds as we see them. The cerulean warbler has a note 5/20/56 Dump. Why he was at the town dump, he didn't say, but there he was like a flying piece of azure sky.

There is one thing we have never been able to do and that is to identify birds by their songs. We have to see them first. The truth is, it is not possible, at least for us, to know who utters "a smooth series of husky-sweet notes." Or "a high, rather nasal yap, yap-yap. Kent, kent." Or "a loud, harshly metallic or wooden rattle." The one easy one is the yellowthroat for he definitely does say "Wichity, wichity, wichity."

Life with birds can never be dull. Last week a pheasant somehow got herself trapped in the long kennel run. We hadn't used this run all winter so we had to wade through four feet of snow to get to the gate. As we floundered along, the pheasant ran frantically

back and forth, beating against the fence. Jill tried laying a track of corn to lure her to the gate but this did not reassure her at all: it drove her mad. Inside the house three cockers and an Irish were charging from window to window, upsetting furniture as they went.

"I'll have to get inside and try to catch her," said Jill.

As she shoveled along, the pheasant gave a last despairing rush and lumbered into the air, barely clearing the fence top and sailing dizzily into the swamp.

"Think of what she'll have to tell the family," I said.

We hadn't forgotten the pheasant when we had more bird trouble. A feckless phoebe started a nest on one of the timbers in the barn. A nest in midwinter. We discovered it when we got to wondering why twigs and feathers were piled on the floor. We looked up and saw the nest and a bit of head sticking up. In summer we were used to swallows in the barn and left the barn door open. But it wasn't like leaving it open in January. The kennels were inside the barn heated with a coal stove. With the barn door open, we were heating part of the back yard. So we tried shutting the doors at night. But that meant the phoebe was shut in for too many hours. We put a pan of bird seed in on Jill's workbench, but it didn't suit her. When the door was opened in the morning, a hysterical small bird dashed past our heads.

We never knew whether she managed to lay an egg or not. In the end, she gave the whole thing up and left. We never saw her again.

The only time we were able to save a bird's life was when a hooded warbler dove into the front window. Fortunately the dogs were busy with a rabbit in the back yard. So I picked him up. He felt weightless in my hand. His eyes were closed but I thought his heart beat faintly. With one finger I massaged his neck for usually birds break their necks when they plunge at a window. After a moment, one eye opened. It looked right at me. I kept on stroking, and I knew in that strange communication that occurs between wild creatures and mankind, that he was not afraid. Finally the other eye opened and he settled more comfortably in my hand.

Eventually I put him gently on the top of a fence post. He sat there some time, perhaps twenty minutes, and then was airborne again. I felt as if I were flying too.

I had finally mastered the dial telephone, I thought. For years I had been able to discuss things with the operator who then got the number. But the dial phone was different. Every time I dialed, our phone rang twice. So I would get the operator and say the phone was out of order. She would tell me to hang up and she called me, and always found nothing wrong. Now I know a telephone is a simple instrument, even a child can work it. In fact, of late, it is the favorite sport of a number of children hereabouts. They call when you are beating egg whites or getting a custard in the oven and when you breathlessly answer, they start to sing a popular tune.

But now I have a new problem. To call a friend in Newtown, I have to dial more figures than I can keep track of. By the time I dial 112 and then try to think of the number I want, I have to hang up and begin again. Then the operator, who has been there all along, I guess, asks me what MY number is.

I called Faith Baldwin the night before this new dial went into effect and told her plainly that from now on, she would have to call me. I called the children in New York and said the same thing. And then I looked gloomily at the notice from the telephone company which said in view of the new convenience, etc., the rates were going up. Sometimes progress is a little too much.

The pile of Christmas books gradually diminishes. I think the test of a fine book is whether you are sorry when you finish it. And plan to read it again soon. One of these is *Born Free* by Joy Adamson. This moving and beautiful story of a lion is a classic. My favorite picture is of Elsa, the lioness, lying on a cot at the Adamsons' camp, but the illustrations would be a book in themselves. Then there is *The Dog Who Came to Stay* by my friend Hal Borland. It is a book to laugh over and cry over.

And topping the list of inspirational books is *Testament of Trust* by Faith Baldwin.

As far as cookbooks go, I choose Myra Waldo's *Modern Gourmet Cook Book*. This is a delight, and belongs on the shelf with the old favorites. It's a beautiful book, too.

I also have Paul Engle's *Poems in Praise,* and this is worthy of the poetry shelf.

Books make wonderful Christmas gifts but these days I note it is well to read them first. Because many of today's books are not suitable to give to anybody. A gift book should have, I think, an underlying quality of serenity, it should enlarge our understanding, and leave a deep sense of satisfaction in the reader. However, few things in life are more personal than books, and everyone has a right to his own taste. Some readers seem to be personally insulted if a book comes out that they disapprove of. There is no law making anyone read a book if they don't want to. There are books enough pouring from the presses to suit every taste. And having written more than thirty books myself, I know how much an author gives to a book so that even if I do not agree with his viewpoint, I do respect his earnest effort.

Now we get daily ski reports, which do not matter to me personally. How much snow is on Mt. Mansfield is interesting to those who launch themselves madly from the top and risk their necks. My one attempt to do this almost landed me in a hospital, and it was only a hilltop, not a mountain, from which I whizzed. I still remember the sickening moment when the ski pole left me, followed by the skis. I made a crash landing, and limped for some time.

It is one of the most beautiful sports to watch, however. This probably means I trust the skiers not to break their necks. And I must say one of our best friends who skis annually, broke her leg while trimming the Christmas tree right in her own living room, and not on the ski slopes!

Snow is a special joy to the dogs. Teddy and Jonquil and Tiki, the cockers, will launch their small bodies recklessly into drifts so deep that they are up to their ears. Holly, the Irish, rolls in it. And yesterday when I looked out, she was dozing with her head pillowed on an ice cake. I could understand this better if they were what is called outdoor dogs but they are not. When the furnace goes out, Holly tries to get under the blankets on my bed and Jonquil moves right into the fireplace where the hearth stones are boiling hot. And after a bath, Teddy shivers as if he were about to collapse, even wrapped in warm towels and in an overheated room.

The cockers are very susceptible to heat in summer. Holly will run happily in the sun when it is ninety degrees. By which I judge that her thermostatic controls are different. The cockers make cool beds for themselves, either undermining the shrubbery or uprooting the best violet beds. But when Holly rests briefly (her rests are always brief) she chooses the hottest part of the yard in full blaze of sun. Possibly the close coat of an Irish insulates.

Dog language is something there has been controversy about, but not by people who live with it. Holly has a wide vocabulary. For instance mail and town. If I say, "I am going for the mail," she resigns herself with a huge sigh. This means a brief trip to the box up the hill, not worth putting on her leash, getting her into the car, getting back in the yard. But if I say, "I am going to town," she nearly knocks the door down, flies to the gate and puts her paws on the latch ready to go.

She knows the rooms in the house. When non-dog people are coming I say, "Go to the back kitchen now." If they are dog people, I say, "Go in my room until they get in the house." She distinguishes between front door and back too. Of course she knows all the Obedience terms as all Obedience dogs do, but the rest of the words she acquired by herself with no effort on our part.

As for her own speech, I know which bark means I must stop everything and give her something to eat. The go-out bark is entirely different. Then there is the "There comes that nice boy down the road." And the ear-splitting shriek, "A horse! A horse!"

What is perhaps more interesting is that the dogs communicate with each other, although cocker language is not like Irish language. It is as if a Frenchman and an American could converse with no lessons in each other's tongue. The cockers can bark their heads off if they are outside and Holly pays no heed. Same old rabbit, she seems to say. But a different bark sends her rushing to the back door. Means Joe or Erma are rounding the corner. They come at different times, in different cars, but no matter.

Joe's bark is like but exactly like Erma's bark, so to speak. Joe feeds them, does chores. So for him it is "I thought you'd never get here! Where have you been?"

For Erma it is a carnival with calliope for they can help hang out the washing, gather fallen branches, and dash in and out for hours.

As for cats, the most verbal one I have had was the seal-point Siamese. And I always understood what she was saying. Tigger, the Manx, was a conservative, spoke little, but to the point. Usually he got his way by just staring at us, but if we ignored his signal, he would hum louder and louder and louder and roll over and over by the door he had picked as an exit.

Aladdin, my Abyssinian, was an ardent purr person, very seldom mewed, but could make plenty of noise if he were shut in. While we were fitting him into the assorted household, he was supposed to sleep in my dressing room in his own basket. The second night he figured how to lift up the latch and came swinging into the room hanging on for dear life. After that, he slept at the foot of my bed.

I never understand why some people do not appreciate cats but

I've come to believe it is partly that they want cats to behave in a human pattern. Dogs, by and large, will do anything, no matter how silly, if their humans so desire. If you want a dog to wear rubbers when it rains, he will wear them. If you want to half-starve him and beat him, he will accept that. He will carry your slippers, fetch part of the mail from the gate and so on.

But cats have a strong feeling for their own individuality and seldom will demean themselves. I think I should not like to see a cat not being a cat. A regimented cat would be a sorry thing.

It is not true that cats select people who hate cats and torture them by sitting on their laps. No respectable cat would bother or care who liked him or not. It does not fit with their attitude to life in any way.

The reason they seek out the non-cat lovers is simple. Such people ignore them, do not make cooing noises, or kitty-kitty calls, or snap fingers to get their attention. Such people, in my long observation, are almost always quiet-voiced and do not make sudden gestures. And the fact that they do not try to gather a cat up and make a fuss means the cat can make the advances.

But dogs have a sure knowledge of whether you like them or not. Cats, perhaps, assume they have to be welcomed by anybody because they are royalty. I never knew a cat that did not feel a slight condescension in making advances. Dogs are just looking for someone who, as Jill said, "thinks like a dog." In a roomful of guests, I have watched Holly skirt past eight people coaxing and calling and trying to pet her. She went directly to one man who had not even said hello, laid her head on his lap. There you are, she seemed to say. And he smiled and said, "I knew."

The same sort of thing often has happened to me in restaurants. Any dog nearby will slip over to me if the leash is long enough, otherwise he or she tries to pull the leash along. How do they know that in a roomful of diners this one is a passionate dog lover? I believe they are psychic. I don't know any other reasonable explanation. It is certainly not due to any superior qualifications of mine. I haven't any. They just look at me and feel like having a reunion.

Now and then they offer to come home with me, and there is

nothing their owners like less. Dog people wish to have an exclusive with their own dogs.

In any area of life, I believe love is a grace fully given, and if fully given is likely to be returned. If even a wild bird momentarily in your hand can accept the fact that you care about him, how much more this is true of human beings. There are many kinds of love, in fact I recently read a category of them. But I think it is better to love than to analyze.

There is a time of enchantment in January when the snow stops falling and there is a pale blossom of color in the sky. Over the frozen pond it is lemon color, over the hills delicate green. As the sun sets, the smooth sea of snow has blue shadows on it. Shadows from the top of the hill flow to the bottom in a long pattern.

Then twilight drops into night between one footstep and another. The snow crunches under my boots as I take a last turn around the yard. It is a clean sound, and the countryside stretches clean and pure as far as I can see. The paw prints of dogs and rabbits are blue in the last afterglow, and bird prints are all around the back door.

"Not too long till spring," says Joe, dropping in to see if we are all right. "Notice the days are getting longer and the pussy buds are swelling."

The true countryman's eye is sharper than mine, I had not noticed. But I am grateful, for by January my heart looks toward spring. Signs are here if my eyes can be trained to observe them. I do notice during the January thaw that the sun has a new warmth and the wellhouse icicles drip on my neck as I go by. And I remember Hal Borland saying that the winter landscape is the ultimate of simplicity, and this may be why in January I take a long look at life. People have seasons too, I think. There is something steadfast about people who withstand the chilling winds of trouble, the sometime storms that assail the heart, and themselves have the endurance and character to wait quietly for an April time.

Inside Stillmeadow on a cold January night, the smell of apple logs is sweet. The kitchen is crowded with four-paws who are interested in what cooks at Stillmeadow this very minute. The first pale moonlight comes in the windows and a heavy weight of snow falling from the roof makes a fall of stars in the light. A brief winter day has ended and the stillness is profound. A special gift to us in winter is the stillness. It is like a quiet hand held out from nature.

We have supper by the fire and slice the dessert apples thin for Jonquil, who adores apples.

"I like to listen to the silence," says Jill.

And at this point all the dogs begin to screech, that is what they do. They have HEARD the snowplough coming down the road.

February

ON a dark February day the crackle of the fire in my Franklin stove has a special pleasure. Actually I am not sure it is true Franklin, but it is very old. We picked it up in pieces at a junk shop, the only things missing were the feet and we had a blacksmith supply two bars for the base. It is small and narrow and fills from one side. In the front there are two curved doors, which, when open, make it resemble a tiny fireplace. But also there are two rectangular upper doors which can be opened, and they make the fire burn slower. The top has two stove lids set in the flat surface, and an intricate grill above topped with a handle which I can only say looks like a medallion or a flower of some kind.

There is a cosy fender for toe-toasting too. In short, it is a treasure and worth all the hours it took Jill to get the rust off and the polish on. This was a job because the whole front and sides are patterned, not plain. The stove stands on a wide hand-hewn hearth and has the fireplace mantel above it.

Of course when we moved in, we opened up the fireplace itself. After all, the house is built around that fourteen-foot-square chimney but evidently the former owners just forgot to open this side up. We found out why the first day Jill started the furnace. Before she could get the fire damped down, my room was so thick with oily smoke that we couldn't breathe in it. Mr. Clark, the mason, came in a hurry and clucked at what he saw.

"Had to use that flue for the furnace," he said, unnecessarily. "No place else for a new chimney."

When he saw how sad I was, he offered the opinion that we could put in a small pipe hole "for one of the old-kind of stoves."

Then he bricked up the opening, replastered, repainted the stone around the plaster, and departed wondering why city folk knew so little, I am sure.

My room had to be painted over because there is nothing like white to absorb soot and smoke. The worst job was the antique radiator which is an enormous one, and it takes perseverance to paint a radiator. I haven't the patience. I helped with the lower woodwork, which is why the upper part looked so much better. I am a splashy painter and impetuous. Jill cheerfully painted the windows, going around the eighty tiny panes without spilling. I spent a good deal of time mopping up the old oak floor where I had small rivulets of white. And then we had white paw marks in the family room since a dog or two always popped in to see what we were up to.

It took us over a year to find the stove; meanwhile Mr. Clark had thoughtfully provided one of those asbestos circular hole-covers. The day the stove went in, we celebrated by bringing in the tea-kettle and making tea in my bedroom.

There is one thing about my stove, however. It will heat the room comfortably if the furnace is off, but I have to keep hopping up to put in more wood, it just eats wood up. There is a small grate inside and we tried burning coal at one time, but the coal just went out. We suspected there wasn't draught enough since the stovepipe is no more than two feet long, if that.

The front-room fireplace will burn coal nicely, which makes our theory more reasonable. We put a grate in that one after the first winter when the "electric" was off for a few days and the fireplaces consumed a whole woodpile. Not to mention the back-kitchen stove.

February is the time we think most about heat and heating problems in the country. After a bad storm, when everyone meets at the village store, the first and constant question is, "Did your pipes freeze?"

We learned how to cope with just plain below-zero weather. Jill got a huge trouble lamp and hooked it in under the sink. It has a wire cage around it and yards and yards of heavy cord which we coil here and there and then try not to trip on. We got an electric panel for the back kitchen, under which there is no cellar and possibly a bit of unmelted glacier lurking. We got several electric heaters to plug in here and there.

And, naturally, blew the fuses out the first time they were all working.

"It would have been all right," Jill said, "if we hadn't had the wafflemaker on too."

The next time it was ten below we did a merry-go-round pushing in and pulling out plugs, alternating.

And of course once the current goes off, all of these aids are life-less. We go right back to wood fires and kerosene lamps and hope for the best.

There is an outside problem also during the winter. The lawn that is such a mowing problem all summer, now becomes a reasonable facsimile of the Arctic. But neither the cockers nor Holly, the Irish, have any idea of hauling us to the gate on dogsleds. It is about a quarter of a block to the gate and that can be a long way. It is two blocks to the kennel for me, one for Jill whose long legs can really cover distance.

To add to the trouble, there is a low place by the front gate which is almost hollow but has enormous flagstones laid on it. These fill up with snow, it melts, and a foot of water is there with no drain-age. Then it freezes and we have a small skating pond, which, in turn, gets flooded but keeps ice underneath.

We know better than to use rock salt. Rock salt is lethal for dogs. I don't know why, but it is. Sand is unavailable and last week Erma felt that strewing cedar shavings would help, which she did. It worked wonderfully until the next melt and then it floated away from the path.

As I write, our neighbor, young Dick Gracy, is chopping away at several inches of ice. And I feel smug. Because I felt that a sharp tool *might* cut the ice.

"Let's use the turf-cutter," I said.

That turf-cutter's days may be numbered but there is a nice chopped-up stretch of ice which can be crossed more easily than Eliza crossed the ice in Harriet Beecher Stowe's *Uncle Tom's Cabin*.

Pending the next sleet storm, all is well!

Now is the time when our city friends urge us to close the house and board the cockers and Holly and come to the city. The theatre and the music and the art exhibitions and museums offer a different world. The city is at its best in midwinter, and there is nothing more beautiful than driving through Central Park in a snowstorm at dusk. The lights glow in the tall buildings and even the ugly structures are lit with enchantment.

There is a fine sense of excitement too in the hurrying crowds, the glamorous shop windows, the vivid flash of skaters over the ice at Rockefeller Center. Everyone seems miraculously young and gay, for the tired and shabby and impoverished and jobless are not as noticeable. They huddle over gas heaters in their dark holes. You have to go on the side streets to find the desolate children hovering over curb fires made of packing cases and the hopeless men hunting cigarette butts.

Fifth Avenue and Times Square and Madison Avenue are breathtaking in color and the throngs make one think there is a festival going on. And in the theatres at night there is the magnificent moment when the curtain goes up and the wonderful smell of grease paint and canvas comes over the footlights as the play begins. Even a bad play has that first excitement which is like nothing else I know of.

Then there are the eating places, softly lit, and with waiters bringing flaming chafing dishes to the tables. All the dishes of all the world may be had right here in one city, French, Italian, Chinese, Indian (oh, the curries), Swedish, Armenian. Yes, the city is gay and full of mystery and magic in winter.

Probably we may be thought peculiar but Jill and I still love the country. We can hardly bear to go to the city at all. We do not think we have any hardships really. Hardships you face yourself with nature are not like city hardships.

Because, in the country, nobody strikes against anybody. In the city when the subway strike is on or the taxicab strike or the wholesalers' strike or a laundry-delivery strike or a garbage-collection strike or a strike of elevator operators, you are absolutely helpless. You are a small nothing in the battle between the employers and the unions. I have frozen numb during a coal-delivery strike in the city.

In the country, you battle cold and snow and sleet in winter and drought in summer and insect pests and so on, but you always have a chance against them. In the city, the hapless consumer or resident is helpless, a victim. Neither Jill nor I ever like to be victims. We would rather have many personal hardships but combat them actively. Because, especially in New York, which we know best, the consumer always loses no matter who wins.

The population is a pawn. There is something terribly wrong about this, to my way of thinking.

The exigencies of nature are more acceptable, at least to the country dweller. We do have life, liberty and the right to the pursuit of happiness. We never have to sit down and wonder how many days it will be before food supplies stop coming in to a beleaguered city.

But then we never have to sit down at all. We have too much to do. And doing is better than waiting for something to happen. And the innocent bystander never even has the right to vote!

The February thaw is a miracle. It is the curtain going down after Act I in New England, for we shall have more winter up to April. But now snow melts, icicles drop from the wellhouse, the air is suddenly silken soft. Out we go wearing no mittens and wearing our summer jackets. A kind of intoxication sets in.

True, we may catch pneumonia, but never mind. We race around with cockers and the Irish and keep thinking the snowdrops will be up any day. Perhaps nature herself is pausing to look toward spring. The snow melts fast, the dogs bring in bones long buried and the lost tennis shoe is retrieved, via Holly. Jonquil drags in a bathing towel. What's left of the pink rabbit Jill's grandson discarded is now in the house, on the sofa. The only thing I mind is Holly's collection of old dog food cans. I do not like them tucked in my bed.

This has nothing to do with our housecleaning. It has to do with Holly's agility. She can snatch a dog food can while you are stirring up the dog meal for the day and then ask to go out. Only as she whisks out do you see that can in her mouth.

It happens with a head of lettuce or cabbage, too, but they wilt down in time and are not observed by guests.

Here our decision about values enters. Is it better to have empty cans in the yard and a happy, happy dog, or to have a dog that gets spanked for lugging them out? We settle for the dog. As Jill says, "We'll get the cans back in the spring."

So far as possible, we have raised all of our dogs with what we felt was enough discipline but not too much. We always ask ourselves what is vital and stick to it. For the rest, if it makes Holly radiant to carry a can around the yard for days, well, why not?

For us, our basic evaluation of how much discipline and not too much, paid off very handsomely with our children. Better, more successful young adults could not be found. They do have a tendency to look down on us as old-fashioned, childish creatures but this is quite natural. We would rather be deeply loved than respected fearfully.

I know it gets more and more difficult to be a parent for so much is written about methods of raising children from birth on.

Young parents now are so informed. They have so many rules to go by. We just muddled along. And made many mistakes, I now see. My worst was a dreadful summer trying to get Dorothy to eat tomatoes for I had read that tomatoes did something for your teeth. I would gladly recall those days if I could. I could probably have persuaded her to take a vitamin pill instead. And meals would have been easier all the way around.

It takes discretion to realize what is vital and what isn't.

But nowadays we have much to-do about juvenile delinquents and it is almost always assumed to be the parents' fault. Part of it may be, but not, I think, all. Part is due to the age we live in, which is souped-up in so many areas, insecure in others. We even have cases in our valley of teen-agers breaking into houses and slashing things up.

But I think of my favorite teen-ager who is helping support the family since his father's death. Dick works part time at the market and does a night shift at a nearby factory besides.

"When do you sleep?" I asked in horror.

"Oh, I catch a nap when I can," he said cheerfully, "and I am holding out all right."

He is as tough and lean as a Western television character. And he is sunny, no job is too much for him. He thanks us. His manners are perfect, he is what might be called a born gentleman.

It makes me wonder whether responsibility isn't pretty important as far as children go. Most of the delinquents seem to drive fast expensive cars or have no home life at all because nobody is at home anyway. They drift, and drifting is dangerous.

I watched Dick drive down our road, down which many adults drive furiously. He gentled his old car. Carefully parked it, as a cherished thing, part of his responsibility. The family owns no other.

As I paid Dick and he counted out the change, I thought how pale he was from lack of sleep. But here was a man and I admired him. Was it all responsibility or an inherent strength of personality? I wondered, as he drove slowly down the road.

The thaw is over so swiftly. Yesterday was balmy, with real warmth in the sunlight. Melted snow ran down the road in rivulets. We went so far as to turn the thermostat down. In the night, the thermometer slid down and down as the long hand of Arctic cold reached out. We got up shivering and built the fire. Yesterday's embers, as always, were hot enough so the logs caught easily. Because we keep a good bed of ashes, embers seem to last indefinitely. Sometimes when Jill plans to lay a fire but not to light it at the time, it begins to burn immediately.

I suppose the attraction of an open fire is a heritage from our earliest ancestors. Fire meant life to them, and judging by my efforts as a Camp Fire Girl to start one by rubbing sticks together, I think they must have guarded a fire with their lives. They had to have shelter too, and in regions where there were no caves must have built something of branches or stones to keep the cold out and give some protection at night.

How man survived at all is a mystery. The weakest, least agile creature of them all, somehow managed to hunt food, protect his young, and develop down the ages into the master of living creatures. And since the caves in France have been discovered, we know he was artistic, for the Lascaux cave paintings are superb. With all man had to do just to stay alive, I wonder how he managed to make his pigments and bring the beauty of the lunging bulls to life. How did he, without tools as we know them, get up to the ceiling of those caves anyway? Did he carry in rocks? If so, how? Or pile dead trees on top of one another? And 18,000 years ago what did he use for brushes? I wonder whether he could have used fur and bound it on a short branch trimmed by burning off the twigs?

As I stand in my own point of time and try to visualize the beginning of man, I feel almost faint with the effort, and of course I have to give it up in the end. Scientists and anthropologists have a special quality of mind which enables them to cast back to the infinite past, but for an ordinary person it is hardly possible.

My father was a geologist and often when we were out hunting Indian arrowheads, he would stop to show me glacier markings on an outcropping of stone. As he talked, the great ice age was more real than the green Wisconsin countryside. He had what I now call pure scientific imagination. It wasn't at all like mine, for he could never see fairies or unicorns or leprechauns. He said I mustn't be silly. Mama never took sides in our stormy arguments. The thing Father simply could not endure was my insistence there might be people on the moon. This maddened him and once or twice he stopped speaking to me.

"But how do you know?" I asked.

Mama advised me to stop upsetting him. She said sensibly that whether there were or were not people on the moon, had better be left to the moon, and why didn't I set the table for there *were* earth people and they had to eat.

I cannot remember Mama ever theorizing about anything, but she may have not done it aloud for fear of setting us off again. Mama was a wise and tranquil woman and did not believe in useless controversy. She had that rare gift, too, of not contradicting people even when they were wrong.

Too many people, I think, are what I call No people. It's a habit which grows like Jack's beanstalk, so that if you even say it is cold, they say at once, "No, it isn't cold. It's just the wind." It's a habit I thoroughly dislike, not that I mind being called wrong on every count, but it is fatiguing. I'm tempted to do the contradicting myself first, just to see what would happen. It usually belongs to people, I note, who cannot bear to be contradicted themselves at all.

I'm afraid I am too much a Yes person. I'm sure this is weak and denotes lack of determination. Jill takes a sensible course, contradicting when it is important, agreeing when it isn't. She is a quiet woman and when she says something, it carries weight.

Actually, the art of conversation has fallen into disuse in our day. Perhaps the conversation of an earlier day only seems so brilliant now because all we have left of it is what came down in letters and books. Sometimes I wonder whether Oscar Wilde always sparkled with bon mots day and night. And did Benjamin Franklin utter pearls of wisdom every time he opened his mouth? Shakespeare, I think, could never have spoken a dull sentence. Sometimes I try to think of him saying, "It is cold today." Would he say, "The footprints of frost fall silent on stone," or something like that?

If I could travel back in time, I think I would like to listen in on a gathering of Keats's friends most of all. I would be blinded just to be in a room with Shakespeare for his genius is too dazzling to contemplate. Keats was more human, I think, although it might be because of his youth. As far as his poetry was concerned, he had the same transcendent quality, but personally he was so embattled that it is impossible to say what would have happened had he reached the presumably healthy maturity of Shakespeare.

But I have said before, and say again, that of the great, I should feel more comfortable with Keats than any. This may be because we have a window seat wide enough for him to sit on, and he liked to curl up on a window seat. It is wide enough for Jonquil and would accommodate Keats very well.

I have wondered whether this favorite habit of his came from his wishing to be part of the group in the room, and yet a little removed from it. However, this is the kind of thing no biographer can ever tell me or anybody else. In fact I view some biographers with doubt. It is possible to choose a great character and develop a basic theme about him or her, according to our new knowledge of psychiatry and then fit everything in as neatly as solving a puzzle. This leads, in turn, to debunking the great figures of the past, and nobody is around to contradict since they are gone.

It even seems silly to me to try to expose Emily Dickinson as a frustrated woman and argue as to who frustrated her. She was a great poet, that should be enough.

But we are a curious people. We always want to know WHY anybody is a poet or an artist or a political figure. We want to understand the causes behind anything. And this is something, I believe, we shall never truly know.

For instance, someone might interpret my tendency to pick up stray dogs and cats, try to save birds fallen from nests and so on, as due to a harsh childhood, so I feel an empathy with all creatures in trouble. But I feel my childhood was pretty special and I was surely as happy as anybody could be while growing up.

I am aware that we are all conditioned by our environment and that it took me some time to live down the fact that I didn't turn out to be a Greek scholar. But I do not think I was damaged by Father's feeling about Greek. I had it too but there were so many other things to be concerned with.

But I doubt whether that relates to my love of all living things and my compassion for troubled human beings. And when I apply the yardstick of my own life to that of others, I feel pretty sure nobody can ever figure out what makes a watch tick one way and not another. The watch manufacturers are near perfection, but even watches can be different. I have had a watch that ran slow no matter what happened, and another watch that ran ten minutes fast no matter how often I took it back. Both were the same make. They just, I think, felt differently about time. There was nothing at all wrong with either, they needed regulating. But they never regulated. They went on ticking as they felt like ticking. One slow, one fast.

If this is true about watches, why do we expect people to tick according to special rules? Shelley was not like Byron because he was not like Byron, and that I understand. They were naturally different. But I do not think we should take them back to the watch factory and try to estimate their peculiar personal difficulties. As long as they both ticked great poetry, let us be thankful.

February cannot be called a restful month in New England. Even before we get the bacon sizzling for breakfast, the wild birds have to be fed. As Jill says, "They are not what I call wild. If they were any tamer, they'd all live in the house."

We keep a new, clean garbage can at the back door, filled with chick scratch feed. Jill stirs in sunflower seed and some regular wild-bird food. A worn-out dog food can acts as a scoop and in bad weather we fill it several times a day. We also use stale bread and cake and keep suet in the suet cages on the sugar maple.

Our birds do not care for raisins, thank you, and none of them eat the rape seeds which abound in the packaged bird food. They love doughnuts hung in the lilac outside my window. We experimented with lettuce leaves and so on but the dogs ate them up, the birds did not touch them. But they all love sunflower seeds which are the most expensive. The ground feeders eat the scratch feed, so do the squirrels, and we try to keep them busy so my window feeder is left for the chickadees, tufted titmice, fox sparrows and of course, squirrels.

We used to make a fantastic mix of melted fat with seeds and crumbs and (innocently) raisins which we molded in juice cans and hung from branches. We gave it up, not because it was such a job so much as because as soon as the birds ate off the top layer, the squirrels took the rest. We tried the prepared suet cakes and they vanished overnight.

"Too easy for the squirrels," said Jill.

As far as the packaged food is concerned, I figure we cannot afford to spend so much for a few sunflower seeds along with all the rest our birds won't eat. We get tired of sweeping that rape seed out of a clogged feeder and fearing it will sprout in the lawn. It makes me wonder why the manufacturers do not put up regional packages. There must be some birds somewhere who will eat rape seed, but not around Stillmeadow. Would it not be a good idea to do a New England package, substituting plain old chick scratch with the sunflower seeds and the little black things that our birds will eat?

Peanut butter we gave up last year. Peanut butter is the passionate love of all squirrels and when they eat a large jar a day, it is enough. If you screen your peanut butter in, they paw it out, and if you put in a smaller screen, the birds get stuck in it. There is really nothing a bird can do that a squirrel cannot do better, except fly, and as I watched our flying squirrel yesterday, I felt he could fly very well.

I am very fond of squirrels, except they eat everything up. My window feeder is just a pane away from my typewriter and when a bright squirrel eye peers at me, I hate to bang at the window. And he pays no attention, except to see what I am at. He goes on cleaning out food enough to supply half a hundred small songsters. And of course he feels anything around is his, since he is bigger and stronger than the competitors. And capable of tight-wire walking besides.

Unfortunately, I seldom get anywhere moralizing. I see the squirrels' side as well as the chickadees'. Why should I blame and discriminate against the squirrel just because he gets most of the seed? That's not fair. Isn't much of our own human economy based on success for the most alert, the strongest, never for the weakest? I think about this a good deal, and then give it up. A countrywoman has to try to feed everybody, I decide. All I can do is to bang at my window at intervals and persuade the squirrel to remove himself from the whole feeder so the small ones can sneak in.

There is one thing about living close to nature and wildlife. You cannot help contemplating. You wonder why one tree grows so tall and not too far away, another tree is hard put to it to survive. In one sunny spot in the yard, the Confederate violets grow thick and in another, same soil, same exposure, they give up. Of course there is a reason, we know there is reason in everything. But sometimes I think the reason for many things is hidden in mystery.

It is not true that nature automatically destroys the weak so as to produce the strong. That is, it is not true in my experience. I would hesitate to have a scientist beside me when I say this. But it is not always the weakest bird that falls from the nest or the spindling seedling that dies. With cockers, over a long period of breeding and raising them, we came to feel that there was more of what I can only call life-force in some than in others. For instance, we could have six puppies exactly alike, born in comfortable quarters (my bedroom) and attended with equal care. Sometimes there would be a least one, sometimes they were like peas in a pod. Two days later, some would be doing better than others, for no foreseeable reason. I could always pick up a puppy and hold it to my cheek and know whether all was well or not.

It didn't matter with ours, for we began supplementary feeding for those that seemed not to care about much. We let the rest fight away for the best milk, the warmest place in the nursery. But we babied the less tonic ones, even before their eyes were open. We encouraged their mother to massage them with her warm sandpaper tongue. She didn't care, for she just licked whoever was nearest.

And suddenly a limp one would take hold of life in a miraculous way.

"Sunbonnet Eyelashes is tonic today," I would call to Jill.

And no more trouble with Sunbonnet from then on.

In fact, when we were raising a lot of puppies, Jill would hand them to me as they were ready to be tucked on the hot water bottle and say, "How's this one?"

"Bouncy," I would say. Or, "Not so good."

For one reason or another, we never lost a puppy unless it was born with a physical deficiency such as a cleft palate. I am reminded of this when I look at Especially Me, for he was a tough problem. He was one of eight, the first-born and unusually big and well boned and plump. But he just could not figure out this nursing business.

He was always under the heap, slowly weakening.

"I think he is not too bright," said Jill in despair, after an hour fitting him to a nursing take-off. "I think maybe he is retarded."

Had he been a kennel dog, he would not have lived. He would never have gotten around to nursing before it was too late.

But Jill made the formula, sterilized the nursing bottle. He was strong enough to fight it off until we discovered the secret. He wanted to eat upside down. Once flat on his back, he gulped happily, paddling his paws, and by the time we were weaning the puppies, he swam in the pan faster than anybody. And as for being retarded, he has been one of the most brilliant of our cockers.

Now we have wondered why. We had no time to wonder at the time for we had seven others to take care of plus a cheerful but not conscientious mother. Was it the extra attention that woke him to the realization life could be a good thing? What made him take hold?

It makes me wonder about babies. Some babies seem born with a terrific push to life, but some do not. Some that I have seen lately squirm and push their heads up and kick off covers. Some are too placid. It is a real problem for parents, I think, not to overstimulate children of any age, but to give them enough attention to encourage them to develop. This is a problem Jill and I never had with our children for they were dynamos from the start.

But recently a friend brought a three- or four-year-old to visit and I had an almost irresistible impulse to say, "Wake up! Let's play a game. Let's have fun with the cockers." For the child was as passive as an unconnected flatiron. She stood quietly, she looked around. Her eyes were alert, she noticed everything. But she lacked the will to take an active part in whatever was around her. She reminded me of Especially Me during the first week of his life.

Maybe, I thought, she just needs to be cherished a little more, to get an extra dividend of love which some need more than others, and who knows why?

In years to come we may know the answers to many questions. Now every question that is answered seems to cause more questions to rise. But I think the basic answer to most questions is love, for with enough love, we gain understanding. And we are forgiven many mistakes we make if we have love.

"Mama didn't understand but she loved me." That is a good saying, and I have heard it often.

Another blizzard Sunday, sleet mixed with snow. The window-panes were pebbled over with ice so I could not see out. Mainly, it troubled Holly, who loves looking out of windows. She kept breathing against the panes, so the inside steamed up. In the midst of the lashing storm, Connie's voice came from the back kitchen.

"Anybody home?" she called.

Curt built up the fire and Muffin was hauled out of various layers of sweaters, snow suit, mittens (two pairs), hoods (two). I turned up the thermostat for I notice city dwellers like a tropical temperature. But I find city apartments chilly and draughty. I think we all adjust to one temperature and like whatever it be.

In the morning, the world was a drift of pearl and the sun shone from an intensely blue sky. Muffin, at a year and a half, had her first experience with pure country snow. In her blue bunny suit, she looked like an indigo bunting as she went out. Her boots had been forgotten, but Connie devised boots of a plastic bowl cover and a plastic bag and tied them on with some leftover Christmas ribbon.

At first, Muffin just stood and stared. Then she sat down in a soft drift, ate some. Then she made miniature brooms of her arms and swept. All the time she said "Whoo—whoo—whoo" like a tiny blue owl. By the time she had gotten both mittens off and her hands were snow-cold, Connie brought her in.

"Whoo—whoo," Muffin said.

When I thought of the world opening up for my granddaughter, the immeasurable experiences, and the things to learn, I felt awed. She was like the first human being in the first snow. Somewhere along the line, we lose the sense of wonder. We look out, and sigh, and say, "It's snowing again."

For adults, it means, in the country, shoveling, stalled cars, more wood-lugging, being housebound until the road crews finally get through. It means empty bird feeders until we make a path. It means an added load. But to Muffin it meant a strange new wonder. Her hands were full of sparkles and then they were gone.

As I watched her being peeled off like an onion, I wished we might all keep the sense of wonder she now has when all life is a mystery, and a whoo—whoo—whoo kind of thing.

Part of our winter chores is helping haul people out of the ditch beyond Stillmeadow. The brook crosses the road there, and the road itself is narrow and obviously only a dead-end dirt one. Walking up, we come to the old orchard, and sometimes I wonder whether old apple trees are not lovelier in snow than at blossoming. The shape of an apple tree is patterned against the pale sky, and the shadows are marked below on the snow in dark blue lines. Deer prints cross the orchard, for the deer come over the brook to eat the frozen windfalls. Rabbit tracks are there too, and delicate bird tracings.

There are countless other tracks of the wild people who do not hibernate snugly during the long cold. And you always feel their presence when you stand by the old rail fence, although the only sound is the falling of snow from branches. Otherwise the silence is silver. In violet time we used to gather morels here, the delicious beefsteak mushrooms. But of late years the morels have vanished. We used to like them broiled in butter and laid gently on crisp toast for breakfast. We were always careful not to gather too many, nevertheless they departed.

There is a giant hemlock at the edge of the orchard, the only one on our forty acres. It is a mystery. How did it, solitary, grow there in the orchard? Now in winter, it provides shelter for the birds, so the whole tree quivers with wings at dusk. The bare apple trees are no shelter but the close-set needles of the hemlock help break the night wind.

Here in the old orchard when it is deep with snow, quiet comes to the heart. The fret and fever of the world die away and for a brief time peace drops as softly as the snow slipping from a branch. When we turn back down the road, we know we have received a gift from God, a special hour of serenity. And even when we see another car in the ditch to be dug out, we do not lose the feeling of tranquillity.

The orchard was planted a long time ago, the trees grew, they bore winy-sweet apples. Dried-apple pies, sweet foamy fresh cider, applesauce and apple cobblers, not to mention apple jelly with a mint leaf in each jar—these helped make good eating in the farm-house.

The trees grew old in time and violets carpeted the ground. Birds nested in ever-increasing knotholes. There were fewer apples. At one time, a neighboring farmer pastured his cows in the orchard, for the rail fence had broken down and it was a nice grassy area that nobody seemed to own. When we came to Stillmeadow, the orchard was deep with fallen branches, which we lugged to the house for a few winters of lovely applewood fires. Jill managed to get the car part way up the hill without being stuck too often and we loaded the trunk and the back seat and most of the front with dead apple limbs. In time, this cleared an open space so we could comfortably picnic there.

There is a flat outcrop of granite close to the brook that hurries past the orchard. We climbed the hill, followed by the children who carried the lighter picnic items. After we ate, we lingered while the children waded in the brook, picked wildflowers, and filled the picnic basket with bouquets. It was a peaceful, innocent time in the quiet old orchard up the hill. Sometimes we talked idly of building a stone fireplace there so we could cook hamburgers and hot dogs, but we really did not want to change the orchard, we wanted it just as it was.

Everyone, I think, needs such a place to bring a sense of magic to life. And for many, it seems impossible. But Mama used the swing in the back yard for hers. She would slip out the kitchen door and sit, swaying gently, for a little while, her shining brown eyes looking at things nobody else could see. My grandmother had a rocking chair and she retreated to that when the household was in an uproar. It was a small rocker, upholstered with needlepoint cushion. Grandmother lived with my Uncle Walter and his family and his wife's mother and the house boiled with activity and, often, with tensions. Grandmother would slip to her room and sit in the rocking chair and sometimes I would tiptoe upstairs and go in.

For she was an island of tranquillity. She was very tiny and elegant. She would be wearing a grey silk dress with white lawn collar and cuffs, a cameo at the neckline. She spoke softly always, as did

Mama and, like Mama, she never criticized anyone for anything. "You must do as you feel best," she always said.

I was very young when she died and I remember very little about it except the sense of strangeness when I went past her room and the little rocker was empty. The room was just a room.

When the Farmer's Almanac says "Watch This Storm" we get ready for it. Last February the big storm to watch came after a day of low skies, windless, a day when everyone felt tense. At the market, people were hurrying to fill the carts to bursting. George Tomey, our market owner, helped rush cartons and bundles to waiting cars.

"Let me know if you get in trouble or need anything," he kept reassuring the more timid of us.

At the feed store, extra pounds of chick scratch feed were loaded in cars of nervous bird feeders. The big storm would be a punishment to the small birds and hard enough on the bluejays and quail and pheasants.

Around two, I went to Seymour to keep the usual appointment with Marilyn, who "does" my hair.

"This is one time I won't argue with you about staying under the dryer," said Marilyn, winding up my hair as if the building were about to collapse. "I'll get you out of here fast enough to suit even you."

For some reason, I cannot bear to sit under the dryer the required amount of time. I watch the relaxed nearby customers and I feel like a race horse held up at the barrier. Even when I occupy myself with a book, I do not really settle down. Often I rise up, and Marilyn firmly puts me back under. But this day when I popped up she sighed and said nothing. For someone had come in to say it was already snowing hard in New York, two inches had fallen.

I came down the hill toward Stillmeadow just as the first indolent innocent flakes drifted down. Within an hour, the air was very bitter and snow swirled against the windows. When we looked out, the world was like white velvet. By suppertime, the wind was piling the drifts and the thermometer stood at zero. The wind seemed to pick up the fallen snow and fling it in the air in great wheels. It was an awesome sight. The snow was so deep by the picket fence that I worried about the cockers and Irish getting over it.

And when Jonquil went out, she vanished to her eyebrows and had to be hauled in before she smothered in snow.

Holly went lunging about, but even she found the deep weight of the snow too much and came in to thaw the snowballs from her paws.

It snowed all night and on into the next day. By then we could only open one door, and not very wide. Joe, who comes every morning to do outside chores, arrived saying he had been four hours trying to dig out and had not reached home from the factory until four in the morning. So he waded to his waist to fill the bird feeders and check the kennel and went home to dig some more.

About two-thirty, when the snow stopped, two high school boys who live down the road came walking through the drifts.

"Thought you might need help," they said.

They spent almost two hours digging, only coming in for ginger ale and cookies once and to thaw their frozen boots. When they left, they said, "any time you need us."

Steve Nies and Allan Griffith were added to our list of very important people, and not so much that their help was so needed as that they were so thoughtful. They noticed the house sitting drifted in by snow, the unopened doors, the buried car which I had left by the gate. And as they walked by, they decided to to something about it.

As they shoveled away, I thought how proud their mothers must be to have such sons. We hear so much about teen-agers nowadays and most of it is discouraging. But there are many, I think, like Steve and Allan and such are the hope of the country. I feel sure they will move into whatever the future holds with a sense of direction.

"Are you sure there is nothing else we can do?" they asked, as they scraped the snow shovels clean.

If I had said they renewed my faith in the youngsters in our country, they would have been horribly embarrassed, but they did. I went back to the typewriter as happy as if spring flowers were blooming! I did not think about what would happen when all the snow began to melt, for this is a problem. Eventually snow does melt. And when five-foot drifts begin to give up, we have more trouble. And somehow the snow got in to the inside of my storm windows, so I looked at snow as I tried to watch the boys go down the road.

The sky was lemon colored as it usually is after a big storm. The snow was blue, dark blue as twilight dropped down. But all was well at Stillmeadow.

During a severe storm, we always defrost the refrigerator. Jill's theory has always been that if you put everything from the frozen department out in the snow, you can defrost without worry. I am appalled at all the odds and ends in the refrigerator. When the children were little, we never had any. In fact, what we put in toward a casserole was never there when we looked for it. But when the children went away to school, we had a real problem with the refrigerator. We were raised never to waste food because there were hungry children in the world.

"Why is it we are always eating leftovers?" Jill asked mildly. "I would think now and then we could start fresh on something."

I pointed out we were used to feeding five.

"Still doesn't explain it," said Jill. "Why don't we throw out the works and begin again?"

"But you can't waste—"

"I know, with hungry children all over the world."

So we ate leftover string beans, spinach, a potato, and some left-over hamburger, plus a green salad to use up half a head of lettuce.

Eventually, we trained ourselves to cook small portions of every-thing. We used our dear friend Louella Shouer's *Quick and Easy Meals for Two*, and found it helped immeasurably. We found we could even have our favorite boiled dinner without contemplating eating it for weeks. Louella's version calls for a tin of ham, which is about right for two, and the ham is laid on top of the onions, carrots, cabbage wedges, after they are almost cooked. As the ham heats, the flavor seeps into the vegetables and the dish is elegant.

But when the children come home, we like to serve our traditional New England boiled dinner with beef we corn ourselves. We use a six-pound brisket or rump of beef and put it down in a crock in brine for thirty-six hours, weighted down with a plate and a clean stone. The brine is made with 8 cups of water, 1 cup of salt, 3 table-spoons of sugar, 6 peppercorns, a clove of garlic, 2 bay leaves, 2 teaspoons of mixed spices. To this we add ¼ teaspoon of saltpeter and ½ cup of warm water.

When the time comes to cook it, we place the corned beef in cold water, add ½ clove of garlic and 6 peppercorns, and cook slowly, skimming when necessary. We allow four to five hours, or until the beef is tender when we stick a fork in. (If the beef is very salty, we drain off the stock once and add fresh water.) When the meat is done, we take it out and in the stock cook 6 carrots, 3 large yellow turnips cut in quarters, 4 small parsnips, 8 small peeled onions. This simmers fifteen minutes, then 6 medium-sized potatoes are added and a head of cabbage, quartered. When the vegetables are done, we return the beef to the pot and reheat it.

We serve the boiled dinner with horse-radish sauce, made by beating fresh-grated horse-radish in sour cream.

I think the first boiled dinner was devised from necessity, like many excellent dinners. The housewife just used the vegetables in the root cellar and cooked everything together because she had a big iron pot. There are, by now, many variations. Many cooks omit the parsnips, and I admit you have to be wary with parsnips because they are sweet and buttery. But the four small ones add flavor.

The timing for the vegetables is the important thing. It's a sorry moment if you lift off the cover and find the potatoes are nothing but mush while the onions are rubbery. The beef should be sliced thin, not served in chunks. We overlap the rich tender slices on the ironstone platter, arrange the vegetables around them, and serve the stock in a soup tureen. We never, never thicken the stock. We just spoon it over the beef and vegetables.

We used to have our own horse-radish growing at the edge of the garden but it vanished suddenly along with, alas, the catnip. So when Barbara and Hal Borland came down from Salisbury one day, they brought a jar of freshly ground horse-radish. Jill spooned it on bread and butter and ate it plain. She also stirred it in cooked spinach, used it on cold meat. For me, it had to have the sour cream added for there is probably nothing as sharp as horse-radish when it is fresh.

Valentine's Day is a sentimental, beribboned and flowery holiday. It is a time to say "I love you" with roses and violets and heart-shaped cakes. And I have said before, and will repeat, that it is not a time to send funny valentines which are neither funny nor suitable. Those who wish to make a joke of Valentine's Day are insensitive as well as ignorant. After all, it is a saint's day, a romantic day. It is for the delicate joy of first love. It is also for an expression of lasting love. Even my father, who didn't believe in foolishness, always gave Mama a potted plant on Valentine's Day, usually a cyclamen.

When I was very young, we made our own valentines with colored paper, paper lace, cut-out roses and bluebirds and violets. Like May baskets, the donor was supposed to be secret. "Guess Who." But after Mama died, I found a packet of valentines in a drawer labeled "Gladys made these herself."

Later, when I acquired my first beau, I hoarded my twenty-five cents a week until I had enough to buy him a book of poetry, which I fear was Laurence Hope's *Songs of India*. Father never increased my allowance for special occasions because he did not wish me to become a spendthrift. So a lot of banana splits and hot fudge sundaes went into that book.

I now believe Father was right, although not for his reason. But sacrifice for your first love is a blessed thing and adds value to the gift. Nowadays a quarter isn't worth what a penny was, but I still view a quarter with fondness. In fact, I often open my purse to find I have only quarters in the change section. I part with a quarter less easily than with a dollar now.

When I went away to college, I received thirty dollars a month with Father's advice, "Make it go as far as possible." Jill got twenty five. Going to Boston to hear our first symphony and to the theatre to see our first real play and to Durgin-Park for our first broiled live lobster took a big piece of our combined funds.

We were always so hungry too. The dormitory food was at a low ebb then and nobody took vitamins. When the end of the month approached, we would just walk past the Tea Shoppe and look at the fudge cakes in the window. Now and then we made some money. I sold my best hat for five lovely dollars and Jill sold some textbooks. No millionaire ever could realize what fun we had with the extra money. We went to Boston to the Pops concert and sat at a round table and ATE while the music nourished the better part of us. We ate up, so to speak, my hat and some of Jill's textbooks.

And on the way to the train, we bought pickled limes, of which Amy in *Little Women* was so fond. Blissfully we sucked the limes as the train creaked away. That was a day to remember.

"I'd like to play a trombone," said Jill, "that's a deep gold sound."

"I'd like to play the big drum," I said, "because just now and then you go bang, bang, bang and it emphasizes the rest."

By the time Jill got some tutoring to do, we felt we were really in business. I was not an asset for I kept buying stamps to send things in to magazines and they came back. Once my hat was gone, I had nothing to sell. Years later, when an editor bought something

of mine and sent a check for it, I couldn't believe it. I thought it
was a mistake. I had the habit of writing because I had to write,
but getting paid was beyond belief.

The effect on my father was catastrophic.

"I suppose it's all right," he said dubiously, "if somebody wants
to pay you for a story. But don't consider it as a permanent thing
like teaching, which is really worth while."

At twilight the sun leaves a pink glow on the snowy meadow.
Then night comes sudden and soon. It is not possible to mark the
moment when it is no longer day. I have tried to but cannot. It is
like the swooping of ebony wings over the sky. The brief warmth of
the sun is gone and the air crackles with cold. As night takes over
the valley, a star stands clear and pure above the chimney. A cold
moon slips above the apple trees, a moon all pearl. Jill clears the
trestle table of the negatives she has been filing and is cross because
the one of Holly carrying a sofa pillow is still missing. I have
learned that the best negatives mysteriously vanish no matter how
carefully they are filed.

After supper we settle down by the fire to read. Reading aloud
is a passion with me but books to read aloud are getting fewer. Jill
is perfectly happy to reread one of Josephine Tey's mysteries or a
Lord Peter Wimsey. She has always been what one would call a
mystery buff. She says the reason I am not is because I always know
who killed who after the opening scene, so it is no fun. I tell her
that I've been a writer for so long, I have to know about plots just
as an engineer knows about machines.

Actually, except for the fact she has so many practical skills, Jill
might be called a pure intellectual. Mysteries are just an escape
and, if I may say so without offending the writers, a rest.

When we let the dogs out for a last run in the deep powdery
snow, we see dark stains on the trunks of the giant sugar maples.
This means the sap is running and soon every tree along the road
will have a sap bucket hanging on it. The buckets look like top
hats upside down and the spills gleam like silver and are, I think,
tin. This is the first promise of spring to come, this running of the
sap. For it means life is waking in the trees, the cycle of growth is

beginning which will lead to green leaves and to blossom, fruit, harvest in autumn. Hal Borland says without winter the year would lack a dimension. But now with the sugaring-off at hand, we are thankful.

Down by the pond the ice cracks. I hear it as I let the snow-feathered cockers and Irish back in to melt on the hearth and on my bed. I sleep damply in February. But snow is cleaner than the mud which March brings.

The housebound days of winter have been good, giving us time to contemplate the meaning of life. But now we look toward spring and Jill has all the seed catalogs spread out on the cobbler's bench and is MAKING LISTS.

After all, the sap is running again!

March

IN our valley, signs of spring come slowly. It is still mitten weather, and will be for some time to come. But when the old stone walls glisten with melting ice and the pond breaks its sheath, we turn toward spring. The stone walls are the signature of New England, written in curving lines up and down the hills. They were built in the early time as the settlers cleared the land, and they served a double purpose, freeing space for growing crops and marking boundaries. They were dry-laid with boulders it often took two or three men to manage. Smaller stones were fitted in between the great ones, and the building was so expert that no stones fell. It is possible even now to walk on top of these walls, except for those whose best stones have been "borrowed" for house foundations, walls, fireplaces.

Flagstone walks were unheard of when we moved to Stillmeadow. "I'll just run up to the old orchard and bring down some good flat stones to fix that hearth," said Mr. Clark, the mason. "And may as well lay a walk by the well while I'm at it."

The old stone walls provide homes for chipmunks, field mice, country cats. Bittersweet grows over them, goldenrod and wild asters flourish in their shelter, and ramblers bloom against the grey in season. In winter, deep with snow, they cast blue shadows, and now in March they have their own color, for they are not just grey, but flecked with greens, pinks and silver. Later the world of lichens and moss takes over.

It is estimated there are, as I write, 300,000 miles of stone fences in New England. But they are vanishing, chewed up by the building of throughways and bulldozed away for developments. Soon they may be as rare as covered bridges and the patient handwork of long ago will exist only in pictures. Bird cover and wildlife refuge and signature of beauty—progress will not leave them.

There is also another enemy. Travelers passing by stop and fill the trunks of their cars with stones. They want them for rock gardens, barbecues, patios. And somehow they never stop to think those stone walls are on someone's land. They demolish the bittersweet, uproot the wildflowers, leave rubble behind them. Jill is fiercely protective of our own stone fences and once drove such a group away by brandishing our Revolutionary musket. It is strange that people who would not go in a neighbor's garden and steal plants or stop casually at the woodpile and remove a carload of the best firewood, will steal, and yes, it is stealing, almost anything in the country.

Steve and Olive discovered one week end that their best evergreens had been dug up and taken off. Several, too big to dig up, were simply topped and the tops carried along. Another friend came home to find someone had dug up most of her best lilies. All of this gives city folk a bad name.

One kind of depredation is, however, strangely, less troubling. Now and then we hear voices in the woods and a kind of chanting. "The fern pickers are back," says Jill.

I always meant to write a story about them, but they are a quick and secret people. Their voices have a foreign sound but nobody I've asked seems to know anything about them except they come in trucks, gather the ferns, and vanish before anyone sees them. I am sure it is not good for the woodland ferns to be taken off, but on the other hand our woods are deep with fern and possibly thinning them out gives room for them to spread.

As I went for the mail this morning, the sun came through a riffle of wind clouds. I sat down on the old stone wall by the brook, feeling the quick warmth of sunshine. The brook crosses the road by Jeremy Swamp and wanders on through the apple orchard. This morning glowed. Osiers, alders, wild blackberry, swamp maples, and many I cannot name were all pulsing new life after the death-sleep of winter. Spring comes first to the swamp, and so does autumn, for the swamp maple is the first to burst into flame.

I made a special prayer of thanks to God. Prayer doesn't have to be in a special place or at a given time. Wherever one is, there also is God. I often stop in the midst of a household chore to speak. But of course praying with someone, as we do in church, gives an added sense of strength.

March is the month of the World Day of Prayer and on the fourth, from sunrise to sunset, countless millions all over the world lift up their hearts and voices to ask God's blessing for our troubled world. They pray for peace on earth, good will to men. Far in the great north, a prayer service is translated for Eskimos. In the Fiji Islands the day comes with bells and the beating of drums. In China, India and Japan Christians observe this day of prayer as we do in America.

When I think of the power of prayer in my personal life, I sense how infinitely more is the power of universal prayer. Rockets and missiles may reach the moon, and bigger and better weapons hold out the promise of complete destruction of our earth. But prayer has no limitation; it reaches beyond any space we know, and it taps the wellspring of all existence. It establishes our relationship with the infinite power of love.

"Be not afraid for I am with thee."

When I came back from the mailbox, the sun went under and the air grew cold. The cockers and the Irish welcomed me wildly, as if I had returned from a far place. They no longer go to the mailbox with us unless they are safely in the car, for Jeremy Swamp Road now has houses along it and autos flash by with no warning. When we came here, it was all farmland and woods, very beautiful and full of quail, pheasant, and deer. It troubles us that the wildlife is being pushed back so fast. When the countryside is nothing but squirreling highways and developments, will the wild-life be extinct?

Jill was in the kitchen starting braised flank steak with vegetables. We have the butcher make shallow cuts crosswise of the grain and then we pound well-seasoned flour into the steak, cut it in serving-size squares and brown them in shortening in the electric frying pan. When it is brown, we cover it with layers of thinly sliced raw potatoes, sliced onions, sliced green pepper and add a cup of canned tomatoes. We simmer this until it is tender, adding more tomato if needed.

This is a one-dish meal that satisfies brisk March appetites and tastes even better warmed up the next day.

Many dishes are improved by "resting," as we say. Pot roasts and beef and vegetable soups gain flavor by resting. Clam chowder needs at least thirty minutes and my recipe for lobster bisque requires overnight resting.

But woe to the soufflé or Yorkshire pudding that has to stand five minutes.

Last week, we adventured in a new cuisine—namely, baby food. Jill's grandson, Jamie, was in residence with his parents, and the amount of baby food a four-month-old boy can consume is startling. The kitchen was jammed with jars, cans, bottles, packages. When they left, a dozen half-empty jars and cans were bequeathed us. I could see why, for an extra pin wouldn't have fitted into the car. Jamie is an adorable, sunny, beautiful baby, and although he is big for his age, he still is "no larger than a breadbox" as the saying goes. But the equipment that goes with him, in this modern day, is staggering.

"I've got everything in," said Don, "but there isn't room for us."

"We ought not to waste all that food," commented Jill.

We found, by experimenting, that the creamed spinach made a fine cream soup, added to cream of chicken soup. The carrot purée went into beef stew. Jill combined the pear and banana and spiked it with lemon and crystallized ginger and came up with an elegant dessert. The strained liver made a paté with grated onion, freshly ground pepper and grated white of hard-cooked egg.

The trick is, of course, in the seasoning, for there is none in the baby foods. In fact, they all tasted pretty much alike until we added various seasonings. But even the strained baked potato made small potato balls, dusted with paprika and parsley and browned lightly in butter. And when Steve and Olive dropped in for tea, we made tiny sandwiches with filling of seasoned tuna fish.

And, as Jill said happily, nothing was wasted!

Being a den mother is no joke, I thought. I looked out of the window and saw our neighbor Bebe plunging along in the rain with her den boys. They were supposed to be taking a nature walk, but what they were doing was to throw sticks at one another, whoop and giggle, push the smaller ones around. They were no more easily managed than a batch of young puppies. They jumped the old stone fence, sloshed in the brook. Probably, I thought, they weren't observing nature much, but they were experiencing the beginning of spring.

Bebe herded them up the hill finally and into the wet woods. I knew that by the time they got back to her house, her husband would have hot cocoa, marshmallows and cookies and also a supply of warm towels to dry them off.

Last summer it fell to Bebe's lot to be a counselor on a camping trip with the boys. I think these were older boys.

"We made a mistake," said Bebe, "pitching the tents on a steep slope. And then we were short a couple of tents, so some campers and counselors bedded down on the ground."

The counselors lucky enough to rate tent space were so crowded they slept with their feet outside the tent.

"That wouldn't have been so bad," said Bebe, "but the worst storm of the season came up in the night, flooding the tents and washing part of the slope away."

"What could you do?" I asked.

"What I did was take my carload home," said Bebe, "at three in the morning. I woke Phil up at four-thirty. 'Get up,' I said, 'I've got eight campers with me.' "

He got up. The campers were dried out, nourished and laid out in ranks on the floor wrapped in blankets. And the only casualty was that Bebe caught a terrible cold and was in bed three days.

The young fathers take their duties seriously here. They tramp around clearing brush with the Boy Scouts, help plant autumn olive by the streams to prevent erosion, oversee the setting out of multiflora roses for wildlife cover. They also are involved in such things as swimming classes, school parties, the Little League. And because this is a rural area and distances are great, both fathers and mothers do a great deal of taxiing. They may take children to the school-bus stop, pick them up after school, take them to music lessons, to parties and to junior choir practice at the church. It's not what one would call a leisurely life. Also, most of us do our own washing, ironing, as well as cooking and shopping. In spare moments there is always a covered-dish supper at the church or the Homemaker's Guild or P.T.A.

The men are busy raising money for the Lions club scholarships or for the ambulance or for the church. Or for the fire department. For both the ambulance service and the fire department are volunteer. The men take turns at being ambulance drivers, with night drivers and day drivers. The firemen, of course, assemble from wherever they are when what we call the sireen sounds.

Many a time when we have the neighbors in for a buffet, the siren has sounded just as the casseroles come to the trestle table. The men drop their napkins and speed to the door. If it is a small fire, they may get back in time to have a warmed-over plate, but if it is a big fire, they may be out all night.

But nobody complains. Perhaps it is our New England temperament. We expect to take care of ourselves ourselves and volunteer is a good word as far as we are concerned. This will change as the village grows and the big highways plunge by bringing more and more visitors to our countryside. Eventually we will have paid firemen, paid ambulance drivers, and something will be lost, some sense of sharing our burdens without any idea of gainful reward.

In a word, I might say we are old-fashioned.

Another word for old-fashioned is, of course, backward. It's all in the point of view. We have no sidewalks in the village, no street lights along the more heavily inhabited roads. We do not want them. Sometimes we wish we had some kind of transportation other than our own cars. A long time ago there was a small railroad station at the top of a hill and freight cars came in on the line with coal. We used to get express packages there, although how express it was, I do not know.

Now we go to the next town, and we are wary of ordering anything too heavy to carry by ourselves. The nicest thing about a real expressman is that he lugs for you. Around Christmas there is always a rush to get to the office before it closes when baskets of fruit are there. If the road is impassable, we imagine our grapefruit and oranges spoiling away in the office. It would be nice, we think wistfully, to have heavy things roll up in a beautiful Railway Express truck and be DELIVERED.

We do have flower delivery, which surprises our city guests. The Pecks have a lovely florist shop and greenhouse in Woodbury, and if this seems strange in the country, it isn't! The garden season is short, and the rest of the year nothing seems lovelier than a dewy-fresh bouquet for Christmas or New Year's or a winter birthday or for a get-well message when one is ill. There are weddings and funerals too. When Connie was married in the 1732 church, a killing frost had blackened the gardens, but the church bloomed under Mrs. Peck's care, all white and gold, and she made an old-fashioned bouquet in my milk glass bowl for the wedding table.

All in all, we feel very fortunate in our valley. And if we do lack some conveniences of city living, we also lack the smog or smoke, the slush in winter, the blowing litter on the curbs in summer. And the noise, the roaring, reverberating, endless noise. I find after living so long in the quietness of the country that the noise of the city is like hammers beating against my temples. I keep unconsciously waiting for it to cease. Most of my city friends speak with raised voices, trying to talk above the clamor, whereas many country folk speak so softly.

But everyone knows that city people complain about the birds in the early morning hours in the country. Which proves that what we are used to, we find easy to live with. And what we are not accustomed to, is difficult. Our city guests wonder why we are never lonely "way off here in the country," and what we find to do. No theatre, no nearby movies, no concerts, no museums, they say.

We do have theatre in New Haven where the Broadway plays are tried out, and occasionally make the two-hour round trip to see something special like Alfred Lunt and Lynn Fontanne, or Shirley Booth. We also occasionally go to the Yale Bowl to a football game, but the last time we went, it took us an hour to locate the car and an hour and a half more to get to the highway and besides we had walked half a mile to get to the seats in the bleachers. My enthusiasm for the game was not dampened, but Jill's was. She said when we finally got home, hungry and cold and tired, that it was a lot to go through with to watch a bunch of boys fling themselves at one another and kick a ball around.

When we gave in and got a television set, I could watch the football games while she painted woodwork or scraped the old church bench just acquired. I submit that the real game, so to speak, with the color and excitement cannot be compared to a game on a screen, but there is a lot to be said for being so comfortable while you watch. You also see the actual plays better than you ever do from the stands.

Television is a controversial subject, as any new medium must be. I can remember when I was growing up just what Father said about radio. He bought one of the first Victrolas in our town, and now that I understand Father better, I can see why he felt a Victrola was all right but radio, when it came along, was a terrible invention. With the Victrola, he could choose the records himself, Caruso, Alda, grand opera and symphonies. But on a radio, he had to take what came along and he didn't like any of it. He felt there was something immoral about popular music and Amos and Andy would have horrified him. He got the news from the newspaper.

He finally allowed me to have a few popular records such as "The Whistler and His Dog," "When You Wore a Tulip," and so on, but I played them when he was at college. It irritated him no end to find I had such low tastes.

This matter of taste is curious. It has always been hard for me to understand it, for I like all kinds of music, various types of writing, much painting. I like traditional and modern furniture. Then too, I equally admire intellectual people and those who obviously are not. Perhaps I lack discrimination, but it is a lovely way to be, because the more in life you can enjoy, the wider the horizon.

I am limited in my understanding of some modern architecture. I looked long and earnestly at the winning drawings for the memorial to be erected to Franklin Delano Roosevelt in Washington. I could make nothing of any of them except one of the runners-up, the Japanese, which used four slender curves of concrete (for the four freedoms) soaring over a heroic statue. This seemed to soar gracefully toward the sky, the curves suggesting a fountain. But the prize-winner was a series of stone slabs shaped like huge book ends, scattered around a bigger book end. If it resembled anything as a whole, it would be a cemetery.

Certainly the serenity and dignity of the Lincoln Memorial is preferable for my taste. But I realize this may simply mean I do not know enough about modern architecture.

Lately I have read a good bit about the idea of city planning, whereby a uniform plan is set up, slums are gradually cleared, new buildings erected in harmony. This has begun in Philadelphia with restoration of part of the historic area. The magnitude of remaking a city staggers me, but think of what it would mean to have our cities stand in beauty, and the poorest inhabitant live in decent housing. Think, too, of parks enough for the children, of tree-lined avenues, of small sit-down areas for tired shoppers. If this is a dream for America, it is a dream worth having.

For some time, a family of skunks has lived under the floor of the storage house. Sometimes we see them moving with dignity past the barberries which grow there. Considering that cockers and

Irish are hunting dogs, I wonder why we have never had trouble. Now and then when Erma hangs out the wash, she calls, "The skunks are out, call the dogs in!"

I believe, with no scientific support, that this skunk family has a truce with our dogs. Otherwise it does not make sense. For once when we were on Cape Cod, Holly met a skunk, and the results were catastrophic. This must have seemed a strange skunk to her, for she advanced with flags flying. I've told this before, but I may say again that separating a firm-minded skunk from an excited Irish setter is quite a deal. It is a further problem to carry the Irish home in the car and the clean-up job is terrific and never really successful.

The classic remedy is to rub tomato juice or canned tomatoes into the dog's coat, standing as far away as you can. A long-handled brush helps. This can be followed with a thorough shampoo, then another shampoo, a good rinse and an airing-out. For a week or so, even then, there is no doubt but that your dog has encountered a skunk.

Left undisturbed, the skunk is a quiet, peaceable animal, and a very handsome one. He is also intelligent, according to our friend Dr. George Whitney, who has made house pets of them from time to time.

It is another wonder of nature that this animal has a weapon peculiarly effective and peculiarly his own.

But consider the strange porcupine that is protected by the murderous quills! Once a dog gets near a porcupine, it is even worse than meeting a skunk for the quills are barbed like fishhooks and often it takes a veterinarian to remove them. One wonders how many quill-ridden wild animals die from them.

Buying a new car is not a project with us, except having the money to pay for it. All we ever do is get a new model of the same make. A car is a friend and once you have a good friend, you are accustomed to the personality. I always view with surprise friends who suddenly turn up with a different make!

Barbara Gardner and I were remembering old cars we had known and my story of the station wagon whose doors had to be roped shut and which had an asbestos stove mat for part of the flooring, paled beside her tale.

"My side of the front seat," she said dreamily, "was supported by a large rock. And when we went across the country, we had to back up over some of the mountains because it wouldn't make them going forward."

"Oh, my," I said.

"And Susie sat in the back seat," Barbara went on, "crooning baby songs and tearing up pieces of toilet tissue and tossing them from the window. It was quite a trip."

It reminded me of a trip with the children and several cockers when we had the trunk packed until we had to tie down the top. It was, we thought, a superb packing job. But when we had to unpack at the side of the road so Jill could get out the spare tire, it wasn't much fun. The jack wouldn't work. And while we struggled the car fairly bounced with restless children (three) and anxious cockers (three).

We had to wait for a man to come by and get the jack screwed up. And then we had, of course, to repack everything.

"We'd be better off in the days of horses," said Jill, as she tied the trunk cover down again.

Afterward, such experiences seem rather gay to remember, although I do not know why. Once we carried an antique chest of drawers from the city to the country. It slid off in Yonkers and again farther up the line. I rode the rest of the way clinging to the ropes that came past my window, hoping to help anchor the monster. Another time we had a harvest table in the back seat (a small station wagon) plus Holly who rode rather like a queen in a howdah. We put it in upside down and inserted her on the under side with the leaves rising around her.

Naturally Holly got bored with the whole thing and had to sit in my lap, and since I already had an antique turkey platter, it was also quite a trip.

One characteristic of mine, which may be unfortunate, is that I do believe anything will go in a car if you put your mind to it. What won't go in can go on top. So we have had strange cargo, such as a whole set of Obedience jumps, which really would not fit in, but did. These are built of substantial lumber and will not fold.

Housekeeping in March in New England can be discouraging. The house smells of wet wool, for one thing, as mittens and jackets steam on the radiators or by the stove. Nobody, so far as I know, has invented lilac-scented woolens, although we have progressed in my time to scented note paper. Rubbers smell too. So does mud.

Jill says I have a sense of smell like the cockers and the Irish and perhaps I do. It can give great delight for a lovely scent is like a bar of music or a lyric poem. It can also be a nuisance. When I sit at my typewriter in the far corner of the house and smell drying wraps in the back kitchen, I wish my sense of smell were less acute.

It's practical when cooking for I also smell what's in the oven, three rooms away. We use a meat thermometer but I do not know why. I just sniff and call to Jill, "The roast is done. Take it out." I can't describe this, I only know a roast smells done when it is done. So does an apple pie. Rolls are easy, they get a brown fragrance. And of course baked beans would be easy for anybody as the rich spicy juice begins to bubble over the top.

Jill has no sense of smell at all, owing to a persistent sinus condition, and she admires me no end for knowing when something is burning up on the stove or a fire is about to start in the trash can. She thinks it remarkable that I can smell snow in the air before it snows at all and regardless of the weather report. It means she gets ready for it, going to the village to lay in supplies. And if I smell a hurricane she runs.

The smell of a hurricane is what I can only call a flat smell. You cannot really describe smells because they are like nothing else in our sensuous experience. So when I say a hurricane is preceded by a flat smell, I'll have to let it go at that. It is not musty, it is flat. And one thing I know, it alerts other senses. The sense of sight, for instance. Everything is suddenly so distinct. Shortly after I smell a hurricane, I begin to think the lawn furniture is so close it will move right in the house. The leaves on the trees are sharply drawn against the blue sky. Every grass blade has importance. Then there is what Keats called "a noiseless noise among the leaves." The stillness is profound and beautiful and ominous. This is partly because the birds know and have retreated to the swamp or the pine woods. If there is a sound at all, it is magnified. We can hear a truck on 67. Which is quite a distance away. And also the ancient house creaks, as if getting ready.

Some of our village friends have hurricane warnings built into their bones. Ed Koch says he gets a pain in the middle of his back. Jim Brown feels it in his knees. Erma gets a pressure in her head. I just smell it.

March brings many things, but not hurricanes. But yesterday it brought a storm and a temperature drop, a farewell gesture from winter. The pipes froze again in the back part of the house. And as I viewed the solidly frozen bath mat in my shower, I felt I could do without any record-breaking statistics. The bath mat had been folded over and was a slab of ice. I tried to pry it up with a broom handle, a shovel. I turned on the hundred-watt light to lend a mellowing influence. This might have worked except the March wind was sweeping icy air in under the floor. (No cellar there.)

The last crisis like this Jill plugged in a fancy electric heater and blew all the fuses. I considered pouring boiling water on the floor but somehow gave that up. I felt the pipes might burst. So I got out the vacuum cleaner and turned the blower on and directed the air on the heap of ice and in two hours I could get the mat up and let it melt in the sink. Then I feared that might freeze the sink pipes again so I put it on the radiator in the plastic water pail.

But I could hardly wait to tell Jill when she got back from the city that I had SOLVED something. And I was particularly pleased to solve anything with the vacuum cleaner. For, although I would not wish to hurt the feelings of the vacuum cleaner manufacturers, I have to report I view a vacuum cleaner with doubt, not to say distrust.

This is a wonderful invention, replacing the sketchy broom and the carpet sweeper and presumably the dust mop. But as far as I am concerned, the greatest talent of our vacuum cleaner is that it thawed my bath mat so I didn't have to wear rubbers when I stepped in the tiny bathroom. There are many types of cleaners and we have worked through and with them all. They are all, I hasten to say, excellent, but not for me. The biggest improvement of late is putting them on wheels or runners. At least I do not haul a lot of dead weight around. But they run into things, they

trip me up, pieces of them fall off. The dust bag fills itself overnight, quietly and secretly. I think little people come along and
stuff things in.

The brushes. I have to comb out the dog hair every few minutes.
The non-brush things will not accommodate themselves to our
uneven floors. They jump. And then if you have to run a cleaner
over several rooms and have only a couple of places to plug it in,
you just skim along and the cleaner gives up. The plug has pulled
out. You wind your way back and put it in again and notice the
cord is frayed so you need a new cord. But that is not simple, because it has to come from a company agent. You cannot just go
to the hardware store in Seymour and ask for a cleaner cord and
plug. Oh no.

Jill never did care for vacuum cleaners. She swept and mopped
when Erma was not with us and shook things out and even, once,
got with great difficulty an old-fashioned carpetbeater which she
exercised briskly.

Erma seems to charm a vacuum. We don't. But lately I saw a
new cleaner advertised on TV which also washed, rinsed and
waxed as well as cleaned, and I wonder. I just wonder. Most of the
newest and best pieces of equipment advertise that even a child
can operate them. What child?

All I wish from the manufacturers is a vacuum cleaner easy
and comfortable for a writer to operate and still have a little
time in which to write. But I do not mean, really, to write a
complaining letter to the editor, so to speak. Just the idea of a
piece of equipment that will suck up embedded dirt is quite
dazzling. All I really mean to say is that modern equipment is
wonderful but any homewife operating it has to be quick and not
to mind when it won't work at all. My worst experience was
when the vacuum cleaner blew everything back. This is discouraging. It was, however, exciting to see a stream of dust and dirt and
dog hair sailing to the ceiling. And when I turned the hose out
of the window, things flew over the lawn.

All that I really mean to say is that at times the modern aids
to homekeeping can cause side-effects, such as great frustration.
And when I read articles about the excess leisure women have

nowadays, I wonder. Do we, really? Quite a lot of our time is spent handing wrenches and things to service men who patiently try to get the dishwasher or clothes washer going again.

This is a thought.

Recently someone wrote me to ask how to make soap. My mother made it now and then, but I have no memory of it. It must have been in the early days of the first war. But it made me realize that in the days of my ancestors, soapmaking was a regular job. So was weaving.

Now I have fine scented soap for my bath and a detergent for the dishes and another for the clothes. I have bluing that just sifts on too. I have bleaches and fresheners, and if things fade, I can add a box of color and have them come out fresh and clear. There are also water softeners, although we do not need them in this area. And there are waxers and polishers and dustcloths that gobble up dust.

It's a wonderful era in many ways. But we take it for granted. Hot and cold running water, electric lights, furnace heat, automatic refrigerators—we seldom consider how fortunate we are to have them.

Any time of year I get mail from people who have adopted dogs and cats tossed out of cars as travelers go by. This is worse in summer when many people acquire a puppy or a kitten just to satisfy the children and then depart without that puppy or kitten when vacation is over. But it also happens in March when nights are so cold a dog or cat can freeze to death. In our valley any puppy or kitten that comes humbly to a back stoop is offered to us. Last year we harbored two very amiable cockers until their ownership could be traced.

"I don't want them any more," said the owner. "I only got them for hunting and I can't hunt now."

I know that many people who toss out dogs and cats think they are good citizens, maybe good church members. In my book, they are murderers. They should have a try at being homeless, half starving or dying of hunger, knowing terror. The lucky ones do find a warmhearted human being, the unlucky do not. They just die inch by inch.

There is no law that says you have to have a dog or a cat. It is a matter of choice. But once you take one, you have a responsibility. A living, loving being is not a toy. And I am sure that God who watches the fall of a sparrow will not easily slip over the dreadful cruelty of abandoning a dog or cat because it is not convenient to take it back to the city.

There are also people who own dogs or cats and neglect them. They leave the hapless pets to scrounge food wherever they can, sleep outdoors in the coldest weather. The nearest thing to a brush is a broom that sweeps them out of the way.

Why? Why?

I've never found anyone who could explain this.

On a day of rain and wind, I decided to poke around in the attic. An attic is a lovely and maddening place for everything is there that you do not know what in the world to do with. In a burst of enthusiasm for clearing it out, we sold five spinning wheels and a carder some years ago. But there are still old chests

full of odds and ends, and that is exactly what they are. I do not mean to say Jill and I are hoarders. We are givers-away. Anything we·do not wear inside of a year is given away because as Jill puts it, "If we didn't need that for a year, someone else does." But there are things like paintings and water colors that are rather old-fashioned. No doubt fifty years from now, they'll be collector's items. Meanwhile we do not know who would like them, so there they are.

Also there are bits and pieces of old furniture that Jill hasn't redone because we have no room for another pin downstairs. But we find few people really love rebuilding a Shaker stand or fixing up a chest of drawers. When you give something away, it has to be in perfect condition.

There are also boxes of very old photographs of people we do not know but who must be our relatives. Now and then we spend a couple of hours wondering who that man is in the Civil War uniform and whether the stern-faced lady in bombazine is Jill's ancestress or mine. In the end, we pack the photographs and daguerreotypes back in the boxes.

But the one thing that is a main problem is the keys. I cannot understand why we have so many old keys. They do not seem to fit anything, so far as we can find out. Some of them are very old, tiny, and delicate, some of them are big enough to lock a barn door. Since neither Jill nor I ever lock anything, we are at a loss to understand what these keys are for. A few of them have faded rose or lilac ribbons attached, so they must be important. Jill points out that since we never lock anything, why not just toss the whole box? And I always say that maybe we might need a key one day. Somehow a key has a fascination for me, except that I would not want to use one. A key is a mystery of a sort. It means something might be unlocked some time.

On the other hand a key may be frustrating. Faith Baldwin came to spend a week with us and forgot to bring the key to her suitcase which had locked automatically.

"Well, it's an old suitcase," she said philosophically, as she smashed the lock.

In our valley, until the last few years, nobody ever locked their houses when they went away. A few timid housewives might say, on going away to visit relatives, that the key was under the cocoa mat for whoever might wish to use it. And when we went to Canada, we did hang the key under the window box by the back door. But when we got home we forgot where we had put it and it was tiresome trying to hunt.

Automobile keys are a hazard too. Our dear friend Helen Beals lost both her regular and spare sets, and this was a real crisis. Since she keeps her car in a garage back in the yard and lives on a relatively quiet road, I felt she would better leave the keys in the car.

We advised Helen just to lock the garage, because she could always climb in the window if the door keys were mislaid. But Jill and I don't follow this advice and often Jill dashes around saying, "Did I leave the car keys in my jacket, or did I wear a jacket? Where is the purse I took?"

There are undoubtedly people who always know just where keys are. We have a special hook for ours, but if the plumber comes just as Jill gets home with the groceries—or the cockers have dug a hole in the fence and are deploying around in the swamp—well, the keys do not get hung on that hook.

The most lethal business with keys is, of course, those keys to the safety-deposit box in the nearest bank. We hide ours so well that they barely turn up in time to get the insurance policies out.

But the collection of keys we have in that attic box really has no sense. And yet, we never take them to the dump. Who knows but that some mysterious use for them might occur? We might have tried them on Faith Baldwin's suitcase. Suppose one of the small ones might unlock a secret treasure box which just turns up (I never figure how)? Inside would be old letters tied with lavender ribbon, a brooch, pressed violets, a lock of golden hair. As I hold the key in my hand, it does unlock my imagination. And that may be better than just one box! For suppose the key would "slide softly in oiléd words" and unlock only love letters, stamped with the pony express stamp? Or a scrap of paper with the signature of a signer of the Declaration of Independence?

When I was very young, I had a treasure box, made of metal which looked like gold, but wasn't. I kept the most important and cherished items in this, and kept the key in a spot where I hoped my father would not find it. When I opened it, a few years ago, I found all of youth in it. I found a dance program filled entirely with one name. I found a high school athletic letter, the football A. I found three sticks of gum tied with pink ribbon. I could NOT remember the significance of these. I found a few letters which really said nothing, and yet breathed of young love as arbutus breathes of spring. And I found a perfectly hideous silk handkerchief with San Antonio, Texas, painted on it. And when I repacked the box, and locked it, I did not even throw away the gum. Some day, I thought, I'll remember why that gum was given to me, and since I never chewed gum, I'll wonder whether I did chew one piece or not!

When I consider keys, I pack them all away and think about other keys. The keys to the Kingdom of Heaven, for instance. When I was growing up I was then, as now, very visual-minded. I could see those massive gold keys unlocking great gates inlaid with pearl and rubies and all kinds of precious jewels. Later on, I began to wonder. Jewels are beautiful but they are not important enough to be the gates of Heaven or the key to it. My own keys to the Kingdom of Heaven are love, compassion, selflessness. You cannot wear these in a bracelet or on a string but they are part of the way to the Kingdom of God.

Then there are the keys to the heart. The heart is a strange country but the most important thing about the heart is that it longs to be unlocked. All of us, I think, go through life longing to have our hearts unlocked. But it is a difficult lock and so many keys do not fit.

There is, I think, only one way to unlock a heart and that is to say, "I love you, I cherish you. Could you let me in?"

A good many broken marriages might be saved by this.

This is equally true of a child's heart. I read much about understanding children, raising children, managing children. In our day there is so much written about the problems with children that it is rather frightening. I am sure all parents make mistakes for they are human, they cannot be else. But no matter how intelligent they may be as to the rules, the rules do not always work. And when a rule fails, one is lost.

It is my opinion, as a simple countrywoman, that what children need is love. One can really make all the mistakes there are but if there is love, the children grow up all right. We live in an age of great stresses and strains, and perhaps all ages were so. I often think the parents in ancient Greece had much the same worries as we have today The times were different, but I am sure the parents worried. This is an integral part of parenthood.

As I took the box of keys back to the place under the eaves in the attic, I thought it a good idea that some secret places do have to have keys, for after all fitting a key into a lock is an act of faith. It means we believe the key will fit, the lock will accept it. And this, in itself, is a wonder. Also, conversely, we sense when a key will not fit.

"I wanted to be friends, so much, but I just could not find the right words to say." I've heard this more than once. I have felt it myself when the magic key to friendship was not there. But then there are times when just a few words unlock a friendship. They are usually very simple words, not words trying to make an impression. But they unlock a door.

I come back down the ladder stairs thinking that I really should have thrown out those keys, along with a good many other things. But every now and then we go to the attic and find something we need, old hand-wrought hinges, a few black-oak hand-cut boards, old picture frames. And if the front door suddenly locks itself, Jill says, "I think there's a key in the attic that might fit."

Yesterday I went to the bank, which is a town away in Seymour. I waited to see Mr. Hummel, the president. I had to have my signature certified on some papers. So I thought about banks. Until we moved to Stillmeadow, I was terrified of banks. I always felt apologetic cashing a check. Cashiers eyed me suspiciously. I was always the last in line and it was time for them to go to lunch. Or perhaps I did not look prosperous enough to have ten dollars.

Now our Seymour bank is a different thing. It is a bank with a warm hospitable personality. Cashiers seem pleased to see people and always thank me for putting them to the trouble of cashing checks or depositing checks. The girls in the savings account section cheerfully run around putting money from savings into checking around tax time. They THANK YOU.

It is not because this is a small bank, it isn't. It services a very wide area, it is an extremely busy bank.

Now on a sunny day, we hear the sound of the last pond ice breaking. The singing of freed water as it pours into the brook is gay. The brook itself is almost a small river, hardly contained in its course. I would like to follow it down to Eight-Mile Brook and on to the river, but much of the way is through wild terrain suitable only for a brook. All I can do is toss a short stick in and watch it sail out of sight.

Which reminds me of Christopher Robin, who tossed sticks over a bridge and was so excited when there they were on the other side of the bridge!

The return of the redwings is the true beginning of the year. They come in and fly around in great circles talking things over. Now this is curious, for in the end, they always light in one particular sugar maple. Just why this maple is better than the others, I cannot decide. I keep walking around and staring at it and it is just like the others to my eyes. But the redwings find it superior. Why? And why do they always discuss it first? And why, when the tree is quivering with them, do they keep changing places? They are very talkative birds at midday. And early in the morning I love to hear their O-ca-lee, O-ca-lee. It is a pure clear liquid note, as easy to identify as the yellowthroat's.

One year they came too soon and a heavy snow fell before they settled in. We put out all the food we could but we worried when we saw them trying to tip along in the snow. The winter birds had no trouble, chickadees sang cheerfully, nuthatches skipped head-down on the maples, juncoes sat in the snow around the ground feeder.

"Those redwings," said Jill, "ought to turn around and fly back to Florida."

Nobody has ever explained to my satisfaction how birds know when to start north. Or, for that matter, when to start south. Is it a change in the light as the sun and earth change? Sometimes the weather has no hint of the seasonal cycle. On a summery golden day in autumn, flocks of small birds may begin wheeling, wheeling, wheeling. I notice that they line up on the electric wires after these flights. They look like a string of beads. I do not think I have ever seen them perch like this on the wires except before migrating. Only occasionally in summer will a redwing pause on a telephone wire or a barn swallow light. It makes me wonder whether lining up on the wires makes it easier to arrange the flight pattern? When they are airborne again, there are always a few stragglers. Will these ever make the trip south? Perhaps they will get part way and stop off. Theirs is a long, dangerous journey and on the day when they are really vanishing, I wave them good-bye with a pang. So small they seem against the bosom of the sky, so fragile, yet so intrepid.

Soon now it will be time to put away the ground feeder and use only the window feeder and the suet cages. Once we forgot to do this and had a nice stand of wild-bird-feed seedlings. Including what looked like corn, although the corn we use is ground fine and should not have come up. But there it was, in the middle of the lawn.

Jill put a hopeful spade down in the garden and came in saying we might never be able to plant at all. I didn't ask how deep the frost was. I just told her it was pork chops baked with cabbage for supper. This made the world look better for it is her favorite dish. She got out the seeds and arranged them in the way she planned to plant. Tomorrow she will have a different garden-pattern. During this period we always eat on trays so the trestle table is available for the imaginary garden.

While the chops baked, I went out with the cockers and the Irish. The cold sky was smoky pearl, the air smelled of damp earth and sap. Teddy got up an obliging rabbit and the other cockers flew in to chase. Holly is at a disadvantage, for she freezes to a point at the sight of game, plumed tail level, motionless, one paw lifted, one elbow bent. She can stand thus, on three legs and with that wagging tail still, for an indefinite period. I have, at times, tried to time her point but she outstays me and I have to go and sit down. The cockers do not freeze to a point, far from it. They have a mind to bring back that rabbit as a lovely present for us. The rabbit nipped into the swamp and Holly gave me a reproachful look. Nobody, she implied, minds the rules of the game except me.

Our cockers and Irish lead frustrated lives in a way since they are not "shot over," as we say in the valley. But Teddy can manage a woodchuck, Jonquil caught a possum, and Holly catches moles. Tiki never gets anything because he barks too soon. But he would train easily and he has an incredible nose. He was playing with Muffin's stuffed bunny and I took it away and put it on the high mantel. I put it there while he was eating the cookie reward for being a good boy. When he got back in the room he lifted his muzzle and air-scented and went directly to the mantel and tried to climb up to get the nice plaything.

The bunny has been gone for some weeks but Tiki still rushes to the mantel when he comes in and hopefully cranes his neck. Then he sits back and cocks his head to the right, to the left, keeping watch to see if that bunny might not come back to the mantel.

Now we have what Hal Borland calls "the hurrying wind." At night I wake and hear it and it sounds as if black stallions were galloping above the roof of the farmhouse. Sometimes I get up and look out hoping to see stars tossed in their manes. The wind is blowing winter away, life is beginning to stir in the earth and I have a sense my own life is renewed. Now I shall put away winter failures, disappointments, frustrations. It is time to take stock of the long cold months, then let the wind blow them into time past. It is time to ready the heart for new flowering. It is a time to consider the meaning of existence.

Faith Baldwin once told me when we were talking about the meaning of life that one must look for the leaf on the bare bough, for the leaf is there, waiting for time to open to spring. Most of us know a winter of the heart at one time or another when the bough seems to have no leaf. But implicit in the branch itself is the green leaf which will come forth in season. We have faith that the maples will be in leaf in May. We need also to have faith that the grace of new growth will be bestowed on us.

As the wind beats against the house, I imagine the last snow-drifts sliding into yesterday. I know farmers in the low part of the valley are worrying about flooding. Those people who have built close to a stream will lie uneasily, wondering whether the bank will cave in. Jill is wondering whether the dam will give way and the pond spread all over the lower fields.

Branches crack down, and often we get up to be sure the last old apple tree is still there in the back yard. The Irish doesn't care, she stirs in her sleep and twitches her paws. The cockers are as close to the hearth as they can be without catching fire from the embers. It is not true that dogs do not worry, they worry every time we leave them to go to get our hair done. They worry dread-fully when they are all shut in the back kitchen because non-dog people are in the house. But weather they do not worry about at all.

When we prowl in the night, we always meet each other in the kitchen. Naturally we have to have something, as do the instantly awake dogs. Sometimes we have mugs of hot soup at midnight, sometimes toasted cheese on pumpernickel. Sometimes a Bermuda-onion sandwich. But we manage to cut off snacks from the roast for the dogs. Then we sit a time by the fireplace discussing whether to put on another log or not. Or we talk about what to give the children for their birthdays. Or we talk about modern poetry and decide we like non-modern poetry best as a rule.

"I like to understand what I read," says Jill.

"There goes the front storm door," I say.

"I'll fix it tomorrow," says Jill, finishing her clam chowder.

We are at such a time an island of peace. It doesn't matter if a few shingles fall off in the hurrying wind. It isn't important that the yard is going to be an inland lake for some time. It doesn't matter too much if a falling branch cuts off the electric.

Spring is on the way and the time of snowdrops is at hand!

SPRING

April

A New England town meeting is a lively affair. This last one was called specially to discuss zoning. We got to the school on time (which is always a mistake) and found people milling about in the corridors, tempers already rising. The gymnasium, where we meet, was not arranged with rows of chairs and the moderator's table. It was arranged with the basketball team practising for a game. It was, in fact, full of whooping boys.

It took half an hour to find some other place for the meeting, and eventually someone opened up a classroom and everyone jammed in. It was unfortunate that it was a classroom for very young children or midgets. Some of the men just stood around the wall. I wedged myself in a child-size desk chair wondering who would haul me out. It took another half hour to get the zoning maps up on the walls. I had time to memorize the verse on the blackboard.

> From all who dwell below the skies
> Let faith and hope and love arise.
> Let beauty, truth, and good be sung
> From every land, from every tongue.

I thought it was a fine message, provided these children would know what beauty is, or truth; they are difficult concepts for many adults. Faith too is something hard to understand, difficult to define. However, I thought, squeezing my knees under the desk, the children probably would know the meaning of "all who dwell below the skies."

By then, some of the maps had fallen down and the zoning

commission kept putting them back up again. They were beautiful, impressive maps but impossible to read. I did discover that what must be Stillmeadow's area was dark grey, although some parts of the maps were pink, which is more cheerful. The meeting had been called to order when a scout reported the gymnasium was now free, so down came the maps, out we went, and we began all over.

Now zoning is a hard subject. Everyone wants it, but not for himself. It's all very well to zone a future business district but a hardheaded Yankee may figure he might want to put up a filling station or a hot-dog stand on his land, which is in the so-called residential section. This is further complicated in our rural area because until lately the residential section consisted of farms. The business area consists of a few buildings, country store, post office (in the store), garage, doctor's office. When we acquired a drugstore we wondered whether we might be getting too citified.

The moderator opened the meeting (when the maps were up) and at last the town meeting was under way. Four or five men jumped up at once and began to argue. They jumped up and some jumped both up and down so the floor vibrated. They all talked at once, as usual, and nobody waited to be recognized by the moderator and given the floor.

The hard-core Yankees declared they had owned their land and paid taxes (taxes are a red flag) and they were not going to be told what to do with it.

"If I want to sell off half an acre," said one, "it's my half acre. Who's to tell me I have to sell in three-acre pieces?"

"If I want to put up a barn, I'm not to be told where I can build and where I can't."

"We've got along all right here since we drove the British out and we'll get along all right as we are without a lot of fancy new rules."

The moderator banged away but it was hard to quiet things down so the head of the commission could answer questions and explain the maps.

"This is one of the very few rural areas left in Connecticut," he spoke firmly. "Circumstance has protected you up to now, namely a lack of transportation facilities. This won't last."

He moved to one of the maps and used his pointer.

"Hartford, New Haven, Waterbury and Bridgeport," he said, "are reaching out already as the new highways go in. You are now eleven minutes from Newtown instead of twenty-five. You will soon be eighteen minutes from Waterbury. Your valley is more accessible every year."

It was a grim picture. Business was bound to come; light industries were already shopping for land. The quiet country farms were already going, and developments would take over. He finished by saying that just how the village developed would depend on us. With proper control, it would grow with beauty and grace.

When he finished, the argument began again. The meeting never really ended, and nobody decided anything. Around midnight people began to drift away. This is typical of a town meeting. After the session, some time elapses in which the argument goes on at the grocery store, at the Grange, after church. Eventually another meeting is called at which everyone is even madder than at the first. I once heard a farmer say furiously to another, "I'll punch you in the head when we get out of here."

"Try it and see," said the other.

But I knew the next day these two would be amiably discussing crops, because that is the way it is in our valley. What sounds like plain murder is just independent Yankees exercising democracy.

The zoning battle was perhaps one of the fiercest. But of course we have to have it. The real problem is that we do not like change and we find progress terrifying. The wooded roads, gentle hills, greening meadows, the clean sweet-running brooks and the historic white houses—these are a precious heritage. Our own forty acres seem like a refuge and not in our day, I hope, will they be cut up into two-acre lots for split-level houses.

Our land is hilly, heavily wooded, with only a few arable pieces. There are two old orchards, two swamps (which we dearly love), a rocky place with great jutting cliffs. There are parts of it which are inaccessible to us, although Joe, our neighbor, can "walk the line," as he says. Sometimes we hear the sound of chopping in our

woods and know Mr. X, who is called "the bandit," is helping
himself to our good trees. But he is too handy with a gun for us
to risk trouble with him, and Jill says comfortably that the woods
need thinning.

From time to time we dream of cleaning up the woods with
professional help, but we always decide not to. What's lost to the
bandit we cannot help, but we prefer to think of our woodland
as belonging to nature herself and to the natural wild inhabitants.
The only time I penetrated it was when my Abyssinian kitten was
lost. That day I climbed cliffs, leaped over fallen trees, skimmed
across ravines. I could never have retraced that route in my right
senses. When I got back, I had a sound scolding from Jill. I was
bedraggled, torn by briars, bruised by a few falls. I did not have
Aladdin either.

But I remember the mystery of the deep woods, the silence, the shadowy light. Even when I was lost for a few moments, I was not afraid. I remembered my father, who could go anywhere without a compass. He had a built-in sense of direction and I decided I had it too. I picked the one that felt best and it was not long before I came out at the edge of the swamp. From there, I could see Stillmeadow, lovely in the spring light and I could hear the excited welcome barking of the dogs. I was coming home to the garden, the lawn, the picket fence, but some of the strangeness remained. As Jill got out the disinfectant, I said, "the woods are so beautiful."

Jill had been hunting along the roads and reported no progress. When I had cleaned up and we had supper, we went out and drove around the countryside, stopping every time we saw the car lights reflected in a cat's eyes. We hunted every day for a week, in fact for some years we never went anywhere without looking for the kitten. We met a great many cats, but none of them were the one and only.

Unlike most cats, Aladdin loved everybody, and we were sure someone whistled him into a car because he was extravagantly beautiful and different. His undercoat was pure apricot, the top was ticked with salt-and-pepper color. His face was wedge-shaped and he had pointed upstanding ears. He charmed everyone, even non-cat people. He followed the dogs everywhere, and this was his undoing because he slipped out that fatal day underneath Jonquil, who has a heavy coat. I thought he was asleep in the lacquer bowl on the cherry table. Jill thought he was, as usual, helping me typewrite, batting the keys and humming away.

A good many people do not think it important when you lose a cat or a dog or a parakeet. But if you lose a being you love, you lose a piece of yourself. We have friends who were in anguish when their parakeet flew through an open door. Their plea in the newspaper was pathetic.

> Lost, parakeet, answers to the name of Philip. He will sit on your hand and say "Hello, my name is Philip. I belong to the Maxwells. They have gone swimming but they'll be back." Please phone Maxwell, 6743, at once.

They got Philip back, and he climbed his miniature ladder,

looked at himself in his mirror, ate a hearty meal, and related his experiences in pure parakeet.

We had a friend who was forced to give away his German shepherd, Brom, for reasons I need not go into. He found Brom a fine home where he would be cherished. Brom was back twenty-four hours later, a little the worse for wear. He was on the back steps when his master came home from work. Perhaps he did not like his new home, thought the owner, so he found another, even better. Three days later, Brom was back, more tired but triumphant. He had traveled forty miles this time to get home. This time he stayed, despite the circumstances.

And then there was the cocker who was left across the river and got on the ferry and rode back for free and went home.

I do not believe in giving dogs away unless they are too young to have become part of the family. Cats are more independent in themselves as a rule but I have known of cats that traveled incredible distances to get back to their own folks. After all, the homing instinct is basic.

April brings spring cleaning, for the mud of March has dried out and the ancient floorboards no longer are patterned with wet paws. I doubt whether many homemakers "turn things out" as they used to. In my childhood fathers had a way of disappearing during this time because the confusion was too much for them. Father did consent to beat carpets on the line, but his beating was so vigorous that Mama feared he would wear the nap off. She replaced him with a college boy who beat idly and carelessly.

It was a time when meals were sketchy and I was asked not to bring my gang home but to play outside. Mama went bustling around, very rosy, her soft dark hair tied up in a kerchief. She never looked prettier than when she was battling the winter's dirt. And this was strange, for Mama was an excellent housekeeper any time of year, and a most efficient one. Somehow she never seemed too busy to sit a while over tea and cinnamon toast with a troubled neighbor. Or to have Father bring home unexpectedly a few of his special students or somebody he happened to meet on campus. Or to read my latest composition.

She never seemed hurried. She did her share of church work
and Red Cross and club work. She also made some of our clothes,
and with the help of a once-weekly cleaning woman all the washing and ironing. The big silver tea service was always polished.
Even the jars of fruit, jelly, preserves, vegetables, in the cellar
were never dusty. What she did not do was garden. She tried
establishing a modest border when we moved into our new house
on the riverbank, but she found out Father kept digging things
up and moving them somewhere else, so she gave that up. She let
Father have his way in the vegetable garden down the hill, which
resulted in our always having tons of one vegetable, such as beans,
but no peas or carrots. When he dedicated himself to tomatoes we
had washbaskets of tomatoes, but that year no beans. He was a
single-minded man.

But spring housecleaning was traditional in our town, and we
spring-housecleaned when everybody else did. And this was pretty
complicated for the time had to be just right. Before the weather
turned really warm but after there was no danger of an April storm.

Came the day when nature was cooperative and all along the
street, banners of carpets and blankets hung out. Mattresses
sunned on porches. Lace curtains on stretchers decorated the
greening lawns. Wash lines were heavy with drapes, damask, satin,
chintz. And husbands and fathers, when they could be caught,
painted the porch furniture.

This was no mean job for most of the furniture was wooden
and had spindle-backs to it. Porch swings were canvas set on an
iron frame which always rusted. The wooden tables were decorated
with fretwork. The truth is, most of the porch furniture was simply
retired house furniture and not designed for porch or yard. A few
families had wrought-iron settees and chairs, admired greatly except by the unfortunate painter.

I think the truth was it was the beginning of America moving
outdoors. Daring souls, like Mama, even served meals on the
porch on hot days. But when we went to the family doctor's we
could, indeed, sit on the big cool screened-in porch but not to
eat. When we ate we went inside to the steaming dining room and
ate privately, out of view of passers-by.

Later came the era of eating in the yard, picnicking, and now we are in the barbecue age, and I fear it is getting pretty civilized. We are overrun with electric gadgets, automatic rotisseries, built-in refrigerator units. This will, I fear, move everyone back into the house eventually. Where the sink is! Some of the most wonderful cookouts we have had have been down by the pond where we built a simple barbecue with iron set in for the grill. The iron was part of the old horse stall in the barn. We put two wide flat stone edges on either side of the fire-hole and that was all. And from this operational base we once gave a clam and lobster dinner for twenty. We used an aluminum folding table and benches because nobody can eat lobster on a paper plate held on the lap. Or nobody but a true Cape Codder who does not really need the plate, just a paper napkin.

As America moved outdoors, the porch furniture became expensive and special, not just castoffs. Some of it is not as comfortable as those old wooden rockers, but it is better looking. The color of chalk-white metal, turquoise or coral plastic upholstery, or lemon and lime canvas is a far cry from the orange and dark green in favor in my childhood. Or even firehouse red. Mama had a sense of color that a decorator might envy and she would never let Father paint the furniture either orange or livid green or red. Ours was usually a modest apple green.

Further, Mama would not have spokes and rockers one color and seat and headrest another.

"No use making it look all chopped up," she said firmly.

During the spring cleaning, she had her annual battle with Father over the storm windows. There were seventy-two and Mama hated them. I have inherited this for I also hate them with a deadly hatred. I do not like to look through two layers, usually clouded, in order to see the outdoors.

But Father was a restless man, to put it gently, and he usually decided to put the storm windows on in September, just to get it over with. This was a fierce job because the house was built at the very edge of a steep hill and it took double extension ladders to get to the upper windows. Father would not hire the job done.

"Can't trust these college boys," he said. And since college boys were THE help for everything in our small college town, that left it up to Father.

But in April, Father had decided that the storm windows might as well stay on because it would be winter again any minute. He conceded the smaller ones because he himself suffocated if the temperature in the house was over sixty. But we had two enormous windows overlooking the swift-flowing Fox River. They were Mama's idea and she had never heard of picture windows but that was what they were. They did not open. They did bring the beautiful drop of the wooded hill and the shining river and the stars and moon practically in the house.

"Now Rufus, you may as well take the storm windows off the big windows," Mama would begin.

"No use," he would say, "I'm going to leave them on this year. Just have to put them back up before you know it."

"But Rufus, nobody leaves storm windows on in summer," Mama would answer.

"I don't care what anybody else does," said Father, and in this he was so right. He never did.

"I don't want to look through two sets of plate glass," Mama pointed out, "besides, I want to wash them."

"I'll hose off the outside," Father offered.

"I want to wash the insides." Mama was firm.

She seldom crossed Father in anything but these storm windows were to her like Custer's last stand.

"You can't get any air there anyway," said Father, "they won't open."

"I told you when we built they should open," said Mama.

"We have enough windows that do open." Father's face was always red at this point.

"I know it's an awful job," Mama would say sweetly, "and I fear it is too much for you. I'll get two of the college boys. It's a two-man job."

At that, with a furious snort, Father would rush down cellar and get out the extension ladders. Fortunately a neighbor always happened by (did Mama call him?) and held the huge windows as Father slid them perilously down.

"I hope you're satisfied," he said savagely to Mama.

By September, Mama began to suggest that these storm windows be left off. The windows didn't open anyway.

"You want to waste all that heat?" Father would say furiously. And back the windows would go.

Spring cleaning was not, really, a peaceful time. Father did not want his study disturbed. "You leave my papers alone," he warned.

"I just want to dust the books."

"I want them just where they are. Don't touch them. And leave my fossils alone too."

Mama chose a time when Father had examinations and was not apt to bolt home for one reason or another. Then she and Mrs. Novak advanced to the sanctum.

"It has to look as if nobody had been in here," said Mama.

In view of the speed necessary, I was enlisted, although usually as a household help, I was a good writer of poetry. I dusted, being careful not to disarrange a single volume. Mrs. Novak did the rug and floor, Mama did the windows and the minerals and fossils. The Indian artifacts got a hasty wipe-off. But the blowfish was a problem. It hung on the wall and was Father's pet. It looked like a very plump porcupine and every spine or quill or whatever caught the dust from our hot-air furnace heat. Cleaning the blowfish was a crisis. And usually just as the job was going on, we would hear Father gunning the motor of the Keeton as he swept into the driveway.

Unfortunately Father had the nose of a bloodhound and as he went into his study he would say, "Somebody's been in here."

"I had to answer the telephone," I would say.

The only telephone in the house was on Father's desk, which enabled him to hear every conversation that went on over it.

"Did that boy call up again?" he would demand.

Now I never lied to Father, I sometimes evaded. The phone had rung while we were madly cleaning, and I was thankful it was not that boy.

"Something about the church," I said.

Mama and Mrs. Novak were scrubbing the kitchen.

"Why don't you stop this infernal fussing?" he asked. "Get out and get some fresh air and exercise." Then he gathered some books up and sped back to his next class.

His final words floated back, "Whole confounded house smells of wax."

So, all in all, spring cleaning was not the most tranquil period in our family life.

I have often discussed whether it is better to have a big spring cleaning and a big fall cleaning, or to clean one room at a time working from top to bottom of the house and then begin again, which might be called cycle cleaning.

There is a particular triumph in having everything done at once, all the curtains, all the rugs, all the floors and all the windows. Spot cleaning does not give this sense of achievement, but it is a lot easier to face four sets of ruffled curtains than fourteen. I do not know how many small windowpanes there are at Stillmeadow, but there are eighty in my room alone. I've just counted them again with disbelief, but there it is. The windows are twelve over eight which means twenty panes to a window. By the time we are through washing them, we have had it. Especially since all the lower panes are smudged with cocker and Irish noses.

The cockers jump to the antique maple day bed and thence to the window sill. They can look down the road and comment on what is happening, and they always press their noses against the glass. Holly can reach the windows from the floor, so that is no problem. The only problem is that I have a clouded view of the road and the swamp.

When Erma comes, she usually goes straight to the windows before she gets out the vacuum cleaner. And Erma can make the windows shine with crystalline clarity, which I never can do. Washing glass is a gift. For me, none of the modern window cleaners does a good job, from which I have to conclude there is something wrong with me as an operator, not with the product. All I can say in my defense is the tiny panes have a lot of corners, and the old bubbly glass ones are a challenge.

As I write, Erma is hanging quilts on the line, and in the pale April sun they glow with color. When they come in they smell of sun and pine, for the clothesline is stretched between two great white pines. The rugs are spread on the young grass to air, but every rug has a recumbent cocker on it. They consider it a special treat.

> He who loves an old house
> Will never love in vain—
> For how can any old house
> Used to sun and rain,
> To lilac and to larkspur,
> To arching trees above,
> Fail to give its answer
> To the heart that gives its love?

A friend sent me these lines, which were found on a wall panel in an old house built before the Revolution in Concord, Massachusetts. Apparently the author did not sign his name or give the date. I should like to have known him. It is possible, of course, the lines were copied from a poet of the time. They sound strangely modern, I suspect they belong to a later period than the house. And also the house must have been already old to have inspired the verse.

In any case, I wish I'd written them, for they are lovely.

There is a special relationship between an old house and the owner. An old house has endured so many storms, sheltered so many people, kept steadfast against time. It speaks of love and happiness and grief, of babies rocked by the great hearth, of young lovers on the settle, of men and women growing old serenely. It speaks of death, for there is the coffin door at the bottom of the steep stairs. The coffin door gives on two stone steps by the wellhouse. The steps are pleasant to sit on in the spring for we have violets on either side, big dark purple and the pale ivory Confederate violets lined with blue. The steps themselves are hand-hewn stone and what a task that must have been, bringing them in and shaping them.

The borning room is sometimes called the birthing room. It is a small room and has no fireplace. I suppose enough heat was thought to come in from the great fireplace in the family room.

But it must have been chilly on winter nights, even with a feather bed. We found the old wooden cradle in the attic. It may not have been the first one, but we like to think it was. It has a sort of wooden hood and the sides are plain slabs of wood. It rocks on hand-carved rockers which are badly worn. Plenty of babies have been rocked in this cradle.

The borning room is now Jill's bedroom and has room for her desk, a pine chest of drawers, a bed, a chair and the bookshelves which line two walls. It is rather small for Jill, who is so tall, broad-shouldered and long of limb. But she says it is cosy and she loves it. When puppies are born, the room goes back to its original use, which is rather interesting. It is the borning room and then the nursery. The small ones stay in a playpen by the radiator with a wooden box at one end lined with shredded newspapers. They sleep in this in a pile of softness, and tumble out to learn the business of walking in the rest of the pen. Jill nailed a double layer of muslin around the pen to prevent draughts. The mother gets in and out when she wishes to, and naps on Jill's bed, which is covered with an old quilt. From this vantage point, she can view her offspring but not be nagged by them!

When the puppies are able to swim in a pan of Pablum, we promote them to the back kitchen, pen and all. And Jill has her own room back. She does not like to sleep in an upstairs bedroom.

"I can't hear what's going on," she says, "can't hear if the furnace goes off or the pump starts pumping for nothing or the puppies get in trouble or anything."

We once tried putting the nursery pen in the front entry which gives off from my bedroom (once a parlor) but my room and the entry are a throughway for all the cockers and Irish and cats and it caused trouble. Jill's room can be shut off. So she resignedly moves upstairs while the puppies are very young.

By the time they are galloping around, climbing the playpen and leading their own lives with vigor, we move them to the kennel to finish housebreaking.

Some people think this is all a silly process. Why not just pop the mother and her babies in the kennel the minute they are born? There are several reasons. In any litter there will be strong puppies who push the smaller ones aside when nursing. If you watch, you see what is happening and pick up the big boys and give the small ones a chance. Then if you have a big litter, as ours usually are (care of the mother?), it is possible for the mother to get distracted and sit down on a little one. And then both Jill and I believe almost any dog is as good as the care and attention he or she gets during the first ten weeks. Kennel-raised puppies seldom have the sunny, secure dispositions that house-raised ones have.

And finally, of course, we just love every minute with the puppies and it is better to have them at hand than in the kennel at the end of the yard. The development of a puppy is a miracle, from the blind squeaking morsel that fits in your palm to the bouncy ball of fur that struggles to get paws coordinated. The day the first puppy has a slit of blue for an eye is a great excitement. The day the two strongest begin to bat at each other is delightful. They wave the raspberry paws, they fall down, they growl fiercely (in a sort of purr). In the end they are both victors and collapse one on top of the other and fall asleep, often with paws outspread. They are "tard out," as Joe says.

When there are more puppies than the mother can manage, we use the nursing bottle and take turns feeding the puppies extra formula every four hours. It makes the difference between a perfect litter or a scraggly one, quite often. And somehow it is well worth staggering up at four in the morning, heating the formula and picking up a morsel of breathing living being. And hearing the busy sucking sound while the paws pad back and forth on your hand. This minute creature has come from a mystery no scientist has yet explained. There is the flat, pushed-in muzzle which will lengthen, there are two ears no bigger than my thumbnail. There are four paws, all provided with velvet pads. And there is the will to live, to grow, to be a big person.

And there is also complete innocence. A four-week-old puppy believes in the world. Love is all he knows. Being held against the neck of a monster is fun. Being kissed is pleasant and right. Even being scrubbed up with lukewarm suds is all right for spilled milk does make a person uncomfortable, it stiffens.

In any litter there are infinite variations of temperament. Jill says it is not true that I can predict what a puppy will become when it is only two days old, but I can. There are always the quick ones, the placid ones, the adventurous ones (who will later get a hole dug under the fence and GET OUT). There are what I call genius types and what I call steady comfortable ones.

As they grow, they tend to fulfill my predictions. When Donna was born, I predicted great things for her and in no time at all she was riding around on the vacuum cleaner. I predicted Especially Me would be placid and easygoing but someone to depend on. (He kills the woodchucks that demolish the garden.) I predicted that Honey and I would never be separated a minute and she turned out to be the best typewriter help I ever had. And I predicted that Linda would have more sheer charm than any puppy we ever had but would be flighty. She was.

How to pick a puppy is the subject of many articles, but I am often asked how to choose one. The way to get the right puppy is to stand quietly and watch all of the litter. If you need a strong, aggressive dog, watch for the one that pounces on the others, bowls them over, gets to the feed pan first, and at once observes YOU. If you wish a gentle, easy puppy, choose the one that sits quietly. A non-pusher and shover. If you wish a difficult but dedicated puppy, ask for the one that stays in the corner of the run and trembles if someone slams a door. For the right owner, such a puppy will be pure delight. For the wrong owner, the puppy will be either abused or brought back to the kennel.

If possible, before you choose a companion for some years, meet the mother and the sire. And watch their behavior. Most children take after their parents, so do most puppies. It is hard to think that many people spend more time choosing a rug or some draperies, which are just things, than in picking out the lovable companion for the family. But often it is true.

However, it may well be the puppy chooses you and you have nothing to say about it. If, out of a bevy, one wiggling morsel suddenly flies to you and looks up with extreme admiration and then begins to chew your shoelaces, this will be it. "You were a long time coming," he or she says.

When we drove to Lexington to visit Paula MacAteer and see

the newest litter sired by the internationally famous Red Star of Hollywood Hills and having Champion Redlog's Strawberry Blonde for a mother, we spent four and a half hours telling each other that we could not have one single solitary dog more.

"It's out of the question," said Jill firmly, as we rolled through Framingham. "Of course it is the best breeding possible in every way, so we should see how the litter has turned out."

"The darlings," I said helpfully.

Paula and Red Star greeted us and Strawberry Blonde, whose call name was Holly, came bounding from the pen and flung her arms around my neck. Red Star, or Rusty, as he was called, withdrew to sit in the biggest armchair. He expected to be photographed. He looked noble.

We went to see the puppies who were six weeks old and all sound asleep except one, who came over instantly and looked at me in THAT WAY. Nothing Paula could say about any other puppy had the slightest effect on me. We went home with Holly. Paula was willing to let us take her at such an early age, though this is seldom advisable. But she decided we had raised so many puppies and knew all about feeding and care, and were a good risk.

This was the hungriest trip we ever had. We were in such a hurry to go and just look, just look, at these puppies that we had a breakfast so light as to be hardly noticed. We had not stopped for lunch. And of course, with our precious cargo, we could not stop a minute on the way back either. If we left her in the car: (A) she might be stolen; (B) the car might be stolen; (C) she would get frightened. So we drove past all the delicious eating places, fortifying ourselves with a cup of coffee from the Thermos.

I had Holly wrapped in a blue blanket and as I carried her into the house, I was really weak with hunger and excitement.

"We better feed her first," said Jill.

It took an hour to feed her, settle her down in her box in my dressing room. Then we scrambled some eggs and had glasses of milk.

It was a quiet night. Usually puppies scream for two or three nights because of the strangeness and the absence of their mother and the rest of the litter. But when Jill came tiptoeing in the next morning, just because she could not stand it another minute, I said calmly, "Everything's just fine."

It was, too. Holly was snuggled in a small red ball on my bed, and she had my second pillow for her head. Her paws were limp and relaxed, and she breathed the quiet breath of security.

"I just picked her up," I said defensively, "because she got lonesome in the dark."

"Well," said Jill, "this is a fine way to begin training her, I must say." And then she delivered the silliest speech of her life. "This is your dog. You will be responsible for her training."

"She just got lonesome," I said.

I may as well admit, she has never been lonesome since. She is now a big Irish, although she made her championship at the exact weight she should be. She sleeps in her accustomed place at the foot of my antique pine bed, but on bitter winter nights she tends to move gradually from her own place.

"Move over," I say.

And these words she understands perfectly. She makes a great to-do about moving over, but she moves. On the other hand when the furnace goes off and the thermometer drops to ten below, I reach out and encourage her to move up so I can warm my freezing hands on her soft clean fur. Since the normal dog temperature is 101, she can be very comforting as snow sifts in on the window sills.

A dog will adjust to almost anything, including living entirely out of doors. Last winter one who did froze to death, and I wonder whether his owners were happy about that. I do not think everyone needs to make dogs members of the family with equal privileges, as we do, but I feel dogs should be warm, have plenty of food, good clean water, and a little affection.

In the end, any relationship we have in this short span of existence depends on what we give to it. On the whole, I would say dogs will put up with more punishment than people. "To him who hath, shall be given" might mean to him who has kindness and loving, shall be given back in double measure.

And what is given back, as far as dogs are concerned, is an undying devotion, an unassailable loyalty, a trust that nothing can destroy. It is almost impossible to make a dog disbelieve in you. And of course this is very wonderful, for you know you have many failings, but not for your dog. To your dog, you are absolutely wonderful. Your cat may criticize you, but never your dog.

Some people do not need to be completely admired, but most of us enjoy the unwavering admiration of the dog we belong to. If a dog sometimes finds you doing very silly things, such as leaving him behind when you go to get your hair done, he only admires you no end for coming home. Oh, joy, there you are back, you wonderful, precious thing.

After all, most of us get enough criticism from friends and relatives. The stresses of the frightening time we live in do not tend to make people easygoing and noncritical. We have become a jumpy nation, living in the shadow of the destruction of the Earth. Sometimes when a group of neighbors gathers, we do not talk of the world situation at all. But we think about it.

Some experts say a dog lives entirely in the present, neither remembering the past nor anticipating the future. This is not true, but it is true a dog savors the delight of any happy moment with no fear that it might be his last. This is something we all would do well to cultivate. The only person I know who can live completely in the moment is Jill. Problems may be pressing, and all sorts of trouble ahead, but as we sit by the fire after supper, with a bowl of apples and mugs of coffee, she invariably gets a shining look in her sea-blue eyes.

"My, I'm happy," she says.

Week-ending begins in spring. City folk feel the ancient urge of mankind to be close to nature again. Besides, the roads are open. There is no danger of sliding into a snowbank or skidding on ice. Jill's daughter and family come early in April. The grandchildren are now five (Stevie) and seven (Betsy). Stevie is a thoughtful dark-eyed thin boy who has a most endearing way of happening to lean against you when he is telling you something about space ships. This makes it easy to slide your arm around him without its being a public affair. He wants to know the WHY of everything, from why the daffodils have different roots from "other things," to why we have a bootjack on the antique pine cabinet. He also wants to know how everything works, and upon being introduced to a folding yardstick spent an hour measuring everything.

Betsy has dark hair but very blue eyes. She thinks like an adult. When her father came home from a business trip she said gravely, "The family isn't complete without you." And when she was describing a cottage the family had rented the summer before, she said, "Now it has no dining room, but the dining area is related to the kitchen."

Most of the time they spend going up and down the stairs.

"Let's climb this mountain," says Stevie.

When resting, Stevie turns the big hearth brush into a horse.

"Look how the world goes up and down for this cowboy," he says.

Betsy watches Jill baste the roast.

"On thinking it over, Grandma," she observed thoughtfully, "I find there is only one thing in the world I do not like, and that happens to be spinach."

Somehow I feel it is a tradition with children not to like spinach, and I wonder when it started. The dislike seems to go from one generation to the next, spurred no doubt by parents who say it is SO GOOD FOR YOU. I think if parents would say, "You are not old enough to eat this," the story might be different. And the truth is, spinach is not what it used to be in most parents' childhood. It is crisp, delicate, savory. I always liked it, but I can remember when you had to cut it with a knife, the leaves were so tough.

But no matter how people feel about spinach, mine is seldom turned down by anybody. I use 1½ cups of chopped cooked spinach, 3 eggs, 1½ cups of grated Cheddar cheese, 2 tablespoons of butter, 2 of flour, ¾ cup of milk and 1 teaspoon of chopped onion. I make a cream sauce with the butter, flour and milk, then when it is smooth, add the onion and cheese and stir until the cheese is melted. I then add the beaten egg yolks and spinach, then fold in the stiffly beaten egg whites. I pour this into a greased casserole and bake in a moderate over (350°) until a knife inserted in the center comes out clean. I set the casserole usually in a pan of hot water since this dish has a lot in common with a custard. It takes usually from forty minutes to fifty-five to bake it. It serves four to six, but three can eat it and not much left over.

This is called spinach soufflé and can be also made with chopped broccoli. It makes a good luncheon dish when company drops in. Especially if you add hot buttermilk biscuits. But it is also good as the main vegetable for supper with country ham and orange and onion salad.

Spinach can be glorified with a spoonful of horse-radish stirred in or one third of a can of mushroom soup. The latter approximates the French way of serving spinach, which I had once in Paris. It had a base of very light fine cream sauce and I do not know what seasonings were added.

April is my birthday month, and Jill cooks my favorite dinner for the day, rock Cornish game hen. She makes a regular stuffing and adds broken pecan meats. The bird is basted with melted

butter and a few spoonfuls of white wine as it roasts. We also like
it with wild rice stuffing but wild rice is pretty expensive nowadays. We have asparagus dressed with lemon butter and a green
salad. Erma bakes an angel-food cake.

And so I fare forth into another year, and it is a good time to
take stock. Have I grown in understanding and love, in patience
and generosity? Have I walked with faith and hope? Have I, in a
small way, contributed to the world? And have I fully appreciated
the wonder and beauty in every day?

One of the most used words in our language is security. What is
security? I remember the innocent days when a war was something
that happened in history, to be studied in books and involved
memorizing dates, which was always a horror to me. So we had
then the security of a world without war. Nobody paid much attention to the Kaiser's carryings-on. And then I remember the day half
the senior class in high school rolled away on a troop train with
Château-Thierry and the Argonne ahead of them. The flags were
flying, the band played, mothers waved, trying not to sob. I ran
along the train to catch a last glimpse of my love, looking beautiful
to me in the ugly uniform of that period. Through the grimy train
window I saw his face, the steady blue eyes, the sunny hair, the
tight mouth.

"It just isn't fair," I cried to myself.

At sixteen the world had exploded and it was NOT fair. We had
grown up in a pattern. We went to school, we went, most of us, to
college, we got married and had babies in due course. Suddenly
that was not the way it was, at all. There was no security in the
world after all. Some came back, lean and hard and with the wrong
kind of memories in their eyes. Some didn't.

And already a new war was a small cloud on the horizon. The
magic excitement of the end of that war was deceptive. Now we
would hardly know how to act without the constant threat of an
earth-destroying war.

There are other kinds of security. Financial security. What this
means is money enough to pay the bills, have the doctor when
needed, go to the hospital. Money enough to educate children,

giving them the best equipment for living. Money enough not to be afraid that next month the mortgage payment cannot be met. We no longer have this. For much of the population, the heavy tax burden and the diminishing dollar spell constant anxiety. The experts all say we are the most prosperous nation on earth, but I know families too proud to ask for welfare aid, and times are very hard for them. Those families who have enough of a backlog of wealth may not shop for stale bread and marked-down soup bones, but they are in trouble too.

"I ought to let most of the help go," said a friend recently. "But what would they do? How would they live?"

It is hardly likely that in our day financial security will be a staple. The struggle to have bigger and better missiles will soak up too much of the national income.

There remains security in love. I realize many people never find this most imperishable security. Those who do are blessed. The one way to possess love is to give it with a whole heart. It always, I think, involves sacrifice of part of oneself. It involves a constantly growing awareness of the loved one. It never involves "making him or her over." It involves discipline. It involves selflessness, very hard to come by.

And there remains security in God, which is an intangible, mysterious proposition. Few of us can envision God. Is He in a place beyond the stellar system or is He a universal force or is He man's imagination built out of need? So far as I know, with the exception of a minority who are able to believe in nothing at all, man has always reached out beyond himself toward the mystery. Belief in the infinite is built into man. Evidently in prehistoric time, men worshiped a spirit which was a glorified animal. The Greeks had many gods but they each had their own sphere and one god ruled.

Possibly a finite spirit cannot understand God. But we do not need to analyze God to have His help. In times of great grief or insupportable trouble, there is an answer when we ask God's help. There is a sense of strength pouring in that only comes from a sense of an infinite being, an infinite power we may avail ourselves of.

With the security of love and the security of God, most of us can manage the alarums and excursions of life.

I woke up yesterday morning to hear the clean sharp sound of an axe in the back yard. In the winter storms, we lost a big maple.

"No use wasting good wood," said Joe, our neighbor. "I'll bring over my saw and take care of it."

What a comfortable sound cutting wood is, I thought, as I started the coffee. In a short time, the branches were piled by the stone fence, and the job of splitting the logs began. There would be enough fireplace material for a season. And the memory of Joe's thoughtfulness would outlast all the fires. I watched him a while, the easy rhythmic swing of the axe, looking so effortless and having such grace. This had been a tall tree with a great trunk. The wood was hard and firm, and it might have lived countless more years, except that it had been sliced open by the force of the storm. We found out why when it came down. It grew, when young, with two forks and in the hollow between the forks decay had set in, weakening the whole structure. Squirrels had secreted nuts in the hole, possibly birds nested there.

Also this one maple stood close to the barn and the fierceness of the barn fire must have affected the side nearest. The tree surgeons had checked all the maples a few years ago but this one, and this one only, had those two main forks and cutting one down would have left a queer half-tree.

I thought it was rather like people who try to shoot off in all directions and do not have a sturdy resistant core. Perhaps trees like people need a single directed growth pattern. It may be better to do a few things well, I thought, than to divide ourselves. We can learn a lot from trees. If this maple had been pruned when it first decided to be two trees, so to speak, it would have had a central trunk firm enough to resist that winter storm as the other maples did. But when it was a sapling, I am sure nobody thought of pruning it. The first owner of Stillmeadow set out the maples (too close to the house these many years later) and then went about the business of clearing enough land for crops.

It may be this maple was not planted except by God for it was outside the gentle circle of giants that guard the house. What we call the house maples were small trees when Paul Revere made his famous ride.

This one was not as old, although we were not able to date it. I am glad to think it was not cut down for a roadway but suffered the natural end of nature. Now and then as we drive around the countryside we see living beautiful trees falling where a development is going up. I always wonder why no trees are left, for later you will see the shocking pink (and it is shocking) and lime green and chocolate houses set close together and never a tree anywhere. I suppose it is cheaper to build if you do not have to go around trees or plan for setting a house with shade trees around it. If you shave the whole land, however, you do not get even a handhold with nature, you just get houses, blinding with heat in summer and windswept in winter.

And it is my observation that people who live in developments do not expect to live there always or to hand the house down as a heritage for their children. So they seldom plant for fifteen or twenty years ahead, they plant quick-growing annuals, put in a few shrubs they can take with them when they go. Of course I shall be accused of unfairness. There are developments where some wooded areas are left, and the slope of the land remains as it was. But these are expensive and many young couples with small children cannot afford them.

Among the millions of laws passed, I would like one which would really regulate developments.

Now the light lengthens as the season moves toward May. Dusk is violet, night cool and tender. Sunrise is luminous. Daffodils star the hill by the pond and bloom in the Quiet Garden. Violets begin to open their pointed buds. We have the tiny white violets in the meadow and the dark purple around the house, and the Confederate violets carpeting the border. The Confederate violets are ivory white streaked with true blue. And by the pond, the dogtooth yellow violets hang their delicate trumpets. In fact, violets love our soil so well that the vegetable garden has hundreds of the purple ones and Jill has to spade them up before planting. I save as many as I can, and must have carried in bushels and bushels, to be set around the giant maple trees, along the picket fence and around the terrace.

At night, the peepers sing away in the swamp, a flutelike sound.

This is the beginning of a new cycle of growth, a quickening of the earth which will only end as the harvest is gathered in the autumn. And as Hal Borland says "Spring is one thing that man has no hand in."

When I go out with the dogs, I feel a quickening in my spirit too. The season of bloom is upon us, and then the green summer days, and at last the ripeness of autumn, all ordered and unchanged by the world's dissensions. It is something to count on.

Humbly I thank God for the eternal miracle of spring.

May

THE magic of May evokes apple blossoms. All down the valley the apple trees explode into beauty. In the early days every settler who cleared his land, built his house, and put in his garden, set out his orchard. In many places now, the house and barn are gone, the cornfields overgrown and the woods crowd closer, but the old orchard remains. On our land there are two such and there were, before one hurricane, fifteen apple trees set behind the house.

Some of the trees bear pink bloom but most of them open into snowy white. They fill the air with sweetness. Later there will be apples, chiefly windfalls but sweet to the taste if you watch for the wormholes. The main crop is the loveliness in May, and well worth it.

There are not as many pear and peach trees, but occasionally a pear blooms by itself in a meadow, straight and silver as a sword. And there are scattered peach trees. There is one commercial orchard not far away, but this is not a countryside for commercial fruit raising such as Dutchess County in New York State. Many people drive there to see the trees in bloom and they are a fine sight, but I prefer the casual ancient orchards. Trees are too businesslike when lined up like ranks of soldiers and pruned to a fare-thee-well.

I felt the same way when we visited California and saw the miles and miles of orange groves. They were spectacular but not a wonder like the trees in our friends' back yards. The groves reminded me of bowling alleys. I think I like natural grace in any area rather than formalization. But as Jill would say, I am not an orchardist trying to make a living from fruit. Scientific methods get bigger and better crops.

In Door County in Wisconsin the cherry trees stretch to the horizon and break in white foam of bloom. When I was growing up, we always went to see the cherry trees blossoming. But all the glory is really in one tree, a tree you know and love, all the mystery of bloom in one branch.

Lilacs are in bloom now, and narcissi. They bloom in almost every dooryard. In fact they bloom where there is no longer a dooryard. Often only a stone chimney may be left where a house once stood.

Who lived here? Where are they gone? Do their spirits come back in lilac time, surely in lilac time, when the air sings with fragrance? Did they build the vanished house for future generations? If so, why was the place abandoned? Lovingly it could have been rebuilt on the same site, for the ancient stone foundation is here. Never mind, the secret belongs to the long ago, and we must not disturb it. It is permissible to gather a few lilacs in memory of those who planted them.

Once Jill and I came upon an ancient house which had not burned. It had four rooms, as I remember, and evidently some sort of ladder arrangement to get to the attic where the children slept. The fireplace was almost as big as the family room. We were invited in by the swinging back door, and spent a brief time furnishing the house and making up its family. By the back door, a stand of lovely iris was blooming. I can only call it pinky and ivory. Jill carefully lifted several.

"I wish I had time to separate them all and replant them all around the house," she said wistfully, "just for whoever put them in. They're choking to death."

We stuffed a broken shingle in the back door to keep it closed. We promised to come back, and we did, in spring, for several years. Then one day when we drove down the rutted grass-grown road, there was nothing there. The house had gone, and all we found was the doorstone. Even the iris had vanished.

"I'm glad I could save a little of it," said Jill.

As I washed the milk glass this morning, I reflected that we are all collectors at heart, whether we are aware of it or not. Now a collection is not something you buy all at once, collecting is an act. When I read of someone buying a whole collection of valuable paintings, I do not call it the buyer's collection. It is the collection of the one who worked at making it. It doesn't really matter what you choose to collect, just so your own activity is involved.

Our milk glass collection began with a single 101 salad-size plate. We loved its translucent white and the filigree edge (it does look like the numbers 101 repeated). Some time later, we found a covered dish, a placid hen sitting on an oval basket-weave bowl. Once when we were in New York, we spent all day getting lost in Brooklyn because a friend said she had seen a swan compote in a junk shop. Her directions were vague, but she said there was an antique quilt in the window of the shop. Brooklyn we found a rather large place in which to find an antique quilt. It was nearly dark when we did, and the proprietor was just locking up, but he let us in when we begged. I think our state of exhaustion moved him, for of course most of the time we had walked. You can't whisk along in a bus and see one quilt in one dusty shop window.

There was the swan compote, glowing in the dingy shop. And we did, between us, have money enough to pay for it. All the way back we were terrified for fear it would be broken. It was elegantly protected by almost enough old newspaper but not quite. And by then, it was the rush hour. I remembered that day as I washed the swan compote and set it back in the corner cupboard. The lacy-edge plates, the swan salts, the blackberry egg cups, all have memories for us. Some of the most cherished pieces, given us by friends, have been a special joy.

Jill has always said that whatever you collect should be used, and there came the time when we had enough to set a table with 101 (and some lacy-edge and the blackberry goblets, but never mind). We broke one of the very rare rope-pattern cups by washing it in too-hot water. After that we used warm water, mild suds, and a careful rinse.

Came the day we finally got the dishwasher. We then began to use the milk glass just for dessert and washed it by hand while the dishwasher boiled away at the sturdy modern china. And we use the nappies (small dishes) for nuts, bonbons or currant jelly. I use the

mugs and spooners and creamers for bouquets. But we no longer serve dinner for six entirely on milk glass, because we weakly admit the dishwasher is a girl's best friend. The milk glass fills the corner cupboard and the old pine cupboard across the family room and at night when the fire burns on the hearth, it sends a pearly glow over the room.

There are many kinds of collections, I thought, carrying the dishpan back to the kitchen. Thoreau, for instance, wouldn't give a fig for our milk glass. Thoreau retreated to his hut at Walden Pond and made his great contribution to mankind in surroundings not suggesting a collector—a bare table, a stool or chair—a pen. In fact the one object he collected was a stone which he found on his ramblings and brought back to the hut. Perhaps it was a chunk of rosy quartz or a piece of granite with glacial scratches. I would like to know. But Thoreau shortly afterward threw it out, for it was a thing extra.

No, he would not collect even a stone. Yet he was a collector who put his life into collecting nature, from sunsets over Walden Pond to the tides on Cape Cod. When he walked the length of Cape Cod, he studied the beach grass, the terns riding the air currents, the dunes, the thickets farther inland. He observed the habits of sea clams and ate one and was quite sick. Food never bothered him except in this instance, for he stopped to eat blueberries or munched an apple as he studied the breaking waves.

In other words, he collected Cape Cod. But I do not think he took a single shell back with him. He didn't need to. He was a great naturalist, a profound philosopher. He has left a priceless heritage in Walden Pond, although this collection has been devastated of late. But Walden Pond as he wrote of it is forever. All the time he collected ideas.

"Time is but the stream I go a-fishing in. I drink at it; but while I drink, I see the sandy bottom and detect how shallow it is. Its thin current slides away, but eternity remains."

Shakespeare was a different kind of collector. He collected individuals with their particular character, tossed by life, reacting to its stresses according to their pattern. His collection was actually mankind, from the trivial Rosencrantz and Guildenstern to the tragic Lear. His characters, so carefully interpreted, so fully evoked, he made immortal.

Few of us may ever be great collectors, and what we collect may not have value for generations to come. Our collection may be personal—my grandmother collected bits of silk from her friends and later made a silk patchwork quilt.

"That was Emily's wedding dress," she would say, pointing to a tiny bit, "and that was your mother's first party dress."

Yes, she had her collection, and I may say, it was an exquisite quilt. It wasn't exactly useful, but it was lined with deep blue silk and edged with wide handmade lace, and sometimes I take it out of the cedar chest and admire the tiny stitching and wish I could remember all the stories about it.

"I wouldn't bother collecting anything," someone once said to me. "I don't like a lot of stuff to take care of."

Nevertheless, she, too, is collecting. She cannot help it. Nobody can live a lifetime without a collection of a kind. The boy collects the color of autumn as he goes to gather butternuts. The father adds the sight of the red fox drifting along the edge of the thicket, brush flying behind. Almost every woman cherishes the sound of the voice of her first love, "My darling."

Some people collect differently. Some collect grudges and take them out from time to time to refurbish them. Some collect self-pity and envy. (I can't afford a fur coat because George never gets a raise though Mr. Barker does.) (Of course the Jewetts have a new car, but WE have the old coupé.)

Then there are the collections of jealousies. These seem to be easy to collect and come in many varieties from the jealousy of a wife when her husband admires another woman to deadly professional jealousy, to name just two.

Like all collections, once you begin them, they grow. Once a single grudge is collected, inevitably more come. And, naturally, children are apt to inherit the parents' collection. It is well to be sure we collect the valuable intangibles which will enrich the small portion of eternity which is our time.

When I went to cut the asparagus this morning, I startled a pair of young rabbits. They were leaping in the air, chasing each other, spinning in half circles, graceful and gay as dancers. They were half-grown bunnies celebrating spring with proper joy. When they saw me, they hopped into the raspberry bed.

"Have fun, Flopsy and Mopsy," I said.

And as I cut the asparagus, I decided they would never go hungry with the vegetable garden at hand. Stillmeadow rabbits are prosperous, what with all the lettuce they can eat, as well as carrot tops and beet tops. Sometimes Jill feels she plants mainly for the rabbits.

"We ought to TAKE STEPS," she says.

But of course we never do. Rabbits are charming and innocent. My favorite is the big buck who lives under the kennel. He comes out to eat sweet clover, of which he is very fond. And he comes out when the yard is full of cockers and when the Irish is only a few leaps away. When they all rush at him, he cocks an ear and retires with dignity to his hole. The remarkable thing is that he does not hurry. He knows exactly how much time he has before Jonquil gets to him. If he is still hungry, he waits until the furor dies down and the dogs have gone off to bark at the milk truck and then he placidly comes out and resumes his clover dinner.

There are times when I think he has an understanding with the dogs. They can have the fun of chasing him, but must not try to dig him out. Because they never do try, although they make endless excavations at the opposite end of the kennel after whoever lives there. I often think if the kennel were lifted up by a hurricane a whole world would be discovered underneath. For the kennel foundation could hardly be called tight. There are field mice, sometimes skunks, probably other rabbits, and—I hesitate to say—perhaps rats who may prefer it to the barn across the road.

The kennel building has had an interesting existence. It was built by former owners who raised fancy pheasants as a hobby. A second building was put up beside it. For a long time we called them pheasant house one and pheasant house two. We stored odds and ends in them. Then Jill remarked they really looked like summer cottages. They are bigger than some summer cottages and had big slide windows on three walls. The flooring was excellent, well laid. And the roofs and siding were good. When I mentioned the foundations, Jill said many summer cottages only had dry stone foundations and as long as these held up the buildings, why worry?

At once the girls seized on the idea and demanded we give them pheasant house one. For some reason there was no evidence that birds had lived in them and we figured the line of smaller pens with chicken houses which occupied part of the meadow, housed the pheasants. There were many mysteries about Stillmeadow owing to the former owner's having murdered his wife and killed himself.

In any case, we painted the inside of pheasant house one and shellacked the floor and furnished it with pieces moved from pheasant house two. We hung curtains of gay chintz, put down a big grass rug. It made a pleasant retreat for the girls until they were ready to move to our world again.

After they went away to school, we used to go out there in late afternoons and sip our mint-cool tea. Just why it had that curious charm, I've often wondered. The furniture ranged from wicker to mahogany. Nothing matched anything. Maybe the windows had something to do with it, for they were enormous and lowered on ropes, so when you let the ropes down, you were looking right at the woods on one side and the swamp on another.

And a New England swamp is beautiful. It has nothing in common with the dark ominous cypress swamps or the great swamps in the Midwest. It is a place of sun and light and color. Hundreds of small bushes find a foothold on the hummocks and in summer it is bright with birds. In autumn it burns with swamp maple, is garnet with huckleberry, scarlet with black alder. From one side of the pheasant house, we could really study the swamp, from the other we watched the birds in the wild berry thicket.

And it was quiet since we were away from the ringing of the party-line telephone. But, in time, we retired it as a summerhouse for a perfectly logical reason. It needed new curtains and new paint and we were working ten hours a day and did not have the energy to redo the place. Some of the screens had rusted out and several of the ropes rotted so we had to go outside and hammer the windows up and down.

But the pheasant house was not done with. A few years later, the barn and kennel burned down, leaving us with a bevy of cockers who were too many to be in the house all at once. Fortunately we did not also have a couple of litters of puppies at that time. And so we called Cliff Hirsch, our friend who is a builder, and inside of a week we had two kennel units built into the front part of the pheasant house. Cliff insulated them, installed good sleeping units, laid a linoleum floor, added two big runs and we put in an electric panel for heat.

Now names are strange, for after all the years, we still call those two buildings pheasant house one and pheasant house two. It is as if identity once established is permanent. This is not, I may say, peculiar to us. When we moved here, our place was called the Oxford Pheasant Farm. Today, years later, we may meet someone who asks where we live and when we describe Jeremy Swamp Road, he says, "I know, you live on the Oxford Pheasant Farm."

And I notice when I ask Erma where the Bannisters live, for instance, she says, "They live in the Bascom house. The Greenes lived there for four years and the Fosters bought it. When Mr. Foster died, Mrs. Foster sold it to the Bannisters." In short, it may have passed through a number of ownerships, but it is still the Bascom house and always will be. This is the reason that we call Victor Borge's house the Wallace Nutting place. (It belonged for years to the Ballentines.)

Sometimes I wonder, famous as he is, whether Victor Borge minds just living in the Wallace Nutting house!

I suspect in future years people will say, "Stillmeadow? You take the first road past the Kettletown Road—it's the Oxford Pheasant Farm." For if thirty years of this being Stillmeadow has not changed the name, it is not likely ever to be changed. Personally, I like this custom, although I do not know why, particularly since it means my dear name, Stillmeadow, will vanish, and it is certainly more euphonious than Oxford Pheasant Farm. One does not have to have reasons for everything.

The true New Englander seldom does give reasons. If you ask, "Why is it called Johnnycake Lane?" He will answer, "It always has been."

I did find out about Witch's Hill for that was where the witch of Woodbury lived. She had a son and they lived in some kind of shack. But I have not yet found out how she became a witch or what became of her. I do know she was not hanged or burned because this would be told.

The terrible fever of Salem did not reach this far and visitors with a taste for horror have to take the highway toward Boston.

They may stop off at Glebe house in Woodbury, which was the home of the first Episcopal bishop ordained to preach in America. The Glebe house is laid out exactly as Stillmeadow is, but is more elegant. The rooms are larger, the stairway more graceful, the bedrooms bigger. As befits the house of the Reverend, it has paneling in the master bedroom, and lovely paneling it is. There is also a secret opening by the parlor fireplace which led to a tunnel which opened probably in the house of a notable Tory, Jabez Bacon. At that time, the bishop was forbidden to minister to his flock. However, since nobody was arrested on Sunday, he preached his sermons in the parlor on Sunday and then slipped into the tunnel. It occurs to me the Tories were admirable. Because he had to be within reasonable distance of the manse to get there every Sunday for the services. So why was he never discovered during the week? True, most of the early houses had secret rooms, but as he was slipped from one to another somebody must have seen him. Perhaps he had more sympathizers than were on record.

However, feeling against the Tories ran high as times grew from bad to worse. The "Committee of Inspection" ordered that no grain should be ground for the Tories, so either grain was ground for them in the name of Whig friends or they were forced to use the same mortars as the early settlers. During the entire war, salt was of prime importance, and the committee seized all that Jabez Bacon had (and he was a shrewd and prosperous merchant; the early books call him "opulent").

The salt was to be distributed (for a price) at the "Hollow Store." The story, as related by William Cothren in his *History of Ancient Woodbury* (1854) may be true, may not be. Mr. Cothren was what I would call an emotional historian.

However, as the crowd lined up for the salt, Dr. Obadiah Wheeler appeared. He, Cothren says, "was understood to entertain AFFECTIONATE FEELINGS for the 'mother country,' and frequently reprehended MOBS."

An ardent Whig cried out, "Ah, Doctor, I thought you were a hater of mobs? Why do you show yourself here?"

"It is true I hate mobs," said the doctor, "like the Devil, but necessity is mother of many shifts. I MUST HAVE SALT!"

I am glad to think the good doctor who retained affectionate feelings for the mother country and hated mobs, did get his portion of salt.

What must have been hard on the women was that mourning dress was restricted to a black crape (*sic*) or riband on the arm for the gentlemen and black riband and necklace for the ladies, and the giving of gloves and scarves at funerals was discontinued.

The first major rallying of men came in September, 1774, when the report came that British ships were cannonading Boston and troops slaying the inhabitants. Two thousand Connecticut men began to march toward Boston. It must have been a strange homecoming when they were turned back by the report that Boston was safe. It was a preview of many marches to come when many did not return.

It was 1784 when the French troops with General Lafayette came down the valley. They camped between Middle Quarter and White Oak and the soldiers whose tents were near the Sherman house are reported to have eaten twelve bushels of apples and drunk seven or eight barrels of new cider. This must have made them merry at the ball given for the officers, for the sound of music and laughter drifting out was better than the sound of cannon.

As the war ground on, some of the Revolutionary soldiers slipped home to help the young boys and women with the crops. Then they would rejoin their regiment and begin fighting again. Eight years after the battle of Lexington, the war was over and I am sure it did not seem believable for war had become a habit. Now the habit of peace meant beginning life all over for those left alive.

By 1854 Southbury was established as a separate town (the second ecclesiastical society of Woodbury was so incorporated). It was then eight miles from east to west and four in width. It had two Congregational societies and two Methodist societies, all worshiping separately. It had about 1,500 inhabitants. It seems incredible they needed four houses of worship for 1,500, but that was the way it was!

Usually in New England this separation rose over the ministers. If one group wished one minister and another group preferred another, they had two churches. Whatever the reason, Southbury had enough places of worship. It also had three taverns, four blacksmith's shops, several shoe shops, a saddler's shop, four gristmills, ten sawmills, one paper mill, a satinet "manufactury" and several others. I have spoken of this before, but I like to think of Southbury in those days, with even a tinware "manufactury" and a shear one (whatever that is), for it would seem that a start was made after the Revolution toward an industrial center, which was later abandoned. The community became a rural country village and only now shows signs of changing.

When we came, it had the general store, with the post office in part of it. It had a garage, in an old wooden structure, and it had what we called the Triangle, a three-sided stand where the best homemade pies and the hottest coffee were served. The church, built in 1732, is one of the loveliest I have ever seen with its simple Colonial lines and perfect spire rising toward the sky. But when I go to the village for groceries, mentally adding Bullett Hill School to my early list—not far from the school I notice where a small grist-mill stood, operated by the stream that crosses the village. Remains of this may be still seen. I would like to go back in time for a few hours and walk around my village as it was during the Revolution. I'd like to know where Captain John Minor, the Town Clerk in 1672, had his office. And I'd like to see a Post rider pulling up his horse and calling out the news of Bunker Hill.

I'd like to go back and be there when the news of the defeat of the British finally reached this remote spot. With the thankfulness

and the triumph, there must have been women weeping, and wondering how to go on alone. And there must have been anxiety about the future and more hard times to come.

And I think the valley looked strange to the men straggling back, bone-weary and hungry, and sick of war. Peaceful with the sweet-running brooks and the fertile fields and green hills. But with so much work to be done, they must have paused, and prayed to God for strength.

Whenever I hear people say, "This will help to pass the time away," I wonder at them. We all have just so much time and just "passing it away" is rather like throwing jewels down a well. For reasonably healthy persons, it is extremely selfish. I doubt whether there is a place in our country where there is nothing at all to do. Someone always needs help. Oddly enough, the handicapped or ill seldom speak of just passing the time away. One of the most-occupied women I ever knew was flat on her back dying of cancer. She was busy all day planning becoming dresses for her friends, and when she received a package of samples of various materials, she used them as a color chart.

"I've saved this violet for you," she would say, "because there is violet in the blue of your eyes."

"This sea-green silk will be just right for you," she would decide, "and a hat in a darker shade, I think."

As it happened, this was when I was growing up, and in the small Wisconsin town many women made their own clothes or called in the gifted dressmaker who made the wedding dresses and such. And Helen had an eye for color and texture. She had a gift, and nobody will ever know what she might have done with it, except for her illness. But when friends came to see her, on the days she could see anyone, they consulted her and she had a thriving business as a planner. Never once did she complain of lying there passing the time away. She kept the swatches of colored material spread on a small table by her bed, and I used to be allowed to help her sort them out.

When she had a spare hour, she planned the planting for the raggedy green in our area from which the light pole sprouted. Everyone contributed the plants she decided on and the green was a place of blossoming from spring until late autumn.

Although she was young when she died, she did not leave a memory of a useless life and of suffering, but a memory of a useful and busy time.

We took a drive this week to Salisbury to spend a few hours with Hal and Barbara Borland. The Borlands live on Weatogue Road in a farmhouse beside the river. Behind the house the land rises to become a moutain, and this gives the homestead what I can only call a snug look, although I am not fond of the word snug. The country seems wilder than ours but that may be because we are not used to it. The road winds along the Housatonic in a timeless sort of fashion.

Inside the house you enter a big, comfortable living room, and beyond it is an addition Hal built which is what I call a sun and winter room. It has comfortable couches, low tables, and a view of the slope. On the other side of the house is a dining room (we have none) and what the magazines call a dream kitchen. And it needs to be, because the Borlands are gardeners who raise everything you can name, freeze and put up annually enough supplies for a siege. And Barbara as a cook deserves that word genius. She also sparkles as she cooks, which is an art in itself.

If there is any skill Hal lacks, we have yet to discover it. Jill is gifted in building and carpentering, repairing plumbing, refinishing antiques, and as a gardener, a good match for Barbara. But how she admires Hal for being also a woodsman, a naturalist, and a man who can lay up stone walls. And she agrees with me that Hal is one of the very, very few writers of our day who continually dazzles and delights. I sometimes say despairingly, "Hal, couldn't you write just ONE average book?"

On this particular day we sat around the Franklin stove for it was cool enough for the "small busy flame" that Keats so loved. At some period, this house lost its fireplace but the Franklin stove has its own charm. Pat was on the Navajo rug and we talked about him, a quiet black and white hound who drifted in during a December snowstorm and came to stay. Pat has great dignity, great reserve, and if I tried to relate even a few of his exploits, I would be copying pages from Hal's book about him, *The Dog Who Came to Stay*.

All Hal says in conversation is, "Pat's a notional dog."

"What do writers talk about?" I am often asked.

Well, for one thing, they do talk, for writing is essentially a lonely affair. When writers do emerge from the necessary isolation during which they talk only to the typewriter, talk reminds me of a freed brook after winter loosens his hold. But the writers I know best, seldom talk about their books. For instance, when we spend a day with Hal and Barbara Borland, they admit they are working on books and I admit I am working on a book. Then we begin to discuss why birds are changing their migratory patterns, what effect man's conquest of space will have on man's view of the universe, and which is the best way to make bouillabaisse.

Hal relates the struggle he had when a skunk got into the cellar and he used Barbara's French perfume to spray into the ducts upstairs. I tell about my experience getting Holly away from a very big skunk who was sitting by the front door when I let her out at night. Jill describes what happened to the tulips when she was advised to plant them with mothballs. (We had a fine crop of mothballs, no tulips.) Barbara talks about the very best new nature book (excluding Hal's).

And when we leave, we drive away in sunset light. Hal stands on the steps waving, smiling his warm quiet smile and Barbara runs out with a carton of such things as wild raspberry jam. Pat may or may not be visible, according to how this notional dog is occupied at the moment, but Holly hangs out of our car wagging her tail.

"It's hard to say good-bye to the Borlands," Jill says.

When Faith Baldwin spends a month with us, I note that the time we spend talking about our work is negligible. But we seem to talk about everything else, past, present, future. I am always hoarse after a day or so.

So what I think is that most writers, at least those I know, find that sharing ideas and feelings and observations is vital. But the writing self is separate, although greatly enriched. I have never seen the manuscript of any writer I know well until it is published. And as far as the profession goes, the most one says is, "I am having a rough time with the middle of this book."

This may be peculiar to writers. I notice lawyers talk about their professional life to other lawyers, doctors do so too. Teachers, in any category of teaching, go right on teaching wherever they are. Business folk are always full of ideas as to business. Painters talk about painting, and that's that—and most interesting. The painters I know are delightfully verbal. And musicians can talk music by the hour.

And of all subjects, gardens call forth the greatest response. Gardeners who meet need no introduction, they plunge in at once. All I can figure out is that writers are rather shy, as a rule. Some of the very young ones do wish to tell how wonderful everything they write is and just WHY. But I notice this is first-book or second-book people.

Sometimes I wish I could talk about what I am working on. But I settle for explaining it to Holly who could not care less!

When the lilacs bloom, I look for my unicorn. Yes, I know the unicorn is a legendary animal, but my unicorn and I do not care about that. We are quite real to each other and isn't that what counts? He comes from the woods, usually at dusk, walks delicately down the hill, cropping the violets as he moves. When he dips his head to drink at the pond, his silver horn catches the last light. I met him first many years ago, on a night of full moon. I went down to the pond to watch the moon in the water, and at first I thought my unicorn was a flowering hawthorn bush at the edge of the woods.

It would be nice if it were a unicorn, I thought.

And so it was. I could even see his silver hooves as he moved down the hill. As he always has, he cropped the violets. Through the years, he has acquired many friends, who ask, "Has the unicorn come yet?" But nobody has ever seen him except me. And, of course, I only see him at this time of year. He goes back to his own country and where it is, I do not know. But he gives me assurance that there is still magic in the world when he comes in lilac time.

Most of us need something beyond bread-and-butter reality. Children come naturally by a sense of wonder, which parents often discourage.

"Mommy, the dark's coming through the door locks," said Jerry Austin, a very special boy. And so it does, if you see it that way.

"My son has an imaginary playmate called Herman," said a friend, "and he won't believe Herman isn't real."

This can be a nuisance for parents. Setting the table for Herman, waiting until he finds his own swimming suit before the family can go to the beach, getting lost in the woods at a picnic and having to be hunted for.

"There's Herman!"

A tired and badgered family may wish that Herman would get lost forever.

But Herman, until he vanishes to comfort some other lonely boy, is an important member of the family.

I was a lonely child, for we moved about so much, owing to Father's being a mining engineer (before he settled down to be a professor). I never had a chance to be part of a group, I was the stranger. This was probably why I passionately loved the town in which we finally did have a house to STAY in. But I had friends who went with me everywhere. I used to tell my mother I had spent the morning under the mock-orange bush, visiting with the fairies. Even now I can close my eyes and see the green tent of the big bush, and smell the rich scent, and feel the happiness when the fairies came. There never was just one fairy, they came in a group, all together and they always were together. They imparted a great deal to me which I wouldn't repeat even if I could, for it was between the fairies and me.

Mama never accused me of "making them up." Also she had the rare gift of never prying so she asked no questions as to what they looked like and what they said to me. And when I acquired my imaginary puppy, she did not ask where he came from. I owned my imaginary puppy for some time, he was a smallish brown curly-haired puppy and he slept at the foot of my bed. If I had bad dreams and woke up, I knew he was there and went back to sleep.

It was not long before Father brought Brownie home. Brownie was an American water spaniel, a smallish, brown curly-haired puppy. In a curious way Brownie seemed to be that other puppy, but everybody saw Brownie, and there were visible evidences of his presence in chewed rubbers, frayed couch covers, empty food dishes. And visitors would say, "Oh, I see you have a puppy!"

Brownie was the first of an unlimited number of dogs in my life. By today's standards, he wasn't spectacular, and I think the American Kennel Club does not recognize the American water spaniel as a separate breed at the moment. He grew to be a size between the cocker and springer spaniel, and he had the disposition of an angel. He was an excellent hunter, good enough so Father didn't complain. When he hunted by himself, he brought home dead fish from the riverbank, moldy bones from some garbage can, and other things worth retrieving.

When Brownie was poisoned, I went into such a state of grief that Father said we would never have another dog. He added he would shoot the dog-poisoner (every town has one) as soon as the police found out who it was. If they did, they were careful not to tell Father, for his temper was well known. Father went around with swollen eyelids himself but kept telling me that crying wouldn't bring Brownie back. This made me cry harder. But eventually he bought me my Irish setter, although it took years to wear him down.

I have had rabbits, canaries, goldfish, and, more important, cats. My first fluffy grey kittens were named Amherst and Johns Hopkins, for Father's alma maters. They constantly climbed the lace curtains then in vogue, tearing out claw patterns. They could go up, but not down. They clung to the curtain rods and screamed, and since the rooms had very high ceilings, it took a ladder to fetch them down. They also climbed the highest tree in the yard and Father was red in the face as he got the long ladder and then worked his way up in the branches. When he got them, they scratched him.

"Confound those cats," he swore. "They've got to be given away. I won't have this sort of thing going on."

But when they got in the furnace flue, he was speechless. It was a hot-air furnace, fortunately not on at the time, and there were registers in every room. The frantic maaowing seemed to come up through every single register. Mama and I hid in the kitchen while Father banged around in the cellar, shaking the whole house. When he came back upstairs with two sooty wild kittens, he looked like a chimney sweep. It's as well not to report the scene that followed. Later, Mama and I discussed how those kittens got in the flue in the first place and, what was more, how Father got in too. He never said.

The rabbits were relatively peaceful pets except for getting out of their pen and being chased by a bulldog. They were so well behaved that when Father was away, Mama let me bring them in the house for an hour or so. They were intoxicated by the fun of racing around the sun porch. Occasionally one would hop to the kitchen.

"Mama, they talk to each other," I said.

They did, too. One would thump several rabbit thumps, then wait. Answering thumps came back from the other part of the house. These thumps would be replied to with either more or fewer raps, depending on what they were saying. They would hold quite a conversation before they hopped back together and I took them out to their pen.

I am sorry for children who grow up without pets. I admit they may be a trouble, they get into things, they need care, they make extra work, and when they die, they break our heart. But they add a richness to a child's life that nothing else does. And if the pet happens to be a dog, the love and loyalty and companionship cannot be exaggerated. There is something sad about a boy or girl who walks alone down the road, and something happy about a boy with a puppy over his shoulder and a girl with a dog skipping ahead.

Naturally not all dogs can accomplish such feats as Lassie does, and I am glad of it. But we all hear tales of dogs who save children from drowning, save people when the house is on fire, and there is the mongrel who leaped in front of his child-owner and took the bite of the deadly snake and gave his life to save his master. But one story I like is of the man waiting for the police to trace his stolen car. The telephone rang, and when he answered a strange voice said, "I'm the man who stole your car, but I don't want it. It runs badly, there isn't enough gas, and I'm tired of hearing your dog whimper even though I spent a dollar and a quarter for meat for him. You'll find your watchdog and car parked at the corner of State Street."

Now it is planting time, and all the packets of seeds that seemed so small in February take on huge proportions. Jill, like most gardeners, cannot resist planting too much. Take beans. You cannot have anything better than freshly picked, very young beans cooked quickly and dressed with butter, freshly ground pepper and salt, with a spoonful of cream or top milk added for sauce. But beans produce madly and comes a time you can hardly face another huge basketful of beans. I have been writing about this for a long time, but no seedsman has come out with beans guaranteed to bear only five beans to a bush. In fact, they go on making them bear MORE.

The layman might say, "Why don't you plant just a short row?"

Ah, but the true gardener gets in a fever of planting. This is the way it goes: I'll put in one more row. We can freeze them. Some of them won't come up anyway, better plant enough. The bean is one of the noblest vegetables when it is very young and very fresh. Who's to say whether the green or the wax is best? Put in enough of each. Must save some seeds for succession planting.

Jill is the gardener but I encourage this sort of thing. "Be sure we have all kinds of squash," I say.

In the beginning, I was supposed to help plant but Jill gave that up when it became apparent that I could never get the seeds along the string stretched across the garden to mark the row. What I planted came up wiggling like a snake, which made hoeing very difficult. Also what I planted came up in clumps.

"You didn't just sift them along evenly," said Jill, which was the understatement of all time. "You keep out of the garden, you can help cook and can and freeze."

Sometimes I was allowed to pick things, which I dearly love to do. But when I picked beans, often the whole bush came right along with the beans. I had worse trouble digging potatoes because the fork always cut the best potatoes in half. Jill would toss up a whole hill with just a few nicks, but this didn't happen to my hill.

My forte is berry-picking. I can fill a pail of blueberries while Jill is still hunting for the right bush. She is slowed also by looking for snakes. I thrash along, singing, on the theory the snakes will go away. Before the land was sold, we used to go blueberrying in about the wildest thickets I've ever tried to negotiate. Not many people went there, either on account of the terrain or the belief there were copperheads there. There were also the biggest and bluest blueberries and huckleberries. Once Jill got lost, but I found her by figuring if I were Jill, which direction would I take? I also felt she would stay as much in the open as she could, where she would see the snakes first.

We went there for some years and I only saw one snake. He was a big prosperous snake, important as a banker, and he must really have been sound asleep not to have heard my singing. I almost stepped on him, and I lost part of a pailful of berries as I leaped back. I did NOT stop to see whether he was a copperhead or an adder or just a plain common snake.

I like to watch Jill plant for she moves so tall and easy along the rows and her face is absorbed and completely happy. I am sure if I called that the house was on fire, she would answer absently that she would be in in a few minutes, just one more row of carrots to go in.

As I went for the mail, I felt the sugar maples were singing for the birds shook the leaves with music. Often our guests from the city cannot sleep when the birds begin so early in the morning. The yellowthroat's Wichety-wichety and the song sparrow's caroling and the redwing's Ocalee-ocalee seem to wake them up. But when we go to the city, the traffic deafens us, I keep waiting for things to quiet down. Which only proves that we all grow accustomed to the sounds among which we live.

To me, country sounds seem surrounded with the largeness of space while city sounds are bottled up, for they have no place to go. Even when there is a severe noise like the snowplough coming at midnight, which sets all the dogs into a frenzy, there is a sense of the profound silence stretching over the valley and up the hills.

However, before we moved to the country, I used to listen to the all-night trucks rolling by and get a great deal of pleasure imagining them bound for far places, riding through the night, companioned by stars. I pictured the sleeping towns and villages they rolled through, the open farmlands and dark hills they passed by, the wide rivers they crossed. It gave me all of our vast mysterious country, as it were, in the furious grind of the gears.

Actually, the only time I rode in a truck, I clung to the window edge hoping my teeth (all my own) wouldn't be jarred out. Also, I was slightly seasick. I'd hardly have been alive after a cross-country ride!

It is difficult not to be sentimental about May. It is like Edna St. Vincent Millay's "I am waylaid by beauty." After a thunderstorm, it is an opalescent world. Lucent drops fall from the lilacs, the young leaves of the maples look polished. The wet grass smells sweet. The cockers and Holly, the Irish, race through fallen apple blossoms and the cocker ears are feathered with pink-white petals. Apple blossoms have so short a stay, and a thunderstorm is hard on them.

I have a few friends who enjoy thunderstorms; I am not addicted to them. In our valley, they are savage. We had the giant maples cabled as soon as we could afford it after we came to Stillmeadow. But lightning brought down a maple in the farmhouse yard across the road, and the tree fell on the house, smashing the upstairs. During that same storm, I was answering the phone when what looked like a ball of fire ran up the ruffled curtains two feet from me and somehow seemed to explode on the stone hearth. To say I was electrified is an understatement. I dropped the phone and ran to the kitchen, although why I thought the kitchen was a refuge, I do not know. A kitchen is so full of wires and pots and pans.

When we went out, after the thunder rolled on over the hills, the yard was deep with fallen branches and part of one apple tree had crashed on the garden fence. I know a thunderstorm shows the magnificence of nature. My father used to go out and just admire the lightning. But I prefer to pull out the floor plugs, shut the windows and lock the doors and sit quietly on the couch. I try to be sensible and trust in God and the lightning rods and the copper cables, and I would not go so far as one friend of ours who has glass casters under the posts of her bed and just gets in bed when the lightning flashes in splendor.

A regular rain in May is something else. You can see everything grow, and after a good rain there will be a fresh crop of asparagus. But if we have, as happens, two days of it, I have had enough. Not the farmers, however, who always say, "Need more rain." The only time a farmer will admit we have rain enough is when there is a flood and the lowland is covered with water.

Some time ago, a friend from the West wrote me. "Does it ever rain in Connecticut? I've been reading your column for ages and you never have it rain."

I had an answer that Connecticut has what the books describe as "humid, moist, Continental climate." But that I liked sun better. What the weather reports call "precipitation" makes it a green part of the country. Grass grows naturally whether you want it to or not. The woods are green, hayfields are tall with green. Only in rare periods of drought do people have to water their lawns. In August, which we call the dry month, Jill does water the vegetables such as squash and cucumbers which have a way of lying down flat unless they have their quota of rain. She carries water in buckets from the pond and this is a mean chore. At that time the hose comes out to water the mock-orange which seems very susceptible to a dry spell.

But I really would not say lack of water is a problem in our countryside. As I write this, the rain is falling so heavily I cannot see the meadow. The windows are a sheet of silver and we have the lights on. Water is standing in that low place by the front gate. Not a bird is stirring. Tomorrow will be blue and gold, and hundreds of weeds will be up in the garden. And the brook will come down the hill like thunder.

As my dearly loved Farmer's Almanac says, "If it rains above as it does below, angels wear raincoats and little boats row." This poses the thought as to there being weather in Heaven or not. I should not like to be without weather myself, just an over-all changeless state of being sounds uninteresting.

In our valley, there are often conflicting weather reports. The weather seems to change from radio station to TV as well as from one hour's prediction to the next. But if people begin to argue as to what is really coming, someone says firmly, "Get the almanac." And whatever the almanac says has to be right.

As I write, the almanac is in its 169th year of continuous publication. Among other things, it has a weather table, for foretelling the weather through all the lunations of each year, forever. This table was taken from the 1849 almanac, which preceded the establishment of the weather bureau. The table itself is beyond my computing abilities, but what I like about it is that firm FOREVER.

This implies that our battered old Earth will presumably be in the same orbit, in relation to the same moon and stars and other planets. It implies that no tearing about in space with deadly missiles and no testing of fatal bombs, releasing the destructive power to wipe man from the earth while merely testing will upset the weather table, which is forever!

The almanac is said to be eighty-five per cent correct as to the weather of now (never mind that forever) but I believe it would add up to more than eighty-five per cent. If anyone tells me it was wrong about a blizzard or hurricane, I rise fiercely to defend it. The one thing that does puzzle me is in a footnote which remarks that a weather journal kept (not by the almanac) from 1767 on, reveals that whenever the new moon has fallen on Saturday, the following twenty days have been wet and windy, nine times out of ten. The reason this bothers me is that Saturdays skip about so, and also how does the new moon discover when it is Saturday anyway?

We country people have no doubt about the influence of the moon. We are near enough to the ocean here to ride over and see the tides. We also know you plant potatoes in the dark of the moon. Some things you do in the full of the moon, such as choosing your love.

In the golden age of Greece, Artemis was the moon goddess. Now more often called by her Roman name, Diana, she was the goddess of virginity and hunting, which seems an odd combination, since in those times, there wasn't, so far as I know, much connection between the two. In any case, the moon has been worshiped, adored by poets and lovers, deferred to by the country-wise. She has been mysterious, waxing and waning in beauty.

"Slowly, silently, now the moon
Walks the night in her silver shoon," says De la Mare.

"The moving moon went up the sky,
And nowhere did abide:

Softly she was going up,
And a star or two beside," says Coleridge.

"Lady, by yonder blessed moon I swear,
That tips with silver all these fruit tree tops," says Romeo.

Now when the moon is a landing station, with the Russians staking off half and the United States another half, there will be no moon magic. It will be just another place to quarrel over with launching pads to fire missiles farther out into space. It will be a fine scientific project. No lover would ever stand by his love and think, "How sweet the moonlight sleeps upon her breast," for he wouldn't be sure it was moonlight or a super atomic ray beamed by the Russians, or an American-made light projectile.

As I think about our own planet, it appears that many dreadful problems are not solved. Have we, I wonder, advanced to such a state of progress that we should attack outer space? It would seem to me that until this earth is reasonably at peace, the starving fed, the innocent protected, our responsibility is right here. Right now we have a grave surplus of grain in our country but after one reporter comments on this, the next reports seeing two hundred men, women and children starve to death in another country. Problems of transportation and so on seem unsolvable in this case. It is apparently more feasible to spend millions getting a man into space. Why?

When I turn off the news, I go out to experience the serenity of the May night. The garden is weeded, the rabbits are already at the young lettuce, the peas are plumping the pods. From this cherished place will come the golden carrots, purple eggplant, scarlet tomatoes, silken-tassled corn and ah, yes, the beans. A countrywoman can stand a long time in the May moonlight, lost in the wonder of earth and the fulness thereof. The power of life that sleeps in the seed is still a mystery, may it always be so. And I observe the moon tips the fruit trees with silver as in Shakespeare's day.

None can plant without faith, and with faith comes the miracle of harvest in due time.

Let us have faith, now and always.

SUMMER

June

SOMETIMES faraway people write to ask me what June is like in New England. I sit for a time, bemused, wondering how to say just what June is in our valley. Well, first there is the weather. The cool, damp nights of May are gone, nights are usually balmy (a word I dislike but that is what they are). The air is so soft you feel you might pick it up in your hand and hold it against your cheek. Days are warm, sometimes hot, but seldom uncomfortable (we save that for July). It is, in short, practically perfect weather. This is a generalization, of course, for we can have a cold June or a July kind of June. But we expect June to be just right.

The apple blossoms and lilacs have gone by, but the rambler roses are in bloom. And they bloom everywhere, on fences, in neglected dooryards, over the old stone walls along the country roads. They climb grey weathered sheds and spill their glory over the broken roofs. They also climb lattices and arbors where they are supposed to. Most of them are pink or red but there are white ones too. There is nothing much prettier than pink, white and red ramblers spilling color over a split-rail fence.

We planted the pink by our picket fence, and put a silver moon by the gate. The silver moon, which we bought at a ten-cent store, has become my favorite. The blooms are small, ivory-white, and open in lovely clusters. I like a bouquet of them in a milk glass spooner.

Now the grass grows high in the meadows and fields. And every lawn is deep velvet. It is the time of the lawn mower, and the smell of newly cut grass fills the air. The gardens are green with lettuce and chard and pea vines, squash is about to bloom, tomato plants are set out, corn is thriving.

Early in June the asparagus goes by and begins to grow tall feathery tops that will bear scarlet berries in fall. But the new peas, cooked with a mint leaf, need no apology. It is the time of strawberries too, big, dark red and juicy. Every roadside stand glows with strawberries.

Jill gave up raising them after three or four years because she said you had to practically lie down to take care of a strawberry bed, and it was a constant battle with the birds. It was easier to buy them from the hermit down the road.

Our hermit is not a religious hermit, just a live-alone hermit. He is neither young nor old, I doubt if anyone can tell his age. He looks just as he did twenty years ago, except for being a trifle more weathered. He is thin, dark, and voluble. He wears khaki work pants and a sweat shirt. I have never seen him in a coat or with a hat. He lives in a shack that looks like a chicken house. A stovepipe sticks through the tarpaper roof, so he must have a stove of some sort. There is a pile of rubbish and junk around the outside so there is barely room to get to the door.

But nobody goes on his land anyway. The etiquette is to stop the car and blow the horn and wait until he slides out from the shack or materializes from the strawberry bed. His berries are the biggest and sweetest and they are no ordinary berries, they are pedigreed. He advised Jill which varieties to plant when she started our own bed, and even parted with a flat of plants.

"You won't take care of them," he said morosely.

Sometimes he sells honey, now and then raspberries. He has a few fruit trees, and a vegetable patch, and may put squash out on a rickety table by the road if he feels in the mood.

He has no chickens—unless he keeps them in the house! Or under one of those strange rubbish piles. So I suspect he is a vegetarian. He walks to the village occasionally but I think he buys flour and salt and that is about all. He has very nearly gone back to basic survival, and one wonders why. But there is one remarkable thing about our village, which is the attitude, live and let live. Perhaps it belongs with the Yankee independence of spirit. He is there, he is a hermit, and it is his own business.

There are times when most of us, I think, would like to live without responsibility, with no social regulations, with no alarm clocks or deadlines. It is the old dream of a desert island. But few of us really want to BE an island. The recluse misses the sound of voices, of laughter, of singing. He has no friendly conversation at dinner. He has, of course, no love, he is protected from love's anguish but also from love's radiance. And he is completely withdrawn from the world of men.

I noticed yesterday when I went up the hill for the mail that Stillmeadow is completely hidden, as if it had been dropped like a white pebble into the summer green. Halfway back, where the brook crosses the road, the house seems to be tossed up by the green sea. The canopies of the great sugar maples break in green waves above the roof. I am reminded of my favorite legend, that of Lyonnesse. This is about the village which sank beneath the waves, the whole village vanishing overnight. Just where it happened is a matter of controversy but I call it off the French coast. One tale is that once a year it rises in the night, exactly as it was, and there have been those who claimed they saw it. On Christmas Eve it rises, and the church bells ring, and there have been those who heard them, sweet and solemn across the water.

And this legend suggests that of the lost Atlantis.

The island of Atlantis is mentioned in classical mythology. It was supposed to lie in the Atlantic Ocean and was west of the Pillars of Hercules. The Pillars of Hercules have been identified as the Straits of Gibraltar. I can't help liking the original name better. The island was west but how far west?

Was it inhabited or not? In any case, it vanished, apparently in the same mysterious way as the town that sank beneath the waves at a much later date. It existed as a legendary island until at some time or other, someone wondered whether there had not been an island to the west of the Pillars of Hercules. Since then, it has been supposedly identified as the Canaries, as Scandanavia, and even as America.

I expect some time the truth will come to light, even as Dr. Schliemann discovered and proved that Troy was not a myth and the whole story of the siege of Troy was probably based on what actually did happen. Of course a discovery of the site caused no end of controversy. Any discovery of antiquity turns men into treasure-seekers and usually governments are embroiled. Where is the missing gold? Where are the priceless artifacts?

But when the furor dies down, the real treasure is the discovery that myths are often true.

There must be the word as a guide. The word may be in hieroglyphics, or cuneiform or an unknown early tongue which puzzled the scholars. But the Greeks left a rich heritage in epic poetry, drama, philosophy. Whereas Stonehenge has no words for a key. The great ominous stone slabs brood in dark silence. How did they come there, when there is no stone like theirs for miles? What did they signify? For what religion did they serve? I saw Stonehenge in the late afternoon, a long-ago summer day in England. I felt suddenly as if I were drowning in a black sea. There was something there—but I did not know what it was, nor what it meant.

I suddenly longed to be at home in Connecticut, which has mysteries, but not like Stonehenge.

In June, the cockers and Holly help with the chores. Their favorite is helping when we cut the dead lilac clusters from the lilac bushes (oh, how many, many lilacs we do have at this time!). As fast as the clippers snip off a tarnished cluster, it is snipped up by a helper. Jonquil whips away, her mouth full of lilac. Tiki and Teddy are after her. Meanwhile Holly helps herself from the basket, and Holly's way with a plaything is to toss it in the air, leap after it, fling it away again, roll on it. This is the reason why the lawn is full of dead lilac clusters.

They also help mow, and if whoever is mowing the lawn bends to remove a twig or fallen branch, it is instantly snatched and borne away. And then dropped so it interferes with the mower later on. Lately we have shut them all in the house during mowing, for fear they will get too near the machine.

Holly waits at the gate to carry in part of the mail. After she has deposited it on my bed (not even damp) she is overcome by her own brillance and collapses, making a sort of singing sound I have never heard any other dog make. She has to be extravagantly praised until she gets over her own achievement. When Erma comes and it is not mail time, Holly has to carry Erma's purse in, which she carries by the handle as a lady should. This also goes on my bed.

Holly has plenty of excitement when we entertain a bevy of dogs and owners between the Hartford and New Haven dog shows. One year we had five Irish and the cockers were retired to the kennel, which I may say was quieter. The last time, Paula, Holly's breeder, came up from Bermuda with a lovely Irish named Rusty (that is, he was called Rusty; I never knew his show name). A Boston friend came with a pointer. Paula had a second Irish to show. The house was really, to a casual eye, full of dogs.

When you entertain dog people, the routine never varies. The dogs come first. They get fed, exercised, brushed a bit. Then the owners can settle down to eat and talk. We stayed up until two, and Holly went right upstairs and spent the night whinnying outside Rusty's bedroom door. It was love at first sight with her. I went up and hauled her down several times, but she went right back up.

"We must get her an Irish of her own," said Jill.

The next morning, while we scrambled eggs and broiled sausage, Holly escorted Rusty outside and gave him a guided tour of the best rabbit haunts, the nicest mole runs, the place where the skunk lives. Had he come out, there would have been one Irish less at the show. The Irish were beautiful, skimming about the yard, moving like music.

They completely ignored the pointer, who sat by the wellhouse and watched wistfully. I was sorry for him, but I couldn't reason with Holly. By the time Paula tried to assemble equipment and dogs, Rusty looked like a ditchdigger and had to be cleaned up (which resulted in almost missing the show deadline for entry).

Holly had won her championship and we were not taking her to the show. But when Rusty was loaded into the station wagon, Holly wailed and tried to get over the picket fence and carried on so that I wished we had entered her just so she could ride along with Rusty. After a time, she consented to clean up the leftover sausage and scrambled eggs and felt better. And when the cockers came out, she dragged Teddy around by the ear as usual. But that night she went upstairs and looked for Rusty, just in case.

This was the first time Holly had ever paid any attention to a strange dog except when we visited Hugh and Janet Cuthrell, who owned her half-sister, Misty. Holly took charge of Misty, almost acting like a herd dog. But it was not like the affair with Rusty, it was definitely supervision.

Living with dogs is an endless adventure. When they do things you do not understand, it is your limitation. For instance, I noticed lately that Jonquil has been going about the house in a different way. Instead of following the regular traffic pattern, she goes between the sofa and the fireplace, a narrow space with light cords and the fireplace set in it. She winds her way through this narrow way, then around the antique black rocker and so to the kitchen. At first I thought she was losing her mind. Not at all. She is suffering from arthritis and she had figured out the way that meant the shortest route. When she comes in my door, she walks behind the television set to get to the family room and it is much shorter. Now if this isn't thinking, I do not know what is. Further, when she jumps down from the couch in the family room, she jumps at the left end so that she lands on the firm rough stone of the hearth instead of on the slippery wax floor. And when she comes in the front

door, she does not jump up the steps but gets on the terrace and
wends her way in with a small hop from the terrace to the threshold.

Other than making these adjustments, Jonquil does not consider
herself slightly stiff and lame. She cannot keep up with Especially
Me, her son, after a rabbit but she can outsnap tidbits before him.
She catches them in mid-air while he is still looking hopeful.

Tiki is the barker. We named him Kon-Tiki for he was a lone
raft on a big sea, being the only puppy Little Sister had. His show
name is High Heritage. We need no doorbell with Tiki, and we can
tell from the way he barks whether there is really someone coming
in the gate or just boys bicycling by. He spent a good deal of time
with small black Linda and from her learned that a laundry truck
is very dangerous. But when the snowplough comes through, his
bark would do justice to a dog the size of a great Dane.

Sometimes when we have guests and the dogs begin to bark, Jill
goes to the door and says firmly, "Linda, stop that this minute. Tiki
be QUIET. Jonquil, hush that."

"You didn't call to Teddy," says Steve.

"He wasn't barking," Jill answers.

"But how do you know who's barking?"

"They just use their own voices," says Jill.

Teddy (Especially Me) is a quiet person, but when he feels it
is his duty to bark, he barks along with whoever is nearest him,
keening like Jonquil or doing a staccato performance with Tiki. But
still, he sounds like himself.

Except when something happens, cockers are quiet dogs. When
they bark, it means something. They have been called "kennel
angels." As a rule, I would say, they take life easier than the Irish
setter. For instance, they mourn when you leave them, but the Irish
indicate that they are at death's door. I am not referring to regular
kennel dogs, but to house dogs.

On the other hand, when Holly has had to be in a kennel we
hear glowing reports of her perfectly wonderful behavior.

"I only wish all dogs were like her," remarks Dr. Whitney.

When we take her for a check-up or an inoculation, she goes
directly to the examining room, leaps on the table, and wags her
plume. Recently we had to take her to board briefly and, as usual,

she flew toward the examining room.

"Not this time, Holly," said the attendant, "this time we are going upstairs."

And off she went, tail waving.

But if I shut her in the back kitchen when non-dog lovers come to visit, it takes half an hour to comfort her after they depart. She sobs almost like a human, then utters a kind of off-key singing note. Finally, with a heavy long sigh she retires to my bed and indicates we will forget all about this and begin again.

When Paula persuaded us to get Holly's championship, she turned out to be a real trouper and enjoyed every moment of it. I might draw some conclusions from this, such as that Holly can get along with me better than I can with her. But some things do not have to be analyzed. They are the way they are.

There have been many dogs in my life, for that I am grateful. Some day I shall write a book just about the dogs I have lived with, for no two dogs are alike. Father felt it was disloyal to have another dog after Timmie died. In a curious way, which many people seem to share, he felt it would be an insult to Timmie's memory.

"We shall never have another," he said.

And he never did. When he came to visit Stillmeadow in later years and the yard was full of cockers, he tightened his lips and tried not to look at them. At that time we had Snow-in-Summer, who was an exquisite red and white gentlewoman cocker. We had been urged to get her championship but we were more interested in Obedience training.

We ate on the lawn that day and Snow went directly to Father and laid her muzzle on his foot. She turned her dark amber eyes up to him, and wagged her tail so hard she shook her whole rear end. Father stood it for some time, he was a strong man. Finally he gave her a pat.

"I suppose she's all right for a scrub dog," he said grudgingly.

Now and then when he wrote, he would add a line, "How's the scrub dog?"

But he never really forgave me for having any dog at all after Timmie.

My position is that love should not be so limited. I did not feel

I was betraying my Honey's memory when Jonquil came along. It is true there will never be another like Honey, but I do not expect Jonquil to be a copy of Honey. Two cockers could hardly differ more, except in the deep golden color of the coat. During the fourteen years I had Honey, Jill used to say my shadow was golden. If I got up from the desk in a hurry to answer the telephone, I had to be careful not to step on her. She was a dedicated cocker, quiet, with no sense of humor. She loved only me, and that was her career.

Jonquil, on the other hand, is merry, outgoing, gay, and everything seems funny to her. She is perfectly happy with anyone and everyone, a completely adjustable dog. She is always the life of the party when we entertain, whereas Honey retired under my bed until the last guest had gone.

I have never felt it necessary to measure the portion of love for each of them.

Sometimes owners will lose a dog and buy another from the same kennel.

"But Nellie is not at all like Bootsie," they complain. "We wanted one just like Bootsie."

Since no two puppies are alike in the same litter, it is hardly to be expected a duplicate may be had. And often the new puppy is returned as unsatisfactory because he or she is NOT a copy of Bootsie. However, the new puppy may have many endearing traits (some of them perhaps Bootsie did not have). And all he or she needs is a chance to develop in his or her own way.

It is possible to acquire a new dog with the same general inherited characteristics, and that is as far as anybody can go. For the law of heredity operates in dogs as well as in human beings. This is one reason, among many others, why it is a mistake to buy a puppy at a pet shop.

"But he was supposed to be a barkless Basenji," one woman wrote to me, "and he seems to be turning into a Collie. What shall we do?"

"Learn to love Collies," is about all I can say.

However, if there is one violent prejudice pervading the heart of dog-folk, it is that in favor of their own breed. It is very difficult for a great dane lover to admit that there is any virtue whatsoever in a Welsh terrier. Poodle lovers consider cockers a waste of time. So, I may add, do the poodles. Those who love the hunting dogs will defend their superiority to the death.

In years of going to dog shows, belonging to dog clubs, working in Obedience classes, I would say there are wonderful dogs in every breed. My intimate dog friends have ranged from a cairn to a Great Dane, from a wire hair to a Maltese terrier. But, of course, there is nothing like the cocker and the Irish setter.

So there you are.

In any case, there are enough breeds recognized by the American Kennel Club to satisfy everyone. If my memory is right, there are around 160 recognized breeds. Therefore anybody who wants a dog has a wide choice!

There is one thing that I think should be illegal, and that is giving away puppies as prizes. A dog is not a commodity. Giveaways may be boats, or jewelry, or radios or silverware. But when I discovered an Irish setter puppy was to be awarded to the person who guessed how long it would take the St. Patrick's Day parade to pass the reviewing stand, I wanted to wring the neck of the publicity boy that thought of it. Just because somebody guessed a number is not any reason to hand over an Irish puppy to the lucky winner.

Presumably the winner would live in a city apartment, and an Irish needs some free-running as a bird needs wings. To confine the fluent, floating grace of an Irish to the end of a short leash in a park is unthinkable cruelty. Of course it seemed to someone who had never known a dog that an Irish would be more suitable for St. Patrick's Day than a Pekingese (originally called in China the sleeve-dog).

One could only hope that those who entered this guessing game, wanted a dog, at least. And maybe had relatives with a yard. A paved run is no good either, for the Irish have been hunting dogs from the beginning. A chance to point, to air-scent, to locate game (even a rabbit) is vital.

But most of all, I would have liked to take that publicity man into the back yard to watch Holly skimming past, ears flying, plume of tail floating. And seeming not to touch the ground at all.

"Would you confine one in a four-room apartment?" I would ask. And there could only be one answer.

In June the snow peas ripen early and this is one crop we never have enough of to freeze. These are also called edible-podded peas, which sounds stodgy, or Chinese peas or early sugar peas. Jill began raising them long ago, and we still remember the day she sent Dorothy out to pick them and Dorothy conscientiously shelled them too. Dorothy never shirked any task. The snow peas are never shelled. The tender sweetness of the pods is the best part of them.

They should be picked just before sunset, rushed to the house to be cleaned, and popped into the kettle with just enough boiling, salted water to keep them from sticking to the pan. We serve them in soup bowls, dressed with butter, salt, freshly ground pepper. Like most, if not all, vegetables, they should be picked when they are very young. If you wait until the peas inside the pods are big enough to bulge, you have wasted your time picking them. The peas should be about the size of a fairy's thimble. The pods will be almost transparent at this stage, and melting sweet.

A neighbor asked me last week why I spoke of seasoned salt and freshly ground pepper. Seasoned salt is what television says of almost every product, "a combination of ingredients." It brings out natural flavors and enhances them and what it does to poached eggs and cheese dishes and soups and stews, not to mention salad dressings, is to lift them from pedestrian food to an exciting dish. We use plain salt for cooking many things too for it is saltier salt. For instance, plain salt is better, we think, for noodles, rice, spaghetti. We keep plain and seasoned salt beside each other.

As for pepper, the true flavor is inside the peppercorn and if it is freshly ground, the true pungent spicy odor comes forth. I always keep sniffing as I grind it. Ready-ground pepper is a great convenience but some of the rich fragrance is lost. We used to pound peppercorns in the mortar using the wooden pestle. I THINK it tastes best of all this way, for no metal comes in contact with it. But this is probably just a romantic idea of mine, because the mortar and pestle are so old.

Like all villages hereabouts, we have a town dump. When there is nothing else to argue about, we argue about the town dump. It was to have been moved to a new site some time ago, but somehow it is still where it has been since we came here thirty years ago. The original gullies have filled up, the dump has spread. Sometimes fire starts up at night after the dump has been burned over. Then it looks like a distant burning city. But it is not distant, it is on the ridge above Jeremy Swamp Road, and twice the fire has swept down the slope destroying a good many of Steve and Olive's treasured pines. Once it nearly set fire to Rudolf's house.

But, so far, the dump stays there for one reason. It is there.

Except for the dump, the slope is one of the loveliest in our area, rising gently, rich with pines. If you take the narrow way to Rudolf's house, you come out midway up the slope, and enter the low white house through Rudolf's studio. There you stop to admire his hand-painted wallpaper panels, for Rudolf is an artist. He is not the kind of artist that suggests modernistic canvases, Bohemian garrets, or smoke-filled apartments. He designs and paints murals, restores decoration in old houses, and produces exquisite panels, delicate and elegant.

He and his wife, Olga, built the house where it is on the supposition that the dump would be moved before the roof was on. Olga was gentle and gay and always reminded me of a Bavarian fairy tale. Rudolf looks to me like a Swiss mountaineer (and he is Swiss). The house is indefinably Swiss too, and from the wide-windowed living room the view of the pines and the steep drop beyond them makes one imagine it is Switzerland outside. Rudolf did the decorating, and they furnished the house with furniture collected here and, I suspect, abroad. But it does not look too elegant, it looks, and is, comfortable. Aside from the danger of the town dump, they settled in happily and when we went there for dinner, we decided it was one of the happiest houses we knew.

But last summer, Olga died very suddenly, and everyone who had come to love them, felt that Rudolf would sell the happy house and go to live with relatives.

"I manage," said Rudolf.

He cleans house, cooks, feeds the birds, does errands for neighbors in trouble. And works at his painting as hard as ever.

He is a modest, as well as courageous man, and if anyone tries to praise him, he blushes and says, "Well, I can cook."

As far as Jill is concerned, she feels the dump is a disgrace, but she enjoys going there to visit with her friend the dump man. Lately a new dump man has appeared, but to her there is only her friend. He is always cheerful, and has many sound comments to make on life. He wears a scarlet fireman's hat with a magenta plastic rose tucked in the brim.

"Somebody else is at the dump," said Jill one day, "and I asked him where my dump man was. He didn't know."

I suppose one would not consider taking care of a dump as a job with a future, come to think of it.

The village is full of interest, what with one thing and another. Last week we were in the market quietly loading the cart with jellied bouillon and black bean soup when a strange, smiling blond man came charging down the aisle and crashed into us.

"I always go wrong way," he caroled. "How are you? How are you? How are you good morning?"

"Who's that?" I asked Jill, after he had bowed and beamed away.

"Oh, that's my Hungarian refugee friend," said Jill. "He has trouble with his English, and I've managed to remember enough of my German to help him out. He's a very nice man."

She said the market was pretty confusing, and I said it certainly was, for it confuses me. I also said so to George, the owner, not critically, for he is a special friend of ours, but wistfully.

"George, why do you keep changing things around?" I asked.

George blushed. "Well, new things keep coming in, and there always seems to be some way we could rearrange things to make more room. But," he added thoughtfully, "there isn't."

The truth is there are too many brands of everything, from crackers to detergents. And I am as guilty as the next customer for with all the mustards jamming the shelf, I asked George why he did NOT have Bahamian mustard.

"I'll get it," he said patiently.

On the way home from the market that day we stopped at the doctor's office for flu shots. Anne, the pretty auburn-haired nurse, was not there, so we asked the substitute nurse whether she was sick.

"No, she's fine," said Miss Kurzrok, "this is her day to be a den mother."

I reflected that in the city, no nurse could ever take a day off to be a den mother!

And I was reminded again of the difference between the city and a small town last spring when a photographer came out from the city to take some pictures of me for a magazine. He was to take an early-morning train on Sunday. Occasional trains do come in to Seymour, which is about nine miles away, and has OUR bank and the beauty parlor and a few stores, in fact it has a Main Street. Marilyn, our hairdresser, found out about my coming ordeal when I asked her to put a net on my hair so it would KEEP longer. Whereupon Marilyn secretly arranged with Jill to bring me early to meet the train.

"But we'll have to sit and wait," I protested.

"No, we won't. Marilyn is coming down to open the shop and fix your hair." Jill was firm.

It meant that Marilyn had to get up early too, on her one free day, and drive from Fox Drive in Oxford to Seymour, open the shop, and comb my hair properly.

"Because," she said firmly, "I knew you'd be a mess, Mrs. Taber, a perfect mess."

She couldn't have been more right. In my lifetime, a good many well-wishers, both hairdressers and friends, have tried to teach me HOW to manage my hair. And every single one, alas, gives up in the end. It is not that I don't try. And Marilyn says my hair is so manageable and easy to do and stays so well.

"Now just brush it," she says.

So I do. My recalcitrant hair then stands up straight in the air as if I had just seen a tiger in the kitchen. Then it goes the wrong way, unwaving itself, so to speak. And always odd fringes fall in front of my ears, suggesting dimly those sideburns the rawhide cowboy wears.

Usually when I go back to the next appointment, Marilyn closes her eyes when she sees me.

Then she tries to comfort me so sweetly. "But I couldn't write a book," she says as she whips my mop into shape.

Sometimes I watch my daughter deftly putting her hair up in pin curls for the night. My admiration is unbounded. Her slender small hands fly in and out winding locks up, sliding the pins in. She even does the back! Whatever she may have inherited from me or my side of the family is not hairdressing skill.

My mother had no knack either but it didn't matter for she just combed her hair back, made a small bun, and put on a net. Flyaway feathers used to escape and she pinned them back before going out. Her hair was such a dark brown, it was almost like night.

On an occasional day of June showers, I sometimes decide to organize the recipe file. I have to feel in a buoyant mood for this is a miserable job. In fact, I wrote two cookbooks with the idea that all the recipes would be right at hand, any time. But right away we began collecting new recipes or inventing new ones. The plight of the recipe collector is a sad one, for always, the one recipe you want is not filed correctly. It is LOST. It is not in the books either, because you discovered it subsequent to the publication of the books.

It turns up, months later when you don't want it anyway, usually tucked inside the cover of one of the cookbooks that jam the shelves. At one time, we had thirty-five cookbooks, and hunting through them was a task in itself.

This spring a friend wrote to say she had lost the wonderful recipe for Teriyaki Meat Balls (which my friend Dawn Emmons sent me from Hawaii). I wrote back that I couldn't locate it just then, but would look for it. I did. I looked in the files, in old manila envelopes stuffed with recipes, in the loose-leaf books. She wrote again, plaintively. I then hunted through all the gourmet cookbooks, although I did not think Dione Lucas would include Teriyaki Meat Balls in her Cordon Bleu book. Apparently the only source of this recipe was Dawn Emmons in Hawaii.

So I wrote saying I was still hunting. And I admit, had it been a recipe of my own invention, I still would have had to have it written down. Unless I am cooking off the cuff, I look up my own recipes as faithfully as I do others'.

I had, of course, mislaid Dawn's address.

Only last week, Mrs. Greco, from Portsmouth, Virginia, wrote to make some lovely comments on my recipes. She had, she said, a COMPLETE file of all of mine. So I wrote hastily to ask her did she have Teriyaki Meat Balls in her files because both Mrs. Watson, in California, and I were going unquietly mad for lack of it. For by now I had decided I could not live without that recipe. I wanted to use it when Steve and Olive came for supper that week end.

Then I just happened to be sorting the Butternut Wisdom files from *Family Circle,* and one page slipped forward. And there I saw plain as day, Teriyaki Meat Balls. So I wrote Mrs. Greco hastily that she need not join the hunt, sent the recipe to Mrs. Watson, and broiled some chops for supper. However, I expect to use that recipe next week end. And here it is.

Make a sauce of 1 cup of soy sauce, ½ cup of water, 2 tablespoons of crushed or powdered ginger, 2 cloves of garlic, chopped fine. Combine this with 3 pounds of finely ground round steak (or hamburger will do). Form into tiny balls no more than an inch across. (Makes about 100.) Place in a large roasting pan and bake for one hour, uncovered, at 275°. Serve warm on a platter with toothpicks for spearing. This is an hors d'oeuvres special but equally good if you are having a smorgasbord buffet.

But what is so frustrating is that it is an easy recipe. What I couldn't remember was the ginger. I knew it wasn't nutmeg or mace or anything usual. So it's ginger, and I am pasting the recipe on the flyleaf of *What Cooks at Stillmeadow.*

Because I love to cook, people are always telling me about their favorite recipes. For some reason, I cannot concentrate or remember a list of ingredients told me at a party. Often I admire some new dish Olive has invented and she says it is very easy to make, you simply take— Olive has perfect recall and I usually have it for everything except recipes.

With recipes, I blank out after the first five ingredients. And even with very simple ones, I find I am at a loss as to whether it is two tablespoons of Worcestershire—or was it soy sauce? Does it call for two eggs or three? My basic difficulty with figures betrays me every time.

Of course anyone who cooks a great deal can fake or make up most recipes, but not all. You may get a perfectly edible dish but not the very special one you wish to duplicate.

I have a spinach recipe which glorifies the pedestrian green. It is supposed to be Indian, though I didn't know they ate spinach in India, but my ideas are hazy for I expect curry to be the main ingredient of any Indian dish. This calls for ground coriander and turmeric, cottage cheese and sour cream. (In short, you don't have too much spinach in the end, but never mind.) I have to look up the amount of the coriander and turmeric every time, because I cannot remember just how much to use.

I could not, either, remember the magic ingredient of my own bread pudding, which Don's wife requested. She reported that no matter how hard she tried, Don said it was not the same. She said she even followed my recipe and still it was not right.

So I began a study of bread puddings, remembering how all the children loved them. But after a time, light dawned. Don was a thin, leggy small boy in the earlier bread pudding era, and he had a terrific appetite. He also had a passion for raisins, and used to hold the box for me when I made the pudding.

Now he is a doctor, finishing his Army stretch, and I am sure the magic ingredient of my bread pudding is no longer available, for the hungry small boy is grown up and nothing is quite the same. It has nothing to do with Anne's cooking, for she is really a gourmet cook, and I imagine her bread pudding is far better than mine ever was.

A young wife often combats memories of childhood. There is a good deal of truth in those worn-out jokes about what Mother used to make. I myself am positive that Mama's chicken fricassee was DIFFERENT. And her Lady Baltimore cake was breath-taking. She cooked without needing a recipe stuck up before her, too. Which is why many of her best dishes are lost to me. She did condescend to write down Grandmother Raybold's English plum pudding and her fruitcake.

"I just put in enough of what's needed," she said.

Inside the house now in daytime, the light is green and shadowy, for the maple shade overhangs the roof. It is a little like living under water, and the milk glass is opalescent as shells. The wide oak floors have a soft glow, and the ruffled curtains are snowy. The house smells of lavender, for Erma has tucked it in with the linens and in the drawers. We have lavender in the border of the Quiet Garden and it is a rewarding herb, lovely when in bloom, fragrant when dried.

At twilight (which I often think is my favorite time) the last ray of the westering sun gives a glow to the sky over the hill. We do not see the whole sunset, because of the hills and woods, but we see the sun begin to slide, and then the afterglow gives a radiance to the swamp. We take supper down by the pond, for the pond also catches the light after the yard is violet with shadow. Jill does extra hamburgers for the cockers and Holly. We find it impossible to enjoy eating with pleading eyes following every forkful from plate to mouth, except when it is to their mouths. Jonquil and Holly have some salad too, Tiki and Especially Me think salad is a rabbit food.

When we come back to the house, the June moon is so bright that it makes shadows of the apple trees. There is a last flurry as Holly finds her teddy bear (which she borrowed from Muffin). In and out, out and in, everywhere Holly goes, the teddy bear goes. She finally locates him where she left him, under the mock-orange bush. We go in, Jill lights the copper lamp. I take a last look at the moon, and breathe the mint-cool air. Another day has ended, a day that will not come again.

But tomorrow will be fair!

Between Seasons

WE were vacationing on Cape Cod in the cottage by the sea. It always reminds me of Byron's "cloudless climes and starry skies." If there were any warnings of disaster, I do not remember them. We were both, we admitted, tired, but we had put in a very busy year and we were justified in being tired. We sat and watched the tide come in and we sat and watched the tide go out. Holly was with us, and she was not tired at all.

She was running the beach all day except when she helped the clammers. When they clammed in deep water, she swam round and round them. If they were in shallow water, she stood up to her nose in the water, and pounced whenever they tossed small clams back. Through the field glasses we could see she was waving her tail as best she could although it was under water.

That night Jill and Holly retired early and I sat up to see the moon lay a gold path across the sea. "And straight was the path of gold for him, and the need of a world of men for me," I thought. But the moon is too feminine. I didn't like Shelley's sad moon climbing with slow steps either, for the moon is not wan and pale or sad. The moon is all things to all men, I thought.

The next morning, after we persuaded Holly to come from the beach and fill the back seat with sand and clam mud, we went across town and to the other side of the Cape to the doctor's to consult him about some minor complaint of mine. I forget what it was.

We had a habit of long standing of going to the doctor together. It began because I am timid about doctors, and Jill went along, and then I began going with her.

So she sat in the waiting room, looking past the salt marshes to the shimmering blue water. The gulls went crying over. The sun was like new gold. There was no wind, which is unusual for the Cape.

The doctor came out to visit with Jill, by then the waiting room had standing room only.

"Come in, I want to see you," he said, and Jill followed him to the inner office.

I hoped the other people in the room would not mind his taking a few minutes to talk to Jill, for they were old friends. I read the *National Geographic* and a couple of children's books. Time went on, and I thought even if he had given her a shot for her asthma, she ought to be out. Holly began to bark at the doctor's ancient springer, so I went out and sat in the car with her. Several people came to talk to me, for the Cape is a place for talking.

When Jill came out, she slid behind the wheel silently and started for home.

"What were you talking about so long?" I asked.

"Oh, he wanted to take a blood count," she said, "I have to have shots for two weeks. But there's no use your coming over with me and wasting time. You stay home and get on with your book."

"What for, a blood count?"

"He thinks I have anemia," she said.

So I went on working on my novel. And Holly spent quite a lot of time sitting in the car outside the doctor's office. The weather grew hot, as it can even on the Cape, a good, baking hot. But nights were all moon-gold and salty-piny air. Jill asked me to hunt up an extra blanket.

I remember those two weeks as an interlude. I worked away on my book half a day every day and then we had lunch outdoors and talked idly about not much. We took Holly for rides, finding new hidden roads, coming suddenly at an end at a different beach. If the beach was a lonely one, Holly chased things a while and we picked up polished bits of driftwood or unbroken clam shells for ashtrays.

When Jill went for her last shot, I was getting ready to go out to dinner with some old friends of mine. I had not seen them for a long time, so I was fussy about which dress to wear. Something, I admitted sadly, was wrong with everything I owned.

Jill was late getting back, it was sunset, and the cottages on the point looked as if they were carved from gold.

"I'm going to the hospital tomorrow," she said, calmly.

Jill always felt that bad news should be told right out, not deviously worked up to. She said it only made it worse to beat around the bush.

I sat down, saying nothing at all.

"I could do with some coffee," she said casually, starting for the kitchen. In the doorway she turned and said, "The shots didn't work." And added apologetically, "I'm sorry you'll have to get up early, I'm supposed to be there at nine-thirty."

"But you can't," I said, "your pajamas aren't ironed!"

I do not know whether this happens to everyone, but I always have channeled great shocks into as many smaller crises as I can think of. It's a natural defense, like throwing up breastworks against the enemy.

Jill has never been subject to this weakness. She gets right at the enemy. Now she said, "Never mind the pajamas."

"And besides," I said, "you have been wearing out old ones all summer."

"All right," she said, and laughed. "I'll tell them at the hospital all about my pajamas."

"We left the good suitcase at home," I said, "and you forgot your good bedroom slippers. Those calico things you got at the drugstore are AWFUL."

We had some sort of supper, probably liver, for we had been eating liver steadily for two weeks.

"The only thing that worries me," said Jill, "is how you and Holly will manage. If she follows anybody away, call up Millie and Ed, don't try to chase her yourself. Better get some extra money out of the bank. I'll only be gone a few days for tests and a check-up, so you can let things go until I get back. Just keep on with your book."

She went to bed early, because she said she wanted to feel fresh in the morning. After she had closed her door, I got out the ironing board and ironed all the pajamas she had. I am probably the world's worst ironer, and we only had a small portable iron with us. I kept telling myself that at least I would smooth those pajamas out, but they kept getting extra wrinkles in them and drops of sweat fell on them although I was numb with cold.

We left the Cape three weeks later on a day so beautiful I could hardly bear it.

"This hasn't been much of a vacation for you," said Jill as we crossed the bridge to the mainland. "But we'll come back and begin again, just as soon as I get through with the specialist. Any time is wonderful at the Cape."

The night before she died, she said, "I wish we'd had time to say good-bye to everyone at the Cape. But we'll go back as soon as I get out of here. I'm sorry I've been such a nuisance."

"I'll be over early in the morning," I said.

Jill does not walk through the gate any more, tall against the sunlight. I do not see her bending over the garden, or hear her humming as she gathers the vegetables. She was a quiet person, and only hummed or whistled when she was gardening or carpentering. I do not hear her steady footsteps on the old floors. I do not find her down by the pond scything the weeds at the swimming steps. The cockers and Holly no longer leap against her as she crosses the yard, they have given up leaving their choicest marrow bones on her bed. They like to be thanked for such attentions.

Where did the years go? Now there is nobody to remember them except me, for the children only remember certain things but not the whole. All the funny things, the wonderful things, the sorrowful things, that make up a shared life, are left to me, alone.

There is, or was for me, an anesthesia of grief for a time. And then I woke up one morning and realized that every morning would be just the same. So would every afternoon and every night. A permanent winter season was in my heart. But this wasn't doing anyone any good. I had a greater responsibility than I had ever had, and the sooner I began to grow into it, the better. What it boiled down to, simply, was that I must live so as to justify Jill's faith in me, and making a world out of grief was not it.

I discovered if you take two steps forward and slip back one, you are still a step ahead, which is a cliché but a true one. I also discovered that if I could just survive the worst hours, there would be relief in the next ones. Like everything in this world, grief has a rhythm, and this is a great help to remember when even drawing the next breath seems an impossible task.

Almost always, during the bad times, Erma would appear and make hot coffee and tell me about the neighbors and the village news. Sometimes we went for a ride over the hills and along the river, and this got me over a silly phobia about leaving the house. I hope others do not have this, it is a hard one.

"Get your coat, we're going for a ride," Erma would say firmly, "and don't argue."

I saw the beloved valley, the low, sheltering hills, the Pomperaug pearling over its rocky bed. I saw the white farmhouses and red barns and the rich meadows. And I realized that the world was wide and wonderful. I waved at children coming home from the swimming hole. And finally we went to the market, Jill's bailiwick for so many years. I am probably sentimental about our community, but the exquisite tact with which I was welcomed would hardly be equaled anywhere. Everyone was just plain glad to see me, but as natural as if I had been in every day.

And so, gradually, I emerged from limbo into life. Fortunately

I have faith in God, and often I wonder how anyone can endure the loss of a loved one without faith. It would be unthinkable. My own praying was not always in words, because I could not find them. But our young minister dropped in frequently. We hear a great deal of criticism of the church these days, and I venture to think the main trouble is there are not enough ministers like ours.

When Hank comes (and we call him that as a term of affection) he watches me make tea and insists that the water boil hard enough. Then we have three or four cups and he eats quite a few cookies and we talk about everything in the world from the Congo problem to remodeling the parish kitchen. We talk of the books we read and of what happened at the town meeting.

And then he says, "Shall we pray?"

Over the teacups, he voices all those words I have not been able to say to God, simply and quietly and with NO oratory. It might be called a practical praying.

And then I brush Holly's hairs from his dark suit and he swings away, thin, smiling, easy.

"I wish I had your tea-and-cookie minister to drop in and pray with me," wrote a friend who had lost her husband.

The children, Jill's two and my one, came with their families for week ends as often as they could manage it. This concerned me at first, for they all have full lives and spare time is not in their vocabulary. They never heard of it. But then I began to realize that perhaps they needed, from me, a reassurance that the family was still a unit. There was, in a way, something to come home to.

And it seemed to me they grew in understanding overnight. Perhaps I hadn't known them before as adults, but now there were moments when they seemed as old as I am. Their children, tumbling around, widened my horizon so that I went ahead into their future in imagination. It's a wonderful thing to dream about the future of a child! It is like day beginning, glowing with sunrise.

As far as immortality is concerned, I think of Emily Dickinson, who wrote after her father's death, "I am glad there is immortality, but would have tested it myself before entrusting him." Some thinkers feel that man invented the idea of immortality as a kind of defense, and invented God because of an irresistible need to have a being to look up to.

Much has been written about death, man's mortality being of special interest in this age when it might be universal and all at once for all mankind. The philosopher Henri Bergson said that man is the only animal who knows that he must die, which should add a quality of creativeness to life.

That word KNOWS, I would argue with. If Bergson meant man has a general vague perception that the undiscovered country of death lies somewhere ahead, that may be. But I do not think most of us (who are not philosophers) ever realize death until it happens personally to us, putting an irrevocable period at the end of the sentence. We have had plenty of chance to realize it in our era, but we still usually go along pretending there isn't any such finality.

It is only, I think, when the focal point of our lives is gone, that we begin to see the shape of death. And we are not prepared. We are no more prepared when the beloved has a long terminal illness than when death takes five minutes in an accident.

And Emily Dickinson summed up the feeling most of us have about what happens after death.

Someone has said we all hope for a cosmic address. Most of us do, and if we have faith that is about all we need to hope for. There are, I would guess, hundreds of different heavens men have dreamed of. There are theories that after death the soul or spirit is absorbed into a sort of general consciousness. There are theories that personality continues to exist.

Some believe that Christ's Resurrection was, in fact, a manifestation of the survival of personality, others believe this was an illusion of his overwrought followers. As more and more of the Bible is discovered to be based on fact, I see no reason to doubt the validity of the Resurrection.

My first exploration of the other side began when I was in college and a visiting minister came for conferences with groups of students. My question had nothing to do with theology.

"Do you think dogs go to Heaven?"

"I see no reason why not," said the famous minister. Possibly he was disposing of me so as to get on to more vital discussion, I shall never know. But I felt much better about the recent death of my Timmie.

Several of my dearest friends have experienced special evidence of survival of personality, when the door to the other side seems to be ajar. Most of us, at one time or another, encounter the supernatural. There are areas beyond the range of normal human experience which may be charted completely ultimately. I could cite evidence of many instances, but not mine.

My only such experience was a long time ago, and could certainly not be proved.

What do I believe? I believe we never lose those we have loved. I believe in God, or if you wish, an infinite power, for otherwise existence is meaningless, a casual happenstance. I believe in the basic goodness of life, and that love is stronger than hate, although often it does not seem so. I believe eventually good overcomes evil, and that we are put on earth for a purpose which has to do with love and with good.

This may be pretty optimistic, but nobody ever accused me of looking on the dark side of life.

I believe in living out our span of life in full appreciation of the best of it, and with compassion for all mankind, not just a special segment of it.

I do not believe those whose life is cut short have to wait around until the end of the world when Judgment Day comes around. I suspect we carry our own Judgment Day within ourselves.

Faith is the evidence of things hoped for, and the substance of living. With faith, we may face the fact of death and not be defeated.

At least, so I have found it.

July

JULY is just plain hot in New England, and there is no use pretending that "this is MOST unusual." It isn't. What is unusual is a cool July, which makes news. It is now corn-growing weather, haying time, ripening time, picnic time. Time to take an early dip in the pond and finish the day with another.

Jill never minded heat but it flattens me. But I've learned never to fight the steaming temperatures, but to melt away with some fortitude. Father never learned this and Mama said he worked up extra heat getting so angry. Father's life with weather was always chancy in any season, for he took it personally, as he did everything else. He expected weather to cooperate with him.

He was an excellent forecaster of weather, and kept records from year to year. In the days before radio broadcasts mixed weather reports in with advertisements for the brand that is not Brand X, our phone rang often as people inquired whether they could plan a picnic safely the next day or whether it would rain on Saturday.

Now that we have weather reports every hour, I sometimes think of Father stamping to the phone to tell the Buchanans that they better call off the garden party. I never even understood the rain gauge, although he tried to explain it to me.

Heat is relative, in a way. When Jill's sister and her family moved from one Arizona town to another not far away (Gene was on a government project) Betty said it was 112 one day and she had to go downtown to get gas in the car. As she chatted with the gas man, nearly fainting with the heat, he asked if she had been in town long.

"No, we just moved from Wellton," she said.

"Well," said he, "you must be glad to be here where it is so much cooler!"

And I notice on the hottest week end, when the children come out from the city, Connie puts on a sweater as soon as the sun casts afternoon shadows on the lawn.

"Lovely and cool in the country," she says.

Conversely, when they come in winter, I put the thermostat up to eighty and hope I won't have a heat stroke.

Most people have theories about ways to beat the heat. Allan, my English friend, was for a number of years a ship's captain. My geography is so shaky that I never figured out just where his ship cruised, but it was in the subtropics where the temperature was blistering.

"Heat is no problem," he told me, "you just drink boiling hot tea."

So I tried it. I found the scalding tea made me break into a heavy perspiration, which maybe was cooling, but made me miserable. I went back to iced tea, cool and clinking with cubes and laced with mint. I went along with him on the tea but not the temperature.

When we used to go to dog shows, I would sit in the broiling sun all day as we waited to go in the ring, and think about iced tea. Jill said I talked about it for sixty miles on the way home and started the kettle as soon as the dogs were taken care of.

My Aunt Minnie, who at eighty still goes deer hunting, always takes a Thermos of tea with her when she takes to the woods. She killed her biggest buck while she was sitting on a stump having her tea. She told me she lost most of the tea.

Some of our neighbors, come mid-July, draw their shades early in the morning, and one of them tacks old newspapers over the windows on the sunny side. This gives the house a queer cavernlike light, and of course there isn't a breath of air. I would rather have even hot air than none.

Connie believes in an electric fan on the floor, blowing away from the window. About all this does is create a draught around your feet. I use the electric fan chiefly to defrost the refrigerator, where it is indispensable.

One year when Jill's asthma was bad, I presented her with a portable room air-conditioner. This is a wonderful gadget. You feed ice cubes into it and lovely cold air comes out. I was charmed with it. But to get the benefit from it, Jill was to stay in her room with doors and windows closed, thus keeping out the pollen. She put up with it exactly half of one night, and then I heard her door banging open and windows going up.

"I don't want to be shut off from everything," she said.

So the air-conditioner now functions in the family room, with four open doors, the fireplace opening and four windows. In spite of this, it does cool the air, but it eats a great many ice cubes.

I do enjoy reading all the magazine articles about keeping cool. Evidently many women have time to lie down with pads (dipped in this or that) over their eyes. To relax completely and think cool thoughts, then take a long cool bath (with Essence of Alpine in the water). This is followed by a light dusting of Neige de Nuit, and the donning of a fresh flowery frock (Pattern Number 19405).

I think about these women sometimes as I am making currant jelly. Jelly-making is one of the hottest of summer occupations for you canNOT leave it, not at any stage, and lie down with pads over your eyes. You hang over the kettle, and the kitchen is hot as the Sahara. You have to watch the berries, so they won't stick to the kettle. They cook just enough so the juice can be extracted, no more, no less. Then after the juice is extracted, you watch the jelly itself. What a difference a few minutes can make!

One year I was careless enough to leave wild blackberry jelly while I answered the phone. The jelly went in the glasses all right, but nothing could ever pry it out again. Another year, Jill was so anxious to get back to the garden, she took the kettle off and poured the jelly in the glasses, sealed them, carried them to the fruit cellar. We found that wild grape sauce was quite good over custards and with cold lamb.

Jill always felt if you ignored the heat, you would not notice it. I said this was because she was not normal, she didn't notice either heat or cold, her internal thermostat was just PECULIAR.

When the children come for a week end, they resemble wilted lettuce. But in a few hours, they look better. After a swim, we eat down by the pond, where it is always cool. The favorite supper is hamburgers and toasted rolls and a green salad. We always have our favorite sauce for the hamburgers, which we call Louell's Goop.

To make this you put 1/4 pound of blue cheese through a sieve and cream well with 1/2 cup of butter (1 stick) and 1/2 clove of crushed garlic. Blend in 2 tablespoons of prepared mustard, add salt and pepper to taste. When you spread this on broiled hamburgers, it melts into licking goodness. If you have a blender, it is even easier, for the advantage of a blender is that it does the work for you.

Connie gave me a blender last Christmas. As usual, I did not read the instructions, my theory being that instructions only confuse me. This blender has a wonderful feature which the old one did not have, namely, you can wash the knives or whatever you call them because the glass top, the knife unit, and the bottom are all separate. It is a great help, but not unless you know about it! My first experience was making bean soup. I blended in a few seasonings, some minced onion, and tasted it. It was about the most delicious bean soup I ever had made, smooth, creamy, savory. So I hummed away as I unscrewed the top. In no time at all I had bean soup flooding the kitchen floor, as well as a lake of it on the counter (I was making enough for two days).

"Did you read the directions?" asked Jill as she waded in from the garden. There really wasn't anything to say to that, and anyway I was too busy mopping up bean soup to speak at all.

I was discouraged, not with the equipment, but with myself and went into what Jill called "a state."

"I do not see how I ever graduated from college," I began. This is the way I always begin in such cases.

"We never studied appliances at Wellesley," said Jill, getting three sponges from the back kitchen.

"I really do not see HOW you can live with anyone as stupid as I am," I said.

"Have I complained?" she asked.

I wiped some bean soup from my chin, and how had it gotten there?

The next day, I addressed the blender.

"I have now read the book," I said. "We are now going to co-operate in making deviled salmon."

I used Mary Meade's recipe, and actually if you follow her Magic Recipe for the Electric Blender, you could practically live with nothing but a blender and a hot plate. The salmon is our favorite. This day, I advanced cautiously, mindful of the directions and I gingerly put in the blender the following:

> 1 cup canned tomato soup, undiluted
> ¼ onion
> ¼ green pepper, diced
> 3 tablespoons butter
> ½ teaspoon salt (I used more)
> 1 teaspoon prepared mustard
> 1 slice lemon, including peel (no seeds)

I ran the blender until everything was mixed (15 seconds) then added 1 pound flaked canned salmon. I put the whole in buttered baking shells, topped each with crumbs and melted butter and a wafer-thin slice of lemon. I baked the salmon at 400° about twenty minutes.

This is supposed to serve six but three can manage very well.

On the subject of how many servings any given dish contains, I am always doubtful. Some recipes that are supposed to serve six would indeed do so, if all six were midgets. Recipes for four usually will keep two from starvation. And in any case, it depends on WHO is eating! I would hate to make anything for six and serve it to Don and my son-in-law and expect a crumb left over for Holly and Jonquil. Whereas Connie barely manages a single piece of chicken.

We have made it a rule, when having company, to double every-thing, unless we are fully conversant with their eating capacity. Now we know Steve is a modest eater, except when it comes to floating island pudding or angel-food cake. We double the first and make two angel-food cakes.

There are few dishes, except soufflés, which cannot be used up one way or another. It is my experience that people who say they will never eat leftovers, will consume them happily as long as they are not labeled leftovers. The term leftover is unfortunate, but I've never invented a better one, for remainders sounds even worse. It is better to say it is just something thought up on the spur of the moment, and this is true for it is thought up when you see what's in the refrigerator!

Of course soup made from whatever is on hand can always be called *"pot au feu"* if you can pronounce it, or *"soupe du jour,"* which is easier. *Pot au feu* is more of a stew, but *soupe du jour* can be anything from chicken broth (with those leftover noodles) to bouillabaisse, which as far as I can see has everything and anything in it.

The latter is a controversial subject, for gourmets argue as to the ONLY correct way to make it. All ways differ, too. The only other recipe as much of a controversy is the correct way to make hush puppies, and also why they got the name. I no longer enter into this, and shall not. Having lived in Virginia seven years, I feel I know the way to make them, but I do not give my recipe to anyone. I once put it in a column and hundreds of agitated readers wrote me to tell me how wrong I was. Everyone to his own version, as far as I am concerned.

The only time I ever enjoyed arguing about anything was when I briefly was on a debating team in high school, but that was like a game. I never get any pleasure in pointing out to people that they are wrong or contradicting them. I know it is a fine way to work out frustrations and aggressions but I have to work mine out whacking away at fallen branches with an axe or rooting up thistles by the kennel.

The most futile arguments seem to be about dates. I can't see that it matters whether somebody went to Florida in 1932 or 1940. The trip is over, I feel, presumably paid for by now.

I did get into a rare argument with Erma over whether something happened last August or not. But this had to do with the serious problem of whether the three mongrels leaping the fence and chasing around the yard were interested in the squirrels or in siring a litter of half-Irish puppies, and on this hinged my having to board Holly briefly or keeping her with me.

In the end, I just looked it up in my Line O Day book and the argument was over.

I admit that I have very strong opinions, all of them wrong according to Connie. But I have never, in my whole life, known of anyone to be argued out of a firm opinion, so I "save my breath to cool my porridge," as Mama used to say.

If people I meet, in that tactful way many people have, tell me they do not see why I love the cockers and Irish so when everybody knows they are nervous dogs, I turn red as a boiled crab and say shortly, "They aren't." But one could argue all day with these people and afterward they might say, "She does not know what her breeds are like. I had a friend who had a very nervous cocker spaniel, very nervous."

If you take an over-all view of life, you realize that no two people ever have exactly the same experience in any area, for no two people are alike. What is true for one, is not usually universal. And it might be a dull world without individual differences. Trying to make everyone agree with you can be pretty tiring too, as well as useless.

Good conversation is possible without a pitched battle, exchange of opinions is stimulating, and exploring the ideas of others can add new dimensions to one's life. It becomes an argument when someone gets angry. This is easy to tell, for people have a way of growing tense, speaking in higher tones, and men generally bang their fists on something. At this point, it is a good idea to turn the conversation to something simple such as the probability of a hurricane or whose well has gone dry last week.

And the best way to quiet down a severe argument is to ask a question such as, "Have you heard what happened in Bridgeport this week?" Or, "Did you read that article about Russia in the last Sunday *Times?*"

This is a curious fact, Russia is not controversial as to what's happening there and what Russia thinks. What we ought to do about Russia is dangerous to bring up. For that gets you into politics faster than a rocket. There seems to be no middle ground, once you get into politics. For the whole world mess is either entirely the fault of mismanagement on the part of the Republicans or it is definitely because of the Democrats. And I doubt whether arguing about the defects of the parties changes any votes when election time comes around.

Just now, I had a conversation with Holly about not chewing up my favorite nylon dusting mop. There wasn't any argument, really, she just shut her mouth tight, so it looked as if she were carrying a blue muff. I opened her mouth and took it away and gave her a bit of cheese and there was no argument about that either!

We live in an age of plastics. Plastics have revolutionized our living. We may wear plastic raincoats, rain bonnets, boots. We slide into the car and it has plastic seat covers. If the car stands out, it may wear a plastic hood. When we sit down in the house, we may sit on plastic cushions. I am sure I brush my teeth with a plastic toothbrush (nylon bristles). We grip plastic handles on the dust mops. Unbreakable plastic dishes are ready for anything.

Razors, hairbrushes and combs come in plastic boxes. The boxes are fine for buttons, hairpins, needles and thread. They are also good for holding wet washcloths when you travel and like a wash cloth. The case on my bedside radio is undoubtedly plastic. My handbag has a plastic handle.

It is a wonderful invention and will soon invade every cranny of our lives. I have, however, reservations, and they have to do with food packaging. When I approach a plastic-wrapped package of cheese, I hesitate. I know what's ahead of me. Since my episode with the electric blender, I now read all labels on everything, right down to every infinitesimal ingredient. I read fervently: "Open the package this easy way." I look at the picture which is easy enough, the cheese seems to unfold itself like magic.

But not for me. I take my knife (which should be sharpened) and holding the package firmly in my left hand try to insert the point in the heavy plastic, which must keep germs out because it also keeps my knife out. I find my first finger less resistant, I get a Band-Aid and remove the plastic from that, apply the Band-Aid and get the kitchen shears. With these, I make a jagged hole and peel off some of the plastic, also peeling off part of a slice of cheese, which I eat, while I think things over. Then I cut off the whole plastic and assemble the battered cheese on a plate.

And then, invariably, Connie comes for a week end and calls to me from the kitchen, where she is rearranging the refrigerator contents.

"MAMA! Don't you KNOW you should keep the cheese wrapped in plastic?"

Some plastic-wrapped products yield gracefully to the screwdriver. Once you get an entry, you are set. Naturally the manufacturers cannot sell automatic openers with every package, I realize that. But I think wistfully of the days when I used to watch the grocer lift the saberlike knife and slice down a creamy wedge of cheese from a great wheel. There were always crumbs to nibble while he weighed it. Sometimes George gets in such a wheel, and lays the wedge on brown paper and ties it with a string.

I am not, believe me, arguing. The infinite variety of cheeses, cheese spreads, cheese flavors, is a most acceptable help to any homekeeper. I am just wishing the wrappings were easier to open! Possibly I am the only one who has difficulty, for I am not dextrous with anything but typewriter keys. And in any case, I can be sure the contents of these impervious packages must be sanitary!

I watch my granddaughter walking from the sofa to the chair. When she falls down, she thinks it highly amusing. Muffin (her name is Alice Elizabeth and this is too much right now for so small a person), Muffin is now exhibiting what I have read was the first stage of the development of man, when he got up from all fours and walked erect. Muffin had, heretofore, traveled rapidly and expertly on all fours. Suddenly she decided to change her method of locomotion, and now there is the miracle of learning to balance, and to walk. She falls down, she weaves a lot, but she walks.

She enjoys this erect position so much that she insists on standing up in her feeding chair while she has her meals. This gives Connie plenty of exercise, and added to it is the fact that Muffin has ideas about feeding herself, so she has one spoon, usually upside down, while her mother tries to get the quota of food down by means of a second spoon. When Muffin is in the mood, she flings her spoon down. Meals are followed by a mopping-up process both on Muffin and the floor and the kitchen counter. Muffin finds this delightful. In fact, Muffin finds most of life highly amusing.

So far as I know, nobody has ever really understood humor, although it is often analyzed, especially by the top comedians. I think being a Joey Bishop or a Sam Levenson would be too hazardous to bear. Sometimes things are funny and sometimes they are not, and it is an unpredictable business. Some men, like the great Fred

Allen, seem to be funny no matter what they say. And Bob Hope seems to have an infallible ability to hit the jackpot in almost every line. I think my favorite is Joey Bishop because he looks so grave and shy. And he seems to have a natural humorous attitude toward life.

I have thought a great deal about humor, and lately, about the beginning of humor in the diaper set. To Muffin, her Daddy's pursing of lips and making a sort of cheeping sound is absolutely riotous. When Connie sings a French song to her, with gestures, Muffin collapses. Where the water goes when the plug is pulled in the bathtub is side-splitting. But the peak of humor is when Connie says, "Where's Alice?"

This is followed by Alice ducking her head, then peeking.

"Oh, THERE's Alice," Connie cries.

At this, both of them rock with mirth.

Why? I would give a lot to understand. I can only say more things seem to be funny to Muffin than to any other young child I have known. I hope she keeps this sense of humor, for it is the best defense against the stress of life. It is truly the saving grace.

Often when dire events happen, it helps to remember they will be a fine source of amusement later on. For instance, we went to a great deal of effort one year to put up brandied peaches. We spent a whole hot day at it. Someone, some time, had said the best treatment for brandied peaches was to bury them in the ground for a time. So we did just that. Jill dug a nice hole in the vegetable garden in a row that was empty.

"I wonder whether they should stay six months or six weeks?" she asked.

"I can't see what the ground does for them that the fruit cellar couldn't do," I said, "it's cold and dark there too."

We finally decided to dig up a jar or two for the Christmas holidays. Jill went out and was gone some time. When she came in she looked discouraged.

"Maybe you don't bury peaches except in tropical climates." She took off her mittens. "Ground's frozen like granite," she said. "Maybe we can have brandied peaches on ice cream for Easter dinner."

Winter passed, the ground thawed. I was peeling potatoes one day when Jill came and stood in the kitchen doorway.

"Thought I'd go out and dig up a jar of those peaches." Her voice was casual.

"Fine. We can use them when Steve and Olive come for dinner."

"Fine." She still stood there, and then said, "By the way, did you watch me when I buried them?"

"No. I was hunting for that missing batch of check stubs you wanted."

"I started to put them at the edge of the asparagus bed," she explained, "but I decided not to, I think."

Now I dropped a potato, which Holly bore off in triumph. She loves to snatch potatoes.

"You mean you can't remember WHERE you buried them?"

"Now, don't get excited. I know the general area."

"Be careful you don't crack the glass," I called after her.

Then I sneaked to the back-kitchen window and looked out. Jill wandered here and there, sometimes sticking the spade in, then pulling it out. She had the abstracted air of a water-dowser. She was certainly in the general area, she was in the vegetable garden, which is the only place in which you can dig. The rest is merely one stone upon a bigger stone. But the vegetable garden was then about a quarter of an acre or more.

I watched her take up a spadeful by the corn patch, then move toward the raspberry rows. It occurred to me with some horror that when the garden was harrowed, our peaches might be harrowed too. By now, Holly was beside me, resting her paws on the window sill and peering out earnestly to see what I was looking at. I persuaded her to go away and I went back to the stove.

When Jill came in, I didn't say a word.

"Some day I suppose this will be funny too," she said fiercely. "But do not mention peaches to me for a long, long time."

It was a bitter blow to her, for she was the organized one, the labeler, the filer of papers, the drawer of garden diagrams.

Now the strange fact is, those peaches never turned up. The garden was ploughed every year, harrowed, raked, planted. Rocks worked their way through the soil every season, as always. I borrowed spadefuls of good dirt every spring for my violet-transplanting project. But not a shred of glass or a peach pit ever made an appearance.

It was a winter evening some years later when we were popping corn over the open fire and talking of projects for next spring. Jill poured melted butter over the popped corn.

"What do YOU think happened to those peaches?" she asked.

"They just went away," I answered. "The Borrowers took them. They must have had a fine party."

"It is kind of funny," she said, and laughed.

After that, it was funny, and became one of our favorite stories. We called it the time the peaches went away.

The Borrowers are those mysterious beings who take one glove, or the big spoon of the salad-serving set. They take that full bottle of pills that was right on the shelf the night before, you not only saw it, you removed a pill. Sometimes they take a favorite handkerchief, and sometimes they make off with a bottle-opener. Now and then it is a book or a special record. Whatever they need, they take, and you never see it again.

The jars of peaches were their biggest haul, and they had to work for them, for they had to dig, and dig in the exact spot.

There was the time the pressure tank blew up. I started up from bed screaming, "A plane crashed in the yard."

Naturally, I had to shake Jill, for when she slept, she was really asleep.

"Nonsense," she said sleepily. This was her standard reply to my infrequent reports that a plane had crashed in the yard. "It's in the house."

She bolted down cellar and I heard her sloshing through the water, shutting things off. When I peered down (the stairs being too steep for me) it looked like a scene from Dante, the cellar being the river Styx, and steam rising and cartons floating about in the semi-dark. She got the water shut off and sloshed back upstairs.

"Cellar ceiling too," she said shortly.

It was a disaster. But eventually this got to be funny too.

"You and your plane crashes," said Jill.

"Well, I wish they wouldn't swoop right down over the roof," I said.

And then there was the time when a gallon of green paint in the trunk of the car overturned. The lid was not on securely and when Jill opened the trunk, an inch of green paint was all over every part of the trunk, even the raised part in the rear. The well where the spare tire rested was a well indeed, of paint.

It took several hours to scoop out enough so she could drive to the gas station for help. She said the state of the trunk created a sensation, and it took everything the gas station had to get the worst of it out. But as Jimmie DeLory pointed out, "It's a good thing it's green, kind of matches the outside of the car."

By the time we turned that car in, we felt the new owner should appreciate the matching painted inside of the trunk. And by then, we felt there was something really funny about the whole thing! Few people pour gallons of paint inside the trunks of their cars.

When Jill blamed herself for not hammering the cover on the can, I reminded her of my slight error with the same car.

"Remember the chromium," I said.

I was driving that particular day and we were off to a late start for a dog show. It was, I think, the Cape Cod show. The grand master of dog shows is Mr. George Foley, and granite is a soft substance compared to Mr. Foley. If you do not enter your dog ON TIME, you can just go on home, even if you have spent two days and nights getting to the show, have had an auto accident on the way, broken a leg, and taken the wrong road. (This is particularly true of Long Island where all the roads seem to be the wrong ones.)

So I was understandably nervous. There was a car parked at one place in a narrow road, with bushes on either side. I didn't wait, I just dashed by. A small bush went down but the boulder under it did not, and the boulder stripped all the chromium from the car on the near side. It is surprising how much chromium a car has and when it hangs down on the road, it is a devastating sight.

"My, you're a quick little thing," said Jill.

She hammered the chromium up in loops so it didn't drag on the ground. We got to the show with ten minutes to spare and Jonquil wouldn't bring in the dumbbell anyway.

"Oh, the darling little cocker," the gallery cried, and Jonquil loved it. She did all sorts of charming things, except bring the dumbbell. It was a long time before I viewed that day in the proper perspective.

But finally someone was telling about crashing into a road sign, and I remarked cheerfully, "Did you know you can strip ALL the chromium off a car in ten seconds?"

Then we added that fatal day to our list of things to remember as amusing in a peculiar way.

We sympathized with Ed Koch when he came in to fix the electric pump. He asked Jill to go down cellar and check the switch for him.

"I lost my glasses down the Drakes' well," he explained.

We all stopped to laugh at this occurrence, although with full sympathy. It is a catastrophe to drop glasses down a well, but rather rare.

"I just leaned over to see how much water they had in the well," said Ed, "and plop, there went my glasses. Forever." He added, "I can't read a thing. This was my only pair because I gave up the bifocals after I fell down the cellar stairs three times with them on."

I knew how he felt, for my life with glasses has been hazardous. I have always been farsighted, and had no difficulty reading signs tacked on telephone poles at a great distance. But I had difficulty getting a book far enough away to be legible. For a long time, I had three pairs of glasses, one for typing, one for chasing around after the dogs (middle distance) and one small elegant blue-rimmed lorgnette for reading menus and theatre programs when I WENT OUT. Ah, vanity!

Now I have one pair of typing glasses and one pair of trifocals, which are supposed to solve everything. It involves tri-motions of my head, I find, in order to look through just the right lens.

A number of the young marrieds we know wear contact lenses. It is easy to tell the wearers, for they keep going out of the room at intervals to remove a dust speck or something. One hapless neighbor lost one of her contact lenses on Fifth Avenue in New York when she went in to shop. Instantly she was surrounded by people who wondered why she was feeling her way around the sidewalk. Those who wore contact lenses understood instantly and formed a cordon around her to keep the minute glass from being stepped on. One man (who had his on) found hers, and saved the day.

A guest at Connie's wedding also lost one of hers, and going to the church was deferred while everyone crawled around. This lens turned up under the bed in the big bedroom, right in the middle, and how did it get there?

I am told contact lenses are the answer to all problems with eyes, but I am satisfied with my obvious turquoise rims. Much easier to find!

Now, on hot afternoons, is the time to read. I have never been a hammock-reader because (A) a hammock makes me dizzy and (B) it dumps me out in a short time. We used to have one slung between two of the old apple trees and it looked inviting, but not to me. The cockers loved it, chewing the fringe and trying to climb in (they fell out too).

A good lounging chair is my choice, and always turns out to be the choice of every cocker on the place. There is room at the bottom for one, who gets pushed off and replaced by a second, who gives way to a third. This keeps the chair from being too steady, and the situation worsens when Especially Me gets on my lap and sits there, bumping my book and fixing his earnest eyes on me.

The dogs do not like me to read. They seem to sense that if I have a book in my hand, I am away from them. How do they know? They are tolerant of most non-dog activities, but never of reading. They paw at me, sigh heavily, shove against the book. Come back, they suggest, from wherever you are! My best reading time is when a helpful rabbit hops along the edge of the swamp and they have things of their own to attend to.

I wonder who started the idea of "light summer reading." I may get awfully hot in July, but my mind is all right. And aside from the cockers and Irish, there is more uninterrupted time in summer. During the hottest part of the day, there is a lull. And any book suitable for winter is suitable for summer, for books have no seasons. I read Bruce Catton's *A Stillness at Appomattox* in summer, John Hersey's *The War Lover*. I read James Gould Cozzens' *By Love Possessed* (so then I had to reread *Guard of Honor*). I like to read historical novels such as Elswyth Thane's *The General's Lady*.

And then I reread Faith Baldwin's *The Juniper Tree,* not her latest but one of my favorites.

Invariably I read Wyman Richardson's *The House on Nauset Marsh.* It belongs on the shelf beside Hal Borland's *This Hill, This Valley,* and that is about the highest recommendation a book could have.

I reread Keats's letters, always finding new treasure. I sometimes think the true measure of the man is in his letters. For Keats was not only a poetic genius, he was a rounded personality, thoughtful, philosophic, witty, full of naturally high spirits, warm in friendship, passionate in love.

Goethe says, "Whatever you cannot understand, you cannot possess."

Therefore, I do not possess much of modern poetry. It confuses me. A few, such as those of Robert Frost, have classic simplicity. I admire Dylan Thomas, but I like best the parts of his poems which run limpid to my understanding. Such as "And once below a time I lordly had the trees and leaves/Trail with daisies and barley/Down the rivers of windfall light."

This grows more beautiful and has more meaning the more you read it, which is the way poetry should be.

I am not a follower of fashion in poetry. And I do not always think the new is better than the old. At least not because it is new. Shelley, Byron, Keats, have been in and out of fashion a number of times. The Pre-Raphaelites had their day and were put in dusty corners. In my day, romantic poets are retired. Who reads Rupert Brooke any more? But one of my cherished poems is his sonnet, "The Treasure," which is about death and ends:

> Still may Time hold some golden space
> Where I'll unpack that scented store
> Of song and flower and sky and face
> And count, and touch, and turn them o'er,
> Musing upon them; as a mother, who
> Has watched her children all the rich day through,
> Sits, quiet-handed, in the fading light,
> When children sleep, ere night.

Edna St. Vincent Millay is known as a poet of the wild candle-burning-at-both-ends Twenties. But no poet, so far as I know, has made a glory out of mathematics as she did in the sonnet "Euclid alone has looked on Beauty bare—" And ends, "Fortunate they/ Who though once only and then but far away,/Have heard her, massive sandal set on stone."

This is not the age of poetry, I am told, but it is a pity. For poetry can express much that is in our hearts, and so doing, eases us and gives us new perception of the meaning of life. Music does this also, but not so specifically. Actually the muse of poetry and music are one.

We are in a period when science seems primary in importance. Particularly the science of missiles. But man can never live on science alone, for the beauty of a machine is limited. It cannot, I think, nourish the soul as the arts can. But I do not intend to argue the point. If anyone says science is enough to make the good life, it is not my province to assail their belief. But I am sorry.

When a severe storm comes in July, the air is breathless as the charcoal clouds pile up. The dogs decide to come in the house, and they have an anxious look. Perhaps the atmospheric pressure warns them to seek refuge, perhaps it is the flat strange light. It is very still, no bird stirs. The leaves look as if they were carved against the sky. I sense the storm by the fact that I smell it, just as I smell a hurricane.

In our valley, the storm comes suddenly, with a roar of wind and a wild surf of rain. Thunder rolls in the hills, and lightning splits the sky. The corn may be flattened. The pond overflows the dam. And suddenly, the clouds roll away and the sky is a startling blue. The grass is shining with wetness and scattered rose petals lie in the border. The air has the bouquet of wine. And I wonder whether we do not need the storms to make the world seem new again.

The sound of peepers is the music of spring. The sound of cicadas is the music of summer. It is harsh rapid chirping, but somehow it emphasizes the hot stillness and the peace of a summer day. I notice that on television, the sound engineers try to duplicate it in all small-town summer scenes. I may say television cicadas do not remotely resemble the real thing. All I can say is that they are shrill noises that sound as if they were made by bending sheets of tin back and forth. I think it were better if they omitted them, because no matter how faithfully the scene is set, the minute those imitation cicadas sound off, the illusion is lost. There are some sounds that cannot be imitated, at least not to the ear of a countrywoman.

Temporarily, a storm breaks the heat, and coolness flows through the house. The "windfall light" drops from the ebbing sun. It is, I think now, my favorite time of day, with colors muted as the light fades and gentle twilight brimming the meadow. If the lawn chairs have dried out, I carry my tray outdoors and watch the sunset and the blaze of afterglow, which is even more beautiful. Whatever I have, I put extra portions on the tray to divide around among the cockers and Holly. Otherwise, I wouldn't get anything to eat myself.

A day, a summer day, with sun and storm, is over. By the time the dishes are done, the moon rises, dipped in melted silver. The stars are white fire. And Keats's "little noiseless noise among the leaves" makes the night magic. So I go outdoors and sit on the terrace, and watch the fireflies carrying their lanterns in the meadow.

Holly comes to lay her head in my lap. "Pretty nice," she tells me. "Is that why they call it dog days?"

August

THIS is the month Faith Baldwin spends with me, as she has for a long time. Our friendship began in an unusual way. We met first at a dinner at Columbia University, after which we spoke in a small auditorium to a group of writers and would-be writers. I was, at that time, a member of the faculty and about ninety of the audience were my students, so I was perfectly at home.

It was probably the first time in her life that Faith was nervous, and she told me so at dinner. Since she was world famous and one of the best public speakers I've ever heard, I could not figure it out. Finally she said, "Well, I've never been to Columbia. Everybody else has."

I told her the only difference between this group and all the others was that each and every person expected to write the Great American Novel. Otherwise, they were quite normal and most of them pretty wonderful to know.

The next time I saw her, I had been asked for tea. Jill was off judging a dog show, so I went alone. I was nervous this time. I was also worn out because the two cockers who had developed a jealousy feud began to fight as I backed the car out, and I had to separate them (white gloves and all). Dogfights always give me semi-heart attacks, and this one was a serious fight because they both wanted to go with me. Evidently they figured the survivor would accompany me. I finally heaved them up to the fence, one on one side, one on the other, where, eventually, they had to LET GO and drop on opposite sides.

I always thought it was the dogfight that caused me to mow down one of Faith's favorite shrubs as I entered the driveway. I went to the front door and when nobody came, I wrenched at the knob, whereupon the door fell out. It had been nailed shut, so I was stronger than I thought.

On this note, I entered shakily. Faith was, as always, immaculate. I was not. I showed signs of wear all right. But Faith has a magic quality of making everyone at ease instantly, so we had a fine visit.

Later, I wrote about the first time she came to Stillmeadow and we had tea in the Quiet Garden. I said we had watercress sandwiches. When this came out in print, Faith pointed out that we did NOT have watercress sandwiches, they were cucumber. Faith has perfect recall, so I didn't argue.

Our friendship did not ripen slowly, it was apparently there always, just waiting for us to meet. Such a friendship is a rare and precious gift and there is really no way to explain or analyze it. We do not try. We just look forward all year to August.

If there is anything we don't talk over, I do not know what it is. And, as Jill always said, we talk all the time. We also picnic, drive around back roads, follow the sunset. At night, we sit by the open fire—and talk. We keep a jigsaw puzzle going and work at it on rainy days. But we do crossword puzzles separately. I do not believe two people can work successfully on the same crossword.

For one thing, no two people can look at it right side up at the same time. For another, it confuses me to have a quick pencil write in a word while I am on another number. We do, occasionally, consult as to some peculiar word.

Sometimes we discuss plots for stories. "We can both use it," says Faith, "it won't come out remotely the same anyway."

Or she gives me a plot. "This is for you, not for me," she says.

And it is true, although we think alike in so many ways, we do not write alike at all. The one thing we have in common in this field is our firm opinion that the other one has a perfect plot sense which we ourselves lack.

"I have no plot sense at all," Faith says firmly, "I am only interested in characters."

Then I tell her about a story I am having trouble with.

"That's easy," she says, "solve it this way—" and she solves it.

This is the season to admire well-organized people. THEY do not get all settled down for a picnic by the trout stream miles from home and find that the basket with the plates, forks, knives and napkins is on the kitchen table at home. They never have to, as we sometimes do, use whittled sticks to eat with. They never have to make plates out of an old newspaper (the print comes off when damp). And they never find the pepper grinder empty.

On the other hand, organization may be carried too far. I had an aunt who loved to "go a-gypsying," as she said. It took two days to line up the equipment. We carried hampers, bags, folding chairs, tablecloth (linen), boxes of table silver, and ready-cut kindling. By the time we got unloaded at the chosen picnic spot, we were all pretty tired. And after we had unpacked and set everything up, and eaten the food, we could never idle around, tossing stones in the stream, or wading, or hunting wildflowers because it was time to pack up and start home.

A perfect picnic depends on having a picnic temperament. And while it is lovely to have everything you need, some of our gayest picnics were those when we just tossed things in a basket and took off. It is hard to open a soft-drink bottle with no opener but there is a sense of triumph when you manage by wedging it in the car door and heaving. If we forgot the matches, someone always had a cigarette lighter.

We learned not to send the children or guests to the nearest village for missing supplies, for they vanished for a couple of hours. They stopped to look at antiques in a quaint shop or to watch a country auction. They, of course, did not get hungry, for they bought ham sandwiches on the way.

The insect world may be a problem, although not to me. Jill often ate her lunch on the wing, as it were, and if there is a solitary bee within miles, he heads for Connie, so she begins to leap about.

But there is still a magic about picnics.

Now it is a golden season in the gardens. How fast things ripen! And I feel, as Thoreau said, "And pray what more can a reasonable man desire, in peaceful times, in ordinary noons, than a sufficient number of ears of green sweet corn boiled, with the addition of salt?"

There is only one way to eat corn. You put the kettle on, a big kettle, with salted water halfway to the top. Then you dash to the garden and pick the corn as fast as you can. By the time you strip it, the water is boiling and in go the ears, for three or four minutes. Then serve on a warm platter, with plenty of butter, salt and pepper. This is not a silly gardener's idea, it is a fact that corn loses its flavor rapidly after being picked.

Naturally everyone cannot have a corn patch at the back door. It is possible to eat corn which has stood around, so to speak, if you must. For this, you add some milk and a spoonful of sugar to the water in the kettle, and you cook the ears longer, testing with a fork for tenderness. The older the corn, the longer it takes to cook.

Cucumbers are my second love, and these, too, should be freshly picked. We buy them in winter, but they seem rubbery. Jill favored cucumber mousse, baked, stuffed cucumbers, and I like cold cucumber soup. Our friend Arthur Torrey invented broiled cucumbers, and they are delicious.

Arthur splits the cucumbers lengthwise, removes seeds and pulp, and slices enough from the bottom of each half so the cucumbers will sit flat. He pares off some of the skin unless the cucumbers are young and fresh-picked. Then he puts the halves, hollow side down, under the broiler and broils just enough to reduce the water content (depends on size and age of cucumbers). Then he turns the boats over, dots well with butter, seasons with freshly ground pepper, salt, and dill and runs them under the broiler briefly.

"Just keep them in long enough, but not too long," says Arthur.

I would say they are done when the cucumbers lose their stiff look and are golden with broiled butter and dill. This isn't much more helpful either.

Then Arthur fills the boats with sour cream, adds a dash of garlic powder and again puts them under the broiler to heat the cream. (Too long will curdle it.)

This recipe is quicker to make than to read and is fine with sliced cold tongue and hot biscuits.

I gave him my Stillmeadow Baked Squash recipe. I use the pattypan (scallop-edged) squash, and parboil it until barely tender. Then

I cut off a piece of the top, reserving it for a cover, scoop out the inside of the squash, discard seeds and mash the tender pulp. To the pulp, I add diced onion, sautéed in butter, diced celery and a little diced green pepper. Then I add diced lobster or canned tuna fish or leftover diced beef or lamb, and pack the whole mixture back in the shell, top with browned crumbs and a dab of butter and bake in a medium hot (375°) oven until bubbling. I put the cover on for the last few minutes.

This is a one-dish meal with a tossed salad, French or Italian bread and coffee.

If you have the very young, small squash, you serve one to a person. A large pattypan may serve four to six. In that case, you slice it down with a pie knife, and serve the wedges.

This is the season when the good smell of pickling spice fills the house. I doubt whether there are any kinds of pickles or relishes we have not made. About our only failure was sauerkraut and I do not know what went wrong, but it never was crisp, it was limp. We had wonderful luck with stuffed pickled peppers. Jill always made apple butter, and I tried catsup. I think the new hot catsup now on the market is just as good. The first batch of catsup I made was hotter—in fact, so hot that we had to serve ice water with it.

We remembered, from childhood, that our mothers made oil pickles, which we used to eat on bread and butter. We never found a recipe like theirs, so maybe the missing ingredient was the same as in the bread pudding, which Don missed. Sweet pepper relish and corn relish never stayed long on the shelves.

The main delight in making pickles, relishes, preserves, is the feeling you have of using nature's bounty, and creating something special from it. And, of course, when you are freezing vegetables, you freeze them when they are young and tender and not when they are too old to have any flavor. Some commercially frozen vegetables are processed at the right time, but not many.

We tried freezing corn on the cob and found it very good, but preferred to cut it from the cob, feeling it kept the flavor better.

Giving away kittens is always a problem, especially in the country, where kittens are a universal product. The local paper often carries wistful ads such as "Three fatherless kittens need homes. Can you help?"

Or "Six well-behaved part-tiger male kittens available at ONCE." They are available all right, and in time will turn out to be females and sponsor more ads. "Lovely, cuddly kittens, just right to go to new homes—"

Unfortunately we cannot take them, but it is a serious temptation for me. Once I nearly brought home a basketful from New Jersey where I had gone to speak to a church group. These were parsonage kittens, black puffballs, putting their minds on being adorable as only kittens can. But at the time, we were feeding seventeen cats that just came to dinner, so I fled.

My dear friend Lois, who lives in New Jersey, wrote me a few years ago to ask if I knew how to get rid of squirrels and cats. She felt, she said, that I knew a lot about dogs and also about wildlife. But I had never said anything about squirrels in the attic. Or cats that just came by the dozen.

She and her husband and daughter and son live, not in the country, but in a New Jersey community. They have what she calls a middle-aged house, a yard, a few trees and that is all. But regularly the cats move in under the inaccessible part of the porch and have kittens. Meanwhile the squirrels race in the attic. As Lois says, "They carry on." They also run up and down inside the walls (insulation does not bother them).

The cats are pretty expensive, for Lois takes the kittens to the nearest animal shelter plus ten dollars for their care. She says apologetically that since she and her husband both work and the children are in school, they are not in a position to run a cat farm. Recently she wrote they were fresh out of cats but in the middle of the letter, her daughter appeared in the doorway with an armload of kittens and her husband came in the back door with more. She said, however, all the squirrels were gone except the few in the corner of the attic over the bedroom.

There is an old Cape Cod saying, which is all I could think of. "You'll get used to it."

It is my theory that once their house was owned by a cat collector who had fifty or more cats and who died, and the cats turned wild but always come back to the house to have their kittens. I see no other explanation.

This does not explain the squirrel situation. But squirrels cannot be turned in for adoption. They are hard to manage, too. A man on Long Island had a squirrel who fell down his chimney into a screened fireplace. He phoned the county police, who told him to catch it in a box and let it loose outside.

He telephoned the police again when he could not get the squirrel into the box and was told to call an oil company (I do not see why the oil company got into it). The oil company referred him to the S.P.C.A., who said he did not live in their district and to call the local dogcatcher. He telephoned the dogcatcher and got no answer. He telephoned again and finally located the dogcatcher who came with a net, caught the squirrel and turned it loose outside.

Then he warned the man NOT to call again because state law prohibited him from catching squirrels!

It would pay this man to put a heavy screen over his chimney.

Kittens are enchanting, except by the dozen lot, when they are a problem. Cats are even better. Cats have character, independence and intelligence. They do love you, contrary to some opinions, but they understand your weaknesses as dogs do not. A cat can convey a message very clearly. "So you thought you could have all that fried chicken while I was outside? Well, I am sitting RIGHT HERE until you serve, and that's that. And if the phone rings, I'll help myself."

A cat takes a logical point of view, which is that anything edible in the house should be shared. Esmé, our Siamese, used to watch us with amusement in her sapphire eyes as we tucked things on high shelves in cupboards. She could get in anywhere except the oven and the refrigerator, and you had to be quick opening and closing those.

She got in the washing machine once, but fortunately we saw her wedge-shaped head framed in the glass before we turned the water on. We never closed a cupboard door without saying, "Where's Esmé?"

She was a peculiar eater. She scorned cat food, but was passion-ate about chicken and lobster. She liked melon but only when it

was ripe. She also liked to eat flowers, especially tulips. Our efforts to feed her a balanced diet, full of vitamins and minerals, was a lost cause, except that she enjoyed dog food when she could take over a cocker's dish. I don't think she liked dog food so much but she liked feeling superior.

I think people who do not like cats just do not understand them. They get frustrated when cats are cats and not ever going to be anything but cats.

Our dear friend Leon Whitney has made a specialty of tropical fish, and while studying genetics, developed guppies that resemble Siamese fighting fish. He lined a whole room with tanks and when we went in, it was like being in a tropical sea. The tiny fish shimmered with color as they darted around, the water plants were emerald, and the tanks caught sun from the windowed walls.

Leon gave us a jar of fish, and we set up a tank in the family room, but they did not do well for us. We knew our well water might not suit them, so we boiled it. We put a thermometer in the tank, which being an electric one, blew some fuses right away. In the end, just as I had grown attached to one I called Horace, he died. I am sure the water, even boiled, was too full of minerals small fish did not like. We soon had to turn the fish tank into a terrarium.

August is hot, although not with the intense heat of July. Reaction to heat is a highly individual matter, as far as dogs and cats are concerned. I have seen Esmé, the Siamese, fold her brown velvet gloves and sit in the hottest part of the yard, and if I picked her up, her fur would almost burn my hands. But she would be purring away. Heat is for cats, she said firmly. Holly is also impervious to heat, as well as cold. She will sit placidly in ninety-degree sunshine or lie down in a snowbank. (The army should study the natural insulation of the Irish setters, I think.)

The cockers differ. Jonquil is like the little salamander. But she shivers if it is a cool day. And in winter, she prefers the window sill over the radiator or the hearth, very close to the fire. Tiki, the black and white boy, begins to pant the minute summer comes. He would be a fine dog for the Arctic. Especially Me can't stand the cold. Jill always said keeping the right temperature for everyone was a full-time occupation.

Now is the time the tide of summer begins to recede in New England. This is a strange thing, for you cannot say that one day is different than the next. The garden is bright with vegetables. Nicotiana makes the air sweet and Mexican zinnias paint the border with color. But we do not have to mow the lawn so often. Days are hot, nights are not, as the Farmer's Almanac says. There is a slanting sunlight and twilight comes sooner.

Jill always stopped hoeing, for she said the vegetables could take care of themselves. Also she found that the weeds would protect them if we had an early frost.

A few early-fallen leaves drift on the pond and algae floats on the surface. The baby frogs have grown and look as if they had been polished with wax. The country roads have a quiet look, for the heaviest summer work is done. At dusk, I like to ride toward the Litchfield hills and watch the lights go on in the houses and think about the families getting ready for supper. The cows come down the driftways, chewing, as cows always do. I have never seen a cow with her mouth completely quiet, which reminds me of some people I know.

The season reminds me of Byron: "The sword outwears its sheath, And the soul wears out the breast, And the heart must pause to breathe, And love itself have rest."

For after the vigorous growth of spring and summer, nature seems to pause, and the countryside has a dreamy look.

We need to pause too, in the midst of pickling and canning and freezing, and let the serenity of the season give us tranquillity. It is necessary before the brisk days of autumn and the work of getting shored up for winter and before the long cold brings shoveling and wood-carrying. It is time to sit quietly in the shade of the apple trees. And to think of Thoreau's words: "Why should we be in such desperate haste to succeed, and in such desperate enterprises? If a man does not keep pace with his companions, perhaps it is because he hears a different drummer. Let him step to the music which he hears, however measured or far away."

There is more to living than the endless activities we all pursue. Most of us indeed seem to live on a wheel which revolves faster and faster but has no true destination. I've got a million things to do. I can't keep up. I never have time to sit down and read. Oh, I love Beethoven but we seldom have a chance to play records these days. We are so busy—so busy—so busy.

But since we have just so much time alloted to us, some of it should be spent in reflecting, and some in pursuits which have nothing to do with our daily lives, such as enriching our spirits with music, nourishing our minds with literature, enlarging our horizons by looking at great painting. Because life isn't a business, it is a precious gift.

Americans are said to be always in a hurry, and I think this is a valid criticism. I suspect that if we hurried less, we should find more time, in a strange reversal of pattern.

That is, we should seem to have time enough for the things we "simply have to get done," and still time for leisure. I think the sense of pressure most of us feel is old-fashioned nervous tension. It is hardly conceivable that we work harder than the women in early Colonial days in New England. For we do not card and spin wool, make our own soap, carry water with which to wash clothes by hand. If we cook over the open fire, we do not get ALL our meals over it, and do the baking in the Dutch oven. We live push-button lives. Even the carpet sweeper has been replaced by the vacuum cleaner. And the telephone presumably saves hours of time.

But we are too busy to contemplate anything but the next day's round of chores. Why? Part of it is the raising of children. I notice children never just go out and play. They "take" sports. They have dancing lessons. They have group activities for ceramics, wood-working, leatherwork, jewelrymaking. Boys no longer go outside and toss a baseball, they belong to the Little League, well organized, and well regimented. And woe to the boy who does not "make" the team.

All of these activities involve endless chauffeuring on the part of the parents, endless waiting around until the game or rehearsal or class is over. If there is an occasional lull, the children do not know what to do, they stand around or they watch television. They never paddle around the edge of a lake until they learn to swim, they have a swimming instructor, and graded classes.

They are getting trained for a life of rushing from one activity to another, but they are not getting a chance to develop their own resources themselves. When they grow up, there is practically nothing they will not know how to do—except use their imagination!

I found, after Jill died, that I was working myself into a severe nervous state because I never could catch up with the daily chores, the kennel jobs, the errands, and futile attempts to keep some sort of books. I added all this to the major job of adjusting to what was, at that time, complete desolation.

One night I was really taking the count. Just putting one foot ahead of the other assumed gigantic proportions. I found I could not decide what to do next. And then, as if Jill spoke to me, I felt the sense of quiet that she always gave me, and it was as if she said, "Just do what you can. Forget what you can't."

I made some fresh coffee and sat by the embers of the fire and faced the fact that I had been living with no plan. Every day was a confusion of things unfinished while more things piled up. Why had I thought one person could do as much as two? Did I expect to have everything at Stillmeadow exactly as it had been when Jill put in an efficient ten-hour day? She was extremely well organized. I never had been, and never would be. She never seemed to hurry but worked with an economy of motion whether she was building a gate or balancing the accounts.

As I considered my difficulties, I felt her presence, encouraging me. My depression lifted, the tension vanished.

"I've been pretty silly," I said aloud.

The next day, I went back to my typewriter, and first I made a list of absolutely essential chores. I put this in the kitchen, and forgot it until I had worked as usual at the typewriter. This meant that I was not worrying all day because of never having time to do my own main job. When I finished my hours for the day, I found that essential list could be taken care of, and I still did not work half the night.

Every woman should have a different list of essential tasks, and a list of jobs that could be skipped most of the time. And much of the planning depends on how much, if any, help she has. Our beloved Erma has come once or twice a week for about nine years, and her wonderful husband, Joe, comes daily to help with the kennel and shovel Stillmeadow out in season. Since I have been alone, their warm devotion has helped to keep what was a very shaky boat under sail. They both do errands. Joe carries in the logs which I cannot lift. Erma takes care of the things I could never do, such as cleaning the ovens (my knees won't bend that much).

But I still have to keep my eye on that essential list. I used, for instance, to wash the milk glass every few weeks. Now I do not. I save several hours by letting it go, although it is a job I have always enjoyed. The silver and copper get polished when Erma can snatch the time, otherwise I let them go. I dearly love to wash, although I cannot iron, but I no longer run a tubful every other day. The daily dusting is abolished. The dust mop only comes out if the cockers track in too much.

Erma keeps up with the garden, but nobody works daily in it. The care of the hundreds of bulbs alone would be a full-time job. The bulbs do not get lifted, separated, replanted. And there are other things.

What is the result? Well, the result is that I am no longer heading for a collapse. I am able to love and enjoy the 1690 house, to have fun with the cockers (who do not get trimmed every week). I do not feel guilty if I have breakfast in bed and play small games with Holly. I feel no pressure if I sit on the terrace and watch the flight of the barn swallows or the way the shadows make patterns on the grass.

If I find myself beginning to worry about a job, I write it down and put it with the essential list. If it doesn't get done today, or tomorrow, or this week, I find the world goes along very well without it. I am not advocating being lazy, I am advocating what might be called budgeted activity. I could, this moment, think of fifty things that once seemed vital, and which are not.

I have one friend who has been unable to face life without her husband. She has, in a way, projected her grief into the burden she feels because she knew nothing of his business and cannot manage it. Rarely can a woman step into her husband's shoes and carry on a business as he did, especially a complicated one. But there are always experts in any field who may be consulted and authorized to do the managing. The mistake is in not looking for them and then LETTING GO of the burden, and spending your energy in fields in which you may competently perform.

We have a responsibility toward those who have gone into God's other room. I believe they are concerned with what we do with our allotted time in this world. I believe they expect us to live as fully as possible and to live constructively. We may fail often, but if we have a goal, we are apt to move toward it.

Sometimes it seems hard to think of goals when we are left alone, but they are there nevertheless.

Finally, no pattern is fixed. As the current of time moves us along, we make changes. Families have one pattern when the children are small, another when the children are away at school, and this changes again when they marry and the grandchildren are born.

There is nothing static. The pattern of relationships changes too. Romantic love is temporary; if it is real, it grows into the rich fulfillment of a successful marriage. This pattern is not the pattern of early romance. It is more complex, more satisfying.

The pattern of a mother's love for her baby changes too. Mothers who try to keep that first pattern lose the child somewhere along the way. The pattern changes, and fortunate mothers find the adult relationship with the child deeper and richer. The same is true of friendship. An exciting friendship unfolds into a steady abiding love, a deep companionship.

We may accept all these changes, but resist any change in pattern when our loved one dies. Unconsciously, we feel if we keep everything exactly the same, we will be closer to a time which cannot come again. We try to hold to it by all sorts of devices, even to keeping the possessions of our loved one in the same place. I understand this, for I felt very emotional about Jill's things. Particularly her gardening things.

But what virtue did they have in themselves? I could hear her say, "I am not using them. Don't be selfish."

The pattern changes. The presence of the loved one is there. We are not left alone, but we must learn the old material pattern is over with and we must live by a new and less tangible one, but one no less real.

After I have spent an hour or so in the yard, I realize there are many things we cannot understand. We take them on faith, but we take many things on faith. As the valley dreams in the sun, I have faith that the leaves will blaze with color in autumn as they always have. I know, even as this air is so soft and warm, that the snow will come, in season, as it always does.

We know what it is to have faith in love—and how lost we are without that faith. Most of us have faith in God, at least in a hazy way. Faith runs like a golden thread through our lives. "I believe" are two good words to live by.

My thinking was interrupted by the arrival of my friend Joan, who came breathless through the gate to announce the discovery of treasure. She is a pretty girl and was really glowing. It seemed she had been peeling wallpaper from her son Bill's room, because it was a dreadful mess, she said, the worst room in the old house. She had peeled three or four layers from one wall and was about to give up for the day when she finally peeled one last length off and there she saw part of a Colonial wall stencil, perfectly preserved, clear in color.

"And we didn't even know the house was that old," she said.

These wall stencils are rare treasures. In Revolutionary days, itinerant artists traveled about painting flowers and urns on walls. I have seen a few examples, never one that was not artistic. The artist would decorate parlors, hallways, sometimes bedrooms. Meanwhile he enjoyed the meals of chicken smothered in gravy, deep-dish green apple pie with sweet cider and buttermilk as needed. When his work was finished, he went on to the next stop, where, I am sure, he told the next prospect how many walls the Brewsters had decorated.

There isn't, so far as I know, any buried treasure in our part of New England. Not gold doubloons and pirates' jewels. But the ex-

citement of discovering the persimmon flowers and graceful urns under seven layers of wallpaper was like finding a hidden gift from the past.

"And right in our own house," said Joan, with awe.

Sometimes beautiful wall paneling turns up after being concealed under coats of plaster. And I remember when a neighbor uncovered a great fireplace, built, like ours, of hand-hewn stone. She had decided there must be one there and she tapped the wall with a hammer, and when a bit of plaster fell off, she could see the opening behind. The whole family dropped everything and began to hack away at the wall. The fireplace had been plastered up with the hand-wrought crane, iron kettles and spiders (frying pans to some) right in it. There was even a heap of ashes—and how old they were, nobody could guess.

The folk who built Stillmeadow were not affluent enough for stenciled walls, we decided, or for paneled walls in the parlor. But we settled for the worn original mantels, the hand-wrought hardware and old batten doors. We also had the oak floors pegged with square hand-wrought nails, and some of the bubbly glass still left in the windows. We felt we had treasure enough!

The amount of treasure doesn't matter, actually. We had a refugee friend who had lost all of his possessions when he fled to America, except two golden goblets which he managed to hide under his coat. They were part of a set which had been in the family for generations, and they were as exquisite as any in a museum. To him, they were a link with the time when his family owned a comfortable estate and lived gently, not hunted like wild animals. He now worked long hours in a laundry, patient, uncomplaining. But at night, after he washed the sweat off and sat down with his wife to a soup supper, he had the goblets set on the table.

I thought they were a visible heritage, much needed, but his own courage would be a greater one for his children. And it happened that he was able to put his children through college and give them the goblets as a wedding present when the time came.

I wish we might all leave a heritage of courage and warmth and appreciation of the beautiful to our children. This is more important than a financial heritage, although it would be foolish to underestimate the importance of money in this era when not only living costs so much, but education and illness have skyrocketed, and presumably will go on doing so. Not to mention taxes.

The blooming of chicory sounds a nostalgic note to me. It is like blue stars scattered along the roadsides. And it is the bluest blue—a color rare in flowers. Most of nature's blue is in the sky. We have a French blue lilac, and once had a fringed gentian in the meadow, but it moved away (or someone stole it). There is blue in the Confederate violets and heavenly blue morning-glories are a true blue. Delphinium is blue—or purple—or pink. But, at least in our valley, a real blue is rare in the flower-color spectrum.

I do not know personally any flower that is chicory blue except chicory. It does not grow here as profusely as it used to grow in Wisconsin, but there is enough to give notice that summer is ending. There was, in my childhood, a road along the top of a cliff on the way to Ephraim in Door County where the whole fields by the road were blue. Far below, the darker blue water of the bay stretched to the blue sky. So the whole world was three shades of blue, and I ached with it. I daresay the road is gone now, the fields full of development houses. But it is still winding there in my memory.

I always insisted on picking a bouquet of chicory although Father told me it would not keep, and it never did. The only thing he willingly stopped for was sweet clover comb honey, and that was not on my chicory road. But even then, when I was anxious to get back to school where I could be treated to "sinkers" by my beau, even then I felt a pang at seeing the chicory in bloom.

Sinkers, incidentally, did not agree with me. They were rock-heavy doughnuts with thick jelly in the center where the hole should be. I choked them down as a pure tribute to love.

The seasons in New England flow almost imperceptibly from one to the other. But August is unpredictable. I have kept a sort of weather Journal for years and note that August has everything. It can turn very cold so the furnace must go on. It can be dark with fog. It can rain like November. And it can be gentle as June. It is as if bits of leftover weather from all the year are stitched into August.

But on the whole, and usually, August is a mellow month. And nights turn cool, so Erma begins to unpack blankets and woolens and hang them in the sun. We have never made a project, as Faith does, of changing the whole house over for summer and changing back for winter. The same curtains and rugs just get cleaned and put back. The same Indian prints that we use for slip-covers get washed and put back. For a house where dogs are at home, these prints are fine for they wash like handkerchiefs, do not run, need no ironing. When they wear out, I get a fresh batch and since I get them by mail, I take whatever is sent. This means we may have blue, brown, beige, or even black backgrounds and almost any pattern. It means the cockers can tuck up on the maple day bed and not be retired to the floor, which isn't nearly as comfortable.

As I went out to the old orchard today at sunset, I wished the world could hold no sound more loud than the drop of the first windfall apple, and that no sky would be darkened except by the natural night after the day ends, and that no wind would come deadly with fallout.

Happy harvest time, I said, for us all, of the good things we now have!

AUTUMN

September

THE goldenrod blooms in the fields and along the roads. If it were not wild, it would be expensive, but since it may be had free for the picking, few stop to admire the bright rich spikes. It was suspect as to hay fever once, but that has been proved to be a false belief. Goldenrod just happens to bloom when a good many other weeds fill the air with pollen. If it is picked just before it opens fully, hung upside down in a cool dark place, it dries well for winter bouquets.

The wild asters bloom now too, and perhaps they are the true flower of September. They star the roadsides with amethyst. There are two tones, one almost light as mauve and one as dark as lilacs. Every floret is buttoned in the center with gold. The gardens are bright with asters too, the big heavy cultivated ones, but I prefer the wildlings. Often when man improves on nature, the result is overdone. The modern varieties of roses are splendid. Peace and Glacier and Spartan are my favorites, but I think the wild roses cannot be surpassed.

The wild roses of Cape Cod are the loveliest I have seen. They grow on tall, thick bushes, and the foliage is dark green and heavy. The blooms are deep pink or ivory, and open four-petaled from long pointed buds. They may only be picked if you wear heavy gloves for they are armored with prickers. Since they grow in clusters, it does not matter that they are transient for as one bloom drops, another opens. When blossom time is over, the bushes bear hips that are Chinese red or orange, and they are as big as crab apples.

Now is the time to finish drying the herbs. An herb plot takes little space and is rewarding. We had apple mint and spearmint growing wild when we came to Stillmeadow, and catnip. Jill planted dill in the vegetable garden and it nearly took over the whole area. It is better to plant dill off by itself somewhere. She put in chives and garlic by the raspberry bed, and in the Quiet Garden she made a plot for sage, rosemary, tarragon, borage and savory, with lavender and parsley as a border.

There are a number of ways to dry herbs but we liked hanging them in the woodshed rather than drying them in the oven. Perhaps the best part is how good the house smells when you package them. Herb vinegars are easy and delicious. We brought the vinegar to a boil, dropped the herbs in, and bottled the infusion. The tarragon and dill are my favorites. Jill liked the mint vinegar with lamb, but I prefer melted currant jelly as a sauce.

The tarragon died out and after several tries we gave it up. Possibly our winters were too cold. The sage spread and throve. So did the parsley. I like parsley in almost everything except pie. The borage has a delicate blue flower, nice to float on punch and it is also pretty in bouquets. Jill never tried bay, but the herb shelf is never without it. I do not think a meat loaf amounts to much without bay leaves pressed in the top.

A pinch of rosemary glorifies green beans, and is fine with sage in stuffings. Savory is good with beans and in salads, stews and ragouts.

Herbs have been used medicinally for generations. William Coles, in *The Art of Simpling*, written in 1656, says, "There is no question that very wonderful effects may be wrought by Vertues which are enveloped within the compasse of the Green Mantles wherewith many Plants are adorned."

I do not know why herbs were called Simples—was it because they were, in early times, picked wild and were simple, or natural, to the land? Herb teas were called tisanes, and were made by pouring boiling water over the herb and steeping ten minutes. They cured almost anything if you understood them. Catnip tea, for instance, strengthened the kidneys, tansy tea was used for rheumatism, boneset was an emetic. When modern scientists found the foxglove contained digitalis, an important heart remedy, I suspect some long-gone herbwoman was saying, "Well, took you a long time to find that out."

Every kitchen can have the magic of herbs nowadays for a number of firms package them as well as spices and they are available in most supermarkets. My herb shelf is by the range where I can reach for a pinch of almost anything. Saffron, allspice, cinnamon and crushed red pepper flakes are helpful in many ways. All herbs and spices should be used within a reasonable length of time or replaced. No matter how well they are packaged, in time they lose their pungency or flavor. About once a year, Erma clears the shelf and I have a fine time poking around the store for replacements.

I look for curry put up by an English firm (they spell it currie) but most curries are excellent. I like the Hungarian sweet paprika when I can get it but this is not always to be had.

Herb butters are made by blending herbs and sweet butter. I use a level tablespoon of minced fresh herbs or half a teaspoon of dried herbs to two ounces of butter. I add a dash of lemon juice. This is good on broiled fish, on asparagus, eggs or broiled meats.

Bottled sauces and mustards complete my seasoning musts. Sauce Robert and Sauce Diable and soy sauce are excellent, along with the Worcestershire sauces, the hot catsups and sweet catsup. I use a dash of one or the other in sauces, soups, stews and on broiled meats. Also in salad dressings. A sprinkle of soy sauce does wonders for broiled pork chops.

My friend Herbert Hayes sends me a Dijon type of mustard from Michigan at Christmas time and it is a smooth pungent mustard. Then I like the sharp-sweet Bahamian mustard (this for cold meat) and the mild regular mustards for salad dressings and sandwiches. There are also some bottled mustard dressings that are very good on hamburgers.

Now that food prices are in the stratosphere, it is still possible to prepare excellent meals at budget prices with herbs and seasonings. And of course, the invention of meat tenderizers makes less costly meats almost fork-tender. They are one of the best additions of our time in the culinary field.

Finally, for elegant sauces, I often use the frozen cream of shrimp soup. And for casseroles the unfrozen cream soups are excellent. Herbs, mustards, sauces, soups, all add to the adventure of cooking.

When the line storm comes in September, and we have cold wind and driving rain, I decide it is time for Smiley Burnette's buttermilk pancakes. A blender is best for these but a rotary beater will do. This recipe calls for 2 cups of flour, 2 cups of buttermilk, 1 teaspoon of soda, 1 teaspoon of baking powder, 1 tablespoon of sugar, ½ teaspoon of salt and 1 egg.

These are mixed in the blender or beaten until smooth. If the buttermilk is very thick, add more until the mixture is of pouring consistency. Pour into a container (a milk bottle is good) and let stand in the refrigerator overnight. In the morning pour small spoonfuls on a hot griddle, cook until the edges are lacy, turn once, cook until bubbles begin to form in the center. Serve at once to six.

With these, I serve maple syrup, the best in the world. This is first-run syrup from Elswyth Thane's Vermont sugar bush. It is light in color, delicate in flavor. Usually the first run of syrup is kept for the family and the darker syrup which you buy is second run. It is a luxury and rightly so for tapping the trees and making the syrup is a difficult heavy task. It takes about forty gallons of sap for a gallon of syrup, and while the sap is boiling down it must boil constantly. Nowadays some modern farmers are using oil for fuel but usually the fire is of wood and someone stays up all night tossing on the logs. The sap buckets have to be watched too, emptied into containers which are hauled to the firing pit on sledges.

And besides the work of making the syrup, it takes forty years, I am told, for a sugar maple to reach the age when it may be tapped. Our giant sugar maples are often streaked with sap when it begins to run, and I am sure a good amount of syrup could be made from them. But our attempt to make our own syrup resulted in two pints after some days of grueling work, and running out in the snow all night long to empty the buckets was too much.

In Wisconsin in the town where I grew up, maple syrup was as scarce as oranges. It was a special Christmas treat when Mama took down the syrup jug and heated some syrup on the stove and let me carry a cupful out and dribble it on the white snow. I lifted the blobs up with a spoon and oh, how delicious!

"I like molasses on pancakes," Jill said, when I rhapsodized over pure maple syrup. "Save the maple for you."

Molasses is not the same, but it is good, especially heated with butter. Powdered sugar is fine too (no pun). And currant jelly, melted.

But for the first pancakes at the end of summer, the pale gold maple syrup is best. And country sausage should go with them. If this is breakfast, lunch can be cottage cheese and fruit to make up for the calories. Or if it is supper, breakfast and lunch can be light.

I do not care what the diet books say, the best eating always, always, has calories.

After the line storm, summer seems to come again. Connie comes with her husband and Muffin to enjoy a balmy week end. I expect most mothers enjoy a brief emergence of the child within the settled-down wife and young mother. I was happy, when we got to the trout stream, to watch Connie run to the water, pull off her slippers and stockings and wade in the swift water. The little girl is still there, I thought, with satisfaction. I am also glad to see that Muffin has no fear of water as some babies have. Her idea of what to do is to whack it.

Maturity is indefinable. It is written about a great deal these days. Articles on divorce often say emotional immaturity causes most broken marriages. But who decides just when an individual is mature? We may go back to the Bible, "By their fruits ye shall know them." Most people are mature some of the time, but few are mature all day every day. The child within may wake, full of resentment at the harsh world. When a person says, "I'm sorry, that was childish of me," it is usually an honest admission.

Perhaps maturity is realizing this childish self but not letting it dominate situations. Or perhaps it lies in accepting life as it is without rebellion. When we are children, we expect everything to be perfect and we want to "live happily ever after." Then we find out, sadly, that there is no ever after. There is only today and what we make of it. We may still be happy, in one sense of the word, but we do not look for perfection ever after. The other side of this coin, is that we value more what happiness we may have instead of dreaming ahead for the ultimate.

It is time now to have the chimneys cleaned out, before the fire burns nightly on the hearth. Last year we were all reminded of this when our neighbor Dorothy started a brisk fire on the first cool night. Suddenly the chimney seemed to explode, with flames bursting down the chimney and smoke billowing out. Only her presence of mind about the fire extinguisher saved the day, but it did not save the room from a thick layer of greasy soot. She had, she said ruefully, finished the fall cleaning the day before.

There is nothing lovelier than an open fire on an old hearth. Fire is a comforter, a friend, but it may also be a deadly enemy. In the country, the sound of the fire siren strikes terror in our hearts. The old houses and the big hay-filled barns can burst into flame in a trice, and wells do not supply enough water for a real fire. If there is a pond or stream nearby, the volunteer firemen run hoses from them and battle the blaze. They also use tanks of extinguishing material. We are fortunate in our valley to have a dedicated and expert volunteer-firemen group, men who give their service day and night, whenever the siren sounds its warning.

Annual clambakes add to the funds for fire-fighting equipment and when the trucks go by, I wonder how many clambakes are riding along!

We are equally proud of our Volunteer Ambulance Association. The nearest hospitals are in Waterbury, Danbury and New Milford, each of which is a good number of miles away. The men sign up for duty on a rotating schedule—and I always hope when Joe and Louis at the market are on night call people will try not to fall ill, for the boys put in very non-union hours at the market except for Sunday. And Sunday, Joe sings in the choir so that is more added.

The ambulance provides service twenty-four hours a day 365 days a year. In 1960, the ambulance mileage was 2,075, or, as they said, a distance equal to that from Southbury to Salt Lake City, Utah. So when city folk ask if it isn't dangerous to be so far away—we look

smug. We can get to a hospital faster than they usually can in the
city. And we are comfortable with the drivers too! After all, the man
at the wheel may have cut our pork chops yesterday.

The year the Lions club began a drive for a new ambulance, our
neighbor Victor Borge contributed his services and for three hours
worked his magic on a breathless audience. Jill and I had been to
New York for his performances there and watched him every time he
appeared on television, but on this night, he gave the best performance of all—for free. In the end, he said, "I hope we shall now have
an ambulance with three wheels instead of two—and that none of us
will ever have to use it!"

I think the evening matched the excitement of the French troops
coming by during the Revolution. I know we all spent a week telling
one another what he said—and everyone able to walk had been
there anyway. It was one of the worst nights of the year with a rain
one could hardly stand against but, as Jill said, you would think the
whole state of Connecticut was there. Some had to stand in the
vestibule, some leaned against the walls. But nobody coughed!

School begins again and children wait at pickup points on Jeremy
Swamp Road. Most of them carry their books slung over their
shoulders with straps. I always carried mine in a bag. And on cool
days I was forced to wear a sweater. Now children do not wear wraps,
they tie them around their waists by the sleeves, so they look as if
they wore woolly aprons in back. I have watched Randy and Steve
Nies in winter coming down the road with storm jackets slung
around the waist in the same manner. It is the style.

When I was in high school I walked both ways, and it must have
been two miles each way. Nobody ever heard of a school bus. And
no parents had a car pool to transport us either. We were never
picked up after school—and my life would have been ruined if we
had been. My best friend, Peggy, and I saved our allowances and
went to the Palace for double chocolate fudge sundaes with NUTS.
This kept our strength up. Then she walked part way home with me
and I walked part way home with her and since we lived at opposite
sides of town, we got quite an extra walk in.

Or my beau met me under the Discus Thrower and we idled on

the school steps until I KNEW I had to start home. He walked to within two blocks of our house, and then I went on alone. Father didn't take to the idea of a girl being walked home from school by "a member of the opposite sex."

With Father's careful discipline, love bloomed as it might not have otherwise. Every stolen hour was honey-sweet. And for a naturally candid girl, I developed great skill in being devious. If I had really spent all the hours after school practising basketball, who knows what I might have turned into? I may say my conscience never bothered me for I knew Mama was aware of every move I made. She was a buffer state between two countries usually in a war alert.

But Father could be magnanimous too for when most of the boys in the senior class went off to war, he drove me to the camp at Sun Prairie to say GOOD-BYE to my hero, even though he said it was silly to make a fuss as the war wouldn't last three months.

Now the high school boys talk of just when they will do their army or navy stint. It is part of our way of life and only as schooltime comes around do I remember how short a time it has been since war and getting ready for war is a matter of course. How I wish today's children could be innocent as we were!

Today's children do not have a sense of security—how could they? By the time they are in their teens, many of them want to rush into marriage, feeling perhaps that will be their security. Too often it isn't and they are not equipped for responsibility as firm as marriage. If the world were at peace, I believe children might regain the carefree years. And have time for romance before beginning to wash dishes and do the laundry.

However, this is just my personal idea and I should leave such analyses to experts.

Last week end I went to the Steves' for dinner. Steve would not let me add a bay window to Stillmeadow because it would not be in the period, but Sugar Hill is what might be called a middle-aged antique, so he felt no qualms about putting a picture window in the kitchen-dining room. The dining table is a lovely round maple antique and the chairs are captain's chairs made extra-comfortable with cushions. The table is directly in front of the window, overlooking a green slope and the trout brook. Beyond the brook, the ground rises steeply to the horizon, and there are some trees there but not enough to obscure the sunset.

Maude and Harry Anderson were there and Rudolf, and we sat down just as the sun slid behind the hill. Steve said grace and began to carve the lamb, when Olive said, "There's that woodchuck!"

So we all got up and flew to the window. It is Steve's opinion that he shot that woodchuck several times, and it is Olive's opinion he missed him. There is no doubt but that he ate all their sweet corn last season, however. Which may be why he is the biggest woodchuck in Connecticut. We ran out to the terrace, and this bothered him, so he vanished before Steve could get his gun.

We sat down again and Olive brought the ironstone gravy boat and her mother, known as Olive T., served the salad.

"There's that bird we can't identify!" Olive cried.

So we all rushed to the window again and Steve brought the binoculars and passed them around. Binoculars do me no good as I have to shut one eye to see anything through them and that isn't much.

Nobody had ever seen this particular bird before and none of us could identify it either, for it flew away.

So we sat down again, but sat sidewise in the chairs, giving a better view just in case the bird came back to the feeder. Olive's elegant dinner was certainly enjoyed but we were up twice more before we finished. I reflected that dinner in the country is far more exciting than in the city. The only reason to go the window in the city is to see which way the fire engines are going.

Maude and Harry are not old residents but all of us feel they have always been here, for they love and appreciate the country as we do. In a sense, they are pioneers for they bought wooded land beyond North Woodbury and built a cabin for week ends while they waited to put up a house. They had a stern initiation last winter when all the new plumbing froze during the twenty-eight-below-zero week.

They both have a quality which is rare nowadays, they are quiet people. They listen to everything that is said and when they speak, they say something important. I have never heard either of them make a sharp critical remark or utter a sweeping generalization.

We all think they are very special people.

Those of us who have been here a long time do tend, I fear, to speak of "those city people" in a condescending way. This is partly because we had to live down being city people before the native residents accepted us. This is easy to understand, for some people come from the city for week ends and complain because, for instance, we have no sidewalks in the village!

Poking around in the garden yesterday, I found a tiny Indian bird arrowhead, white quartz. So far as I know, there is no white quartz around here, so it must have been brought from a distance. I turned it over in my palm, wondering what dark hands had patiently shaped it. It was strangely comforting to feel the continuity of life from the days when the Indians camped by the brook until today. It seemed to me unlikely the world would end now, when this tiny arrowhead had come down unscathed a couple of hundred years.

The Indians in this valley were friendly and innocent. They traded some prime land for a kettle and the road next to mine is still called Kettletown Road. At one time the road past Stillmeadow led to Kettletown and is still called the Old Kettletown Road. Now the upper end runs into fields and woods. Once we explored beyond the road and came upon an ancient cemetery. We made out on a few slabs the names of Revolutionary soldiers buried there. We only found it once but it was not a dream, for we could feel the stone and the ground was irregular as it is in old cemeteries.

I like to think the white people in this area traded with the Indians and at least gave something for the fertile land, even though only a kettle. The history of the white man in our country has black pages. The main dealings with the Indians consisted in many parts of the country of killing them off. Perhaps one of the worst instances was when the Sioux made a last stand against the white invaders in Minnesota. In December, 1862, after they lost a battle, thirty-eight Sioux were hanged in Mankato. There is a monument recording the event. I do not know of any other monument marking a shameful event.

Sometimes I feel we should not be so smug about our nation. We

invaded the country which did not belong to us and we almost wiped out those to whom it did belong. And it is not much of an excuse that the ways of the Indian were not our ways. They were a brave, proud people and they fought back with their only weapons, the arrow, the tomahawk, the fire. With what were then modern weapons, we drove them back farther and farther westward, and in the end, confined them in crowded reservations.

And when an Indian, who had died for our country a hero, was refused burial in the cemetery in his town, it would seem we have not changed much in the years. He was buried in Arlington, where he sleeps honored by the government, but this does not erase the rejection by that local cemetery board.

I suppose prejudice is the worst sin of mankind. Why do we feel we are superior to anyone not of our race or religion? This is a mystery to me. And if we do, why do we also say we believe in God? Most religions preach the brotherhood of man, few people practice it.

I have a deep-rooted prejudice too, it is against prejudice in any form. When someone says, "Of course, some of my best friends are—" I feel a cold wind blowing. This implies such a superiority, that it is really noble to condescend. Nobody is born with prejudice, it is built in by parents and the immediate social group. And it is an evil destructive attitude which enriches no life ever.

It is customary in our valley to decorate the houses for harvest time. Pumpkins stand on each side of the front steps, or piles of colored gourds. Sheaves of corn hang on the doors, and are often also tied to the lamp posts by the gate. Some enthusiasts have beautiful decorations with cattails, dried goldenrod, broom spikes, and other wildlings. But even the simple ears of corn, red and gold, are lovely. The countryside takes on a festive air.

Celebrating the harvest began about as far back in time as we have records. The pagan festivals combined worship of the gods with the merrymaking. I like to think that when we decorate our doorways, we are also being thankful to God for the bounty of harvest.

The decorations stay up until time for the Christmas wreaths. The pumpkins do not, as we learned the hard way. We had two enormous ones, brilliant orange, one year. One night we had a sudden drop in temperature and they burst in the night. It made quite a mess.

The roadside stands are well worth seeing, with late mums and dried strawflowers and bittersweet, as well as red and green apples, pumpkins and blue Hubbard squash and strings of sweet peppers. Also fresh eggs, crusty loaves of bread, jars of pickles, relishes and jellies. And baskets of gourds.

Jill raised gourds for a few years and we had bushels of them. The first year I shellacked enough for the wooden dough tray and a copper bowl and in a short time they looked like sponges. So we tried pricking holes in them and drying them before shellacking. Then we tried waxing them. They never kept well for us but they were lovely for a while, with their Mexican colors and varied shapes.

The Indians used them for dippers and bowls and I wonder how they preserved them. And they are used as musical instruments in some countries where somehow the pulp is removed and the seeds left in. The rattling seeds make an excellent percussion instrument. Somewhere, sometime in my childhood I drank from a gourd dipper, but I cannot remember where I was.

We also tried preserving fall leaves by ironing them between layers of waxed paper. I ruined one ironing board cover, burned my hand, gummed up the iron, and gave it up. After that, we just put the sprays of scarlet and gold leaves in water in a stoneware jug and enjoyed them as they were in their natural state.

Generally, things are better left alone. In my childhood, it was the custom to gild or silver milkweed pods, dye stalks of ripe grain, and have a stiff hideous bouquet on the scarf that decorated the piano. Mama never did this or put shawls or scarves on the piano. She said that wasn't what the piano was for. She did like sprays of pine, with the cones, for the mantel, and branches of maple on the hearth.

But we never had a Rogers Group either and I used to go to the neighbors to admire theirs. We never had a lamp with a green glass shade (rectangular) and a bead fringe. Nor a cosy corner. We got through the mission period with no mission furniture. I feel sure, as I think of the era, that these evidences of elegance belonged to an earlier time, but they persisted.

Jill had a set of bird's-eye maple for her bedroom, which I greatly admired. But my bedroom was furnished with antique walnut. And we never had a Brussels carpet with roses all over it.

I didn't pay much attention to the fact that our house was different than many of my friends' houses. It was a many-windowed house, uncluttered (except for my room) and restful. And I consider Mama was a genius to make any house seem restful with Father and me inhabiting it. She did a great deal of picking-up after us. But the only complaint she made was about Father's sleeping with a big ugly blue-barreled revolver under his pillow. He said it was handy there in case anybody got in the house.

"But you might shoot somebody," said Mama.

"Of course I would," he agreed, "and I never miss."

I do not know where he got this idea—except perhaps from his years managing a silver mine in the mountains of Mexico. I do not think there was ever a burglary in our town, and I never heard of prowlers either. Now and then, in spring, a few hoboes came through and most people fed them a hearty meal in return for raking the yard. After they finished their apple pie and third cup of coffee, they would move on. They were shabby men, but I do not think anyone ever was afraid of them.

There was a rumor that they marked the houses where they were most welcome so others following them would find the best reception, but although my friends and I searched annually, we never found a mark anywhere on our houses. So it must have been like an Indian sign.

In our valley, we are visited by the Mormon missionaries. They come walking down the road, always a pair of them, and they are fine, respectable men. They never ask for anything but they will leave Mormon leaflets. I admire them for being willing to serve their faith although it is a strange one to me.

We also have frequent opportunities to subscribe to magazines to put so-called veterans through school. Judging by the age of most of them, they must have entered service at thirteen. Joe, our neighbor, subscribed once via one of these and got a receipt but never got the magazine. Some of them are bona fide, I am sure, but I would take more kindly to their approach if they did not begin the old army routine. The last one to come to Stillmeadow shouted at me and waved his arms.

"So you have no loyalty to your country?" he demanded.

I opened the door and let four dogs out, and he stopped arguing. In fact, he ran to the gate and vanished down the road.

It is difficult for me to say no, but I have had to learn to since Jill cannot forestall the callers. After the time I bought a new vacuum cleaner so the salesman could win a silver service which his wife wanted badly, Jill never trusted me. She pointed out we didn't need a new vacuum cleaner as the old one was in perfect shape.

There is one type of selling which really enrages me, and this is soliciting by telephone. The phone rings just as I am shampooing a cocker, for instance, and I struggle to persuade the victim to stay RIGHT THERE in the tub. I dash to the phone and a smooth voice informs me I have been selected to receive a free year's subscription to this or that to celebrate the opening of a new office in

Hartford, New Haven or Bridgeport. I cannot see why I should celebrate it, but before I can say anything, the voice purrs along and I find I do pay for half a dozen other magazines in order to get the free issues of one I do not like.

I think solicitation by telephone is an unwarranted invasion of the privacy of my home, and while I am sorry for the girls who make their living in such a way, I still would not buy so much as a toothbrush in this manner.

My way of subscribing to magazines is to take the address from a copy and send in a check. This seems to work very well and I am never charged less or more. I pay the going price, which seems fair to me.

Food sales are frequent in our valley, and are profitable. You have to get there early or everything is already sold. Church strawberry festivals help raise money, as do occasional benefit concerts. And church suppers not only raise money but are occasions for get-togethers for the congregations. The Lions club raises money for the scholarship fund by selling light bulbs, brooms, or fire extinguishers.

Otherwise we have many chances to support the heart fund, the cancer fund, the mental health fund, the Red Cross, the crippled children's fund and many others. A Community Chest would be a better idea, I think, with a single drive instead of many.

This is the season to visit Cape Cod, when it quiets down from the summer explosion of vacationers. The Cape Codders are patient and polite to summer people, who do, after all, provide a livelihood for the Cape. But there is an air of relaxation after Labor Day. The village dreams in the sun. The great beach which Thoreau walked (it stretches for forty miles) now has only a few earnest fishermen surf-casting. The surf rolls in along the curved shore line, crested with silver. When a wind comes up, sand blows like a golden mist from the dunes.

Inland the cranberry bogs are garnet, and the slopes are glowing with rose hips, and grey-blue where the bayberries are. Gardens are still in bloom, for the Cape climate is mild until winter. The Cape people say roses often grow until December. The Cape goldenrod is short-stemmed and the bloom is not a yellow gold, but more coppery. The sea-lavender has gone by, but the faint tinge of purple is still there, and if we pick it, the sea-lavender will last like this all winter. It makes a delicate bouquet, especially with bayberry with it.

The bayberry is a low bush with dark green leaves and a pattern of branching almost like that of an old appletree. The berries are waxy and set in clusters near the tips of the branches. They have a spicy odor, although not as strong as when they are used in bayberry candles. Once, Faith brought back a carton of bayberry (we cut it carefully as if pruning and never damage the bushes), and it kept for several years. Then one day, she walked past the bouquet and it exploded, she says, the berries all at once disintegrating to grey dust. We never were able to keep it more than two seasons but that is because things get knocked around at Stillmeadow, what with dogs and cats and visiting babies.

Some people find the Cape desolate, I find it next door to Paradise.

Once you get down-Cape beyond Hyannis Port, it is not yet ruined by leaning towers of Pizza, Barefoot Trader shops and so on. The villages have the tranquillity of great age with the typical weathered Cape houses and village greens. The early houses were unpainted and weathered in the salt air to soft grey. There are two variations, the red cedar used for some turns to a color I can only call grey-cinnamon, those of white cedar are grey as a gull's wing. The characteristic trim is white although green is used, and occasionally charcoal.

Many of the oldest houses have low picket fences around the front yard and the garden blooms along the fence. Whatever grows at all in the sandy soil bears bigger and brighter flowers than inland. But if anyone wishes to grow flowers that need real soil, he can buy soil in bushel baskets at a nursery. I remember how the idea of paying for soil fascinated Jill.

"We could make a fortune if we had our garden soil here," she observed.

Apparently when the Pilgrims came, the Cape was heavy with forests, but now the trees are chiefly scrub pine. Some of the villages have elms, and if you come on them suddenly, the elms seem as tall as skyscrapers. The elms in our valley at home were killed by the elm tree blight a number of years ago, so the graceful canopied elms seem like a rare treasure.

The Cape Codders are wise and kind people and quiet, as those who live with the sea seem to be. It has been fashionable for some writers to spend a year or so on the Cape and write about the Cape "characters." I think the chief quality of Cape Codders is a determined individuality. They will not be regimented, and they do look on the Cape as a country by itself. The mainland is foreign soil. They wish to govern the Cape with no interference from outsiders.

They also are willing for anyone coming to the Cape to behave as they wish, and this may be one reason why the Cape is a haven for writers and painters. Nobody is special on the Cape and everyone minds his own business. I should think the true Cape Codders will not bother Mr. Kennedy at all, only the tourists.

Shirley Booth lives in Chatham when she is between plays, and while there she is an individual, coming and going as she wishes, with no crowd of autograph-hunters trailing after her.

The Cape has a Portuguese population as well as the descendants of the early settlers such as the Snows, Eldredges, Nickersons and Mayos. The fishing fleet that puts out from Provincetown is operated mainly by Portuguese, and finer sailors never battled the seas.

Coming off the Cape, the land is sandy and flat for miles and the Cape vegetation persists. When you come to the Connecticut state line, the hills rise darkly blue and the woodlands are flaming in late fall. In September they begin to turn as if someone were painting them with color. The fertile valleys are protected by the rolling hills and you cannot drive far without finding streams, lakes, or rivers. It is always an amazement to me to think how infinitely varied America is in scenery.

After our being away, Stillmeadow always looked unreal to me. It still does, if I am even away for a day. I walk around inside the house, seeing everything as if for the first time. It is touched with new enchantment. Holly always checks everything and when she is sure all is well, drinks heavily from the water pan. Then she races around in the yard, being sure no invaders have been in her favorite spots. I suspect the best thing about a trip is the coming home again.

I shall not wait for November to be thankful, because I am thankful as I look from my window and see the first blaze of the swamp maple, a promise of the splendor to come. I am thankful for the postman's horn, for cockers and Irish running in the soft September moonlight, for the last zinnias. As I walk across the yard, I notice the lawn has received the message from nature for the grass grows close and short as the roots gather strength against the winter. How does the grass KNOW, when it still feels like summer? How do the birds know it is time to circle, making trial flights? What a mystery fall is!

May all be well with all of us as summer ends.

October

THE upland pastures are blue with autumn haze now. The sugar maples around Stillmeadow burn bright with color. The whole world seems to be gold and scarlet and wine. No two trees are exactly alike and the variations in tone are limitless. There is one sugar maple which is a pinky-red and I like to stand under it and just feel the color. No two trees turn at the same time, either. We have one maple which refuses to believe it is not summer long after the other trees nearby are blazing away.

All shades of red and gold are in the swamp too as the bushes are kindled by autumn. Now I wish I could paint with brushes and pigment and not depend on words for there just are no words to describe some of the colors. There is one thing I have not read about in any descriptions of our autumn and that is the way the leaves actually seem to give forth a brilliant light, so that even on a grey day the sun seems to be shining.

The country roads wind along the valleys and up the low hills (ours are the beginning of the Litchfield hills). The pasture grass is still green and the hills fold away in blue haze and there are the trees massed at the ends of the pastures, glowing. We have some pine woods, not many, and they strike a note of dark green in the country-side. White houses and grey or red or pale yellow barns add accent notes. I am reminded of Edna St. Vincent Millay's "O World, I cannot hold thee close enough!"

Days are still warm enough for picnics, and woods-picnics are best. Beyond the old orchard there is an open space where a spring bubbles and a flat grey ledge makes a natural picnic table. In this place there are butternut trees and hickory and plenty of nuts unless the squirrels get there first. There are always a few wild asters and goldenrod which have escaped the black frost, and wintergreen grows in one special place. Princess pine or pipsissewa carpets a hidden part of the woods, and so far nobody has ripped it up. It is on our land but that might not matter.

There used to be a great deal of princess pine hereabouts but it was destroyed by predatory people. It is now on the conservation list along with dogwood and azalea, but there are always those who pay no attention to the law.

Every golden day is an extra dividend from summer for soon the time of storm jackets, warm wool slacks, mittens and furred boots will be upon us. I don't mind boots too much but I hate rubbers and I go through life simply drying my shoes out. I think I wore rubbers often enough when I was growing up to last my lifetime.

"Have you got your rubbers?" was a constant refrain.

I never wear mittens unless it is ten below zero. And I carry gloves to church, but do not put them on. I like my hands to be free and mittens and gloves make them stiff.

I do not own an umbrella. If I get caught in a downpour, I usually can bend a newspaper over my head. I have several of the plastic rain bonnets in case of emergency. In winter I go bareheaded, resisting all suggestions that I will "catch my death of cold." Only last last winter did I succumb, when my darling Lois Klakring sent me a feather-light, down-soft white hood and a pair of white gloves delicate as mist. They are knitted, not of wool but of one of the new synthetic yarns. I save them for use when it is below zero and I find they are so light that I do not feel confined in them, but I do feel a gentle warmth.

Umbrellas always act like unfurled sails when I carry them, and I am blown along like a rudderless boat. I always poke people with the tip, and if I close the umbrella and still must carry it, I manage to trip myself. We used to carry an umbrella in the car for dog shows, because as Jill said, it always rains harder at dog shows than anywhere else. She used to try to persuade me to get under it with her and then the water ran down my neck. So she settled for holding it over the dogs.

I had a plastic rain coat at one show in Massachusetts. That was the day the heavens opened, the tents blew down and the field ran with water. Holly was getting her championship and Art Baines, who was showing her, left us while he showed a pointer. I took my raincoat off and put it on Holly, tying the arms around her neck and holding the hood on her head. She went in the ring dry but I squshed when I sat down.

New England weather is erratic. You can be out in the yard in a sun suit and before you reach the house, it is pouring. You may go off on a hot day for a picnic and turn pale blue with cold before you get back. And in July comes a day when you turn the furnace on and build a fire on the hearth. This keeps you alert, we say.

With these qualifying remarks, I may say that June and October are our MOST equable months. And the weather in both is apt to be flawless as crystal. October has a crisp, stimulating air but not raw and damp. Nights are brisk but not shivery. In the village store, we argue as to whether this is the best time of year or whether May or June is better. I am not much good at making a case, for I like best whatever season it is. I even enjoy winter, provided it doesn't overdo it, as it did the winter of 1960–61.

The market is a fine place for visiting. Yesterday I spent some time discussing the state of education with George, the owner. I admit I am always distracted talking to George for he is one of the most beautiful men I have ever known. I do not say handsome, for that implies to me a kind of slickness, and good-looking is not enough. There is no true reason for confining the word beautiful to things feminine that I can see anyway. George is slim and dark and with eyes as blue as the October sky. He is tired-looking, quiet, and with a radiant smile.

His older son graduated from Colby and the younger son is in school here.

"Do you think television is responsible," he began, "for the fact that young people don't seem to read?"

"Partly," I said, "not all."

"Well," he sighed, "I had a time trying to teach my boy last night the difference between illusion and delusion. How would you tell him?"

"Well," I said, "I think some illusions are delusions, if that helps."

We both agreed that when we were growing up, we read voluntarily, not just for assignments. And that few students nowadays seem to have a passion for classic literature.

"I read Shakespeare when I was a boy," said George.

"Partly it is overemphasis on science," I said. "It's more important now to advance in science than to acquire the richness of a cultural background."

George finally got called away by a salesman and I was so busy thinking about education that I forgot to consult my list and went home without milk, fruit, butter and bread. I walked right past them planning a television hour in prime time (sounds like roast beef) which would encourage reading. Dr. Frank Baxter would run it. It would not be a course with credits, it would be intended simply to create excitement about reading and reading the best. I do not like the word classics for it sounds dull and formal, I would call it something like "There's Magic in Books."

Country folk are busy in October, but the wine-bright air makes work easier. The vegetables that have survived the frost must be taken care of, cornstalks and rubbish burned, woodshed filled to the roofs. In order to burn off the garden, one must get a permit, which we call a perMIT, from the fire warden, preferably after a rain. Summer lawn furniture must be painted, now that the insects won't get painted into it, repaired and stored. It is time to plant bulbs.

Erma begins to wax and polish the floors, wash the nose-marks from the windows, do up the curtains for she says it will be Thanksgiving before we know it. It will, too, for days go faster and faster as winter approaches. I think subconsciously we know snowfall will soon be here, and have a sense of urgency that we lack the rest of the year.

Actually we may have snow flurries in October but the snow melts like dew in the first sun. And the weather turns warm again afterward. I notice another sign of what's to come as the cockers and the Irish begin to acquire more fur. Jonquil looks like a golden

puffball and even Especially Me, who has a flat coat, grows heavier feathers on his legs.

All of the dogs are busy helping in the yard, which means they dig furiously wherever anyone else digs and play ball with extra bulbs. The quality of assistance may be dubious but the companionship is a joy.

A group of us were talking about the relationship of people and pets the other night, and I thought Helen Beals settled the question.

When her son, young Joe (who is still called young Joe, although he has four children), had to board his rabbit, he was disconsolate. But the family was going on a trip and the rabbit had to be boarded. They got back late at night and no sooner had they unlocked the door than young Joe suggested they go and fetch his rabbit.

"It's too late," said Helen.

"I want my rabbit," he said, "I want my rabbit now."

"But everybody will be in bed."

"I'd like my rabbit," said Joe.

Finally they gave in, and drove to the boarding place. The man said, "I don't have any lights in the hutch, and I don't know where your rabbit is."

"I want my rabbit," said Joe patiently, "let me go and get him."

"But I don't know which pen he is in," objected the man, "and I have a lot of rabbits out there. You better come back tomorrow."

"I'll find him," said Joe.

In the end, they went out to the rabbit quarters with a dim flashlight. Young Joe started down the line to cages. He went slowly, thoughtfully. He picked up a rabbit, put him back, picked up a second rabbit, put him back. Then he picked up a third, felt him carefully, rubbed the rabbit's ears.

"This is my rabbit," he said definitely.

All the rabbits looked exactly alike, Helen said, especially in the dark. But young Joe carried this one rabbit to the car in his arms and they drove home.

Now this was Joe's own rabbit and they were sure of it when they put him in his house, for the house had a main room, a bedroom, and a corner bathroom. The rabbit hopped at once to his bathroom, then whisked into his bedroom and flopped onto his bed. Somehow the boy and his rabbit had a communication that was no mystery to them but surprised everyone else.

Of course, the dogs communicate with me, but they bark. Holly also squeaks and chants in a contralto singsong.

"Jonquil wants some lettuce," Jill used to call, "can I give her what's left?"

Or, "Linda says the laundryman has just turned the corner."

Or, "Holly says there is a lovely man at the gate but she does not know him, but let him in!" (We sometimes feel a bit jealous at her adoration of men.)

It is a great help at night to know just what is going on outside. Loud, emphatic welcome sounds mean Erma is coming over, happy-happy sounds signal the arrival of Steve and Olive. Lower, rapid barks mean a stranger is in the yard and the attack-barks are a sure sign a possum has wandered in from the woods. There is, fortunately, a very special whoop which gets me out of bed in a hurry. There is a note of wonder or fear in the announcement that a skunk is on the grounds and I get the dogs in in nothing flat. So far, the only one to get involved is Holly who is so curious she had to get up to see what this thing was! She saw.

Getting the dogs ready for winter means a good shampoo and grooming on a benign day. The house smells of wet fur and shampoo. The minute Erma uncorks the shampoo, we suddenly have no dogs at all. We can hear them arguing under the bed. "You go first."

"No, you go first."

"I think it is not my turn."

Once they get in the tub, they enjoy it. We have never had a dog that did not like to be clean. After they are dried with warm towels they act as if they were at a party, leaping around and wagging and racing in circles around the yard. Then they settle down to find one place in the yard where there is no grass so they can roll in it and come back in with sand and gravel on their washed selves.

I admit we use a special human shampoo advertised to leave the hair soft, lustrous and so-o-o easy to manage. It does give fur a soft, lustrous look and smells better than some dog shampoos. I am always sorry for dogs who never get a good bath.

I note in Stephen Vincent Benét's "Western Star" that two dogs came over on the Mayflower, a spaniel and a mastiff. They helped hunt. And when the Pilgrims first explored Provincetown, the Indians who met them had a dog with them. I doubt whether any of these dogs ever had a shampoo, however.

The spaniel is a breed which dates back at least to 1386 when it was called the spanyell. Originally there were two types, land spaniels and water spaniels, which later were divided into several additional groups.

The cocker is the smallest of the sporting group but does not take a back seat in the field, in fact the cocker can get through brush which the larger breeds cannot manage. He quarters the field when hunting, angling back and forth to cover the territory. When he has flushed game, he drops and waits for the command to retrieve after the game is shot. Since the cocker has a soft mouth, he can even carry an egg without breaking it. It is not ethical to shift his hold on the bird and I once saw a cocker bring in a bird which he held by the tip of one wing so that he could barely walk, but he made it.

The Irish setter became popular early in the eighteenth century in, of course, Ireland. The dog books call him one of the handsomest as well as most useful dogs, exceptionally hardy, vigorous, and long-lived. He is gentle and loyal, in fact the only criticism of him as a hunter is that he may pay too much attention to his handler. In the field he is fast, has great endurance, and judging from my experience (not as a hunter), has an unparalleled nose.

The dog books do not say the Irish has a fine sense of humor, is emotional, and can track a piece of cheese to the top shelf in the cupboard. Or can bring the mail without even dampening a letter.

Living with cockers and Irish, I have learned the cockers are easier to deceive. With them, I can pretend I am not going anywhere. But Holly knows I am before I even get up from my typewriter and is at the door making Let's Go noises as they do in the Westerns. And if I must leave them, the cockers are more patient about it. They grieve but not with such abandon. Holly dies a small death if I go away.

There is great devotion between Holly and Teddy. He was a puppy when she was and although she now looms over him, she still wants to play games with him. He follows valiantly when she skims across the yard, but never catches up unless she stops and waits for him. By nature he is one of the quietest most thoughtful cockers we ever had, and sometimes he decides it is silly to play tag or haul at one end of a towel. He retires to the house and gets under my bed. Holly then sticks her head under as far as she can and begs him to come out.

She never tries to play games with the other cockers, in fact she hardly notices them. But if she and Teddy are parted, she droops. She is willing for him to lie on the day bed with her, but objects if the others want to be there. It's off limits.

My non-dog friends cannot see why I am willing to have a bevy underfoot all the time. And it reminds me of one time when I had to make a trip to Philadelphia and stayed in a hotel several days. I felt morose. The last day I saw a woman get out of the elevator with a black cocker and I nearly knocked a man down getting there to greet him. I felt fine until he and his mistress went out of the hotel. Then I checked the hours until I would get back to my own.

That time when I got back, Honey was not there at the gate to meet me. Her tired heart had simply stopped beating, and although she was well over fourteen, I wondered whether perhaps she had missed me too much. It would have been utterly selfish to wish her back but I couldn't help wishing she might have been there to meet me. The fourteen years seemed suddenly a very short time. I had helped her be born and held the tiny soft ball of satin in my palm. Even just three minutes old, she began to wiggle, and paddle the air with minute raspberry paws. She felt tonic, and the life instinct pulsed through her. An instinct is not supposed to pulse but that was the way I thought of it.

She was not a beautiful puppy but I felt we belonged together. Later, after we had called her a wind-hound for some time, she suddenly blossomed into a facsimile of her Champion Cream Pie sire. She was wheat-gold with low-set long ears and dark amber eyes. She had a blocky muzzle, with a dark nose. And she followed me like a golden shadow. We had a good life together, but as I say it seemed very short.

I often know she walks beside me, especially at Christmas. She was very fond of Christmas, especially of what went on in the kitchen. But she enjoyed the tree too and sat looking at it often. She always had, as they all did, her own present and she appreciated it although she never played with toys the way Tiki and Jonquil do.

There is a truth about love which one learns by having a companion such as Honey. My devotion to her was very special but never prevented me from cherishing Little Sister or any others we ever had. There was always room in my heart. And this, I believe, is the way it should be.

My young neighbors down the road are worrying because they get no mail from their son, newly off to prep school. He seems to have dropped into a vacuum. It reminded me of the first time Don went to camp and we fretted for the same reason. Jill phoned now and then to check on him. When he came home and we unpacked his suitcase, we found two dozen postcards addressed to us and everyone saying, "Hi, I am fine. Love, Don." He admitted sheepishly that he had written them all before he left home and it just happened that he forgot to mail them!

I do not know why a postcard should be an impossible chore, but it seems to be. The one thing that sparks correspondence is when money runs short.

With adults too, the time of letter-writing is past. Very few people sit down and write long thoughtful letters or gay and witty ones. I've thought about why this is so, and I do not think it is due to lack of time. I think it is because leisure has gone out of our lives. I can remember when I used to write my mother what were really informal essays and she wrote me her reflections on life. Now, I notice my own letters are wedged into small bits of time and I sometimes say, "I could write pages about this but—"

Much of the mail I receive begins, "I have a few minutes because I am in bed with a virus—" Or, "I am laid up with a broken leg so I have some time to write a few letters."

I reflect it is a pity that in order to have time to write letters one has to be either ill or laid up by an accident.

Aside from lack of leisure, I think the lack of correspondence has to do with our having so many newspapers, magazines, books and television. In former times, letters were something to read and reread. Fortunately many people saved theirs, and some of the best literature we now have is contained in volumes of letters. Some of Katherine Mansfield's best writing is in the letters, and the letters of George Bernard Shaw are a treasure-trove for Shaw addicts. A great deal of history lives in letters too.

In Keats's time, letters were exchanged between people in the same town or city and Keats even wrote letters to Fanny Brawne when they lived in the same house. I am glad he had no extension telephone. The telephone has had a great deal to do with killing correspondence. The difficulty is that what's said over the phone is ephemeral, and also must be relatively brief. "Your three minutes are up," generally shortens a conversation.

I know a few intrepid souls who talk on and on and on, but it is more of a monologue than an exchange. The telephone has a paralyzing effect on me so that I never remember what I called about.

When Connie calls up, she talks a few minutes and then says doubtfully, "Mama, are you still there?"

"Yes," I answer.

"Can't you think of anything to say?"

I can't.

I didn't know, until I looked it up, that Columbus first saw land at two in the morning of October 12. I had always imagined it as being high noon. How strange and mysterious the land must have looked, unreal and shadowy. When I try to imagine it, I think the man who saw it must have felt numb. And when the ships sailed closer, the forests must have astonished the voyagers.

It now appears that Columbus was not the first to cross the ocean, that some of the Vikings came. There is a spot on Cape Cod where, it is said, ships were moored, holes being dug in the rocks for mooring lines. And in Ephraim, when I was summering there as a child, there was a great to-do about a Norse stone being found. A man came to see Father about it and Father went off to inspect the inscriptions but he left me at home, I am sorry to say. Father said it was all nonsense.

Nevertheless, Columbus is the hero we honor and I suppose it doesn't greatly matter whether he was first or not.

Now we are getting a man off into space—perhaps it will be attempted before I finish writing about it. He will go alone, with only instruments and dials and if anything goes wrong, he will be lost in space. There will never have been a human being so isolated, and I suppose his survival will be a great triumph of science over nature. But I wonder why man could not use his skill first to make the world a better place? Our own planet is not anything to brag about.

And the billions spent on space would do a great deal to help the billions of earth-bound people!

Now the wild geese go over, flying south. I have never seen them, but Joe turns up one morning to say, "The geese went over." They fly high and fast, and they are a symbol of autumn. I do not know why they seem more mysterious and exciting than other birds, but I wish, just once, I might see them. When the songbirds go, the yard seems empty, but not for long. The chickadees and juncoes come in, and the woodpeckers and nuthatches. In winter the evening grosbeaks flash their dramatic color at the feeder and the mourning doves wake me in the early hours with their melancholy music.

Toward the end of October, the small animals begin to hibernate, and as I contemplate them, snug and asleep, it seems a good way to wait out the long bitter cold. How they keep alive in this semi-death I do not know, they neither eat nor drink water. To all intents and purposes, they are in a catatonic state. In February, the ground hogs are supposed to come out and look around, but if the signs are not right, they go back to wait out six more weeks of winter.

And why don't squirrels hibernate too? I seem to have about twenty-five who live near the bird feeders and eat all day. Weasels do not hibernate either, possibly hunting is better in winter. Now and then I have seen a weasel running along the stone fence, but they are rare since chicken-raisers have killed them off. A weasel looks like a liquid shadow flowing along. Once, a long time ago, our neighbor Willie reported seeing an otter in the brook below the pond, and there are beavers and muskrats, but all of these wild creatures are disappearing as the woodlands are cut down.

The fireplace comes into its own cool evenings. There is a special comfort about an open fire, it gives a sense of security. A successful fire is not easy to build unless you know how. I have often watched city guests eagerly flinging in an armful of kindling, throwing in a wad of newspaper and heaving a lone log on top. The paper burns, the kindling flares up and that is that. A good fire needs two logs, touching each other, well back on the andirons. A small amount of shredded paper goes below them on the hearth, with a few pieces of kindling arranged crisscross above the paper.

For a winter fire that you want to hold overnight, it helps to have one log of unseasoned wood which you lay on top when the fire has begun to burn well. The unseasoned wood burns slowly and will last longer, once it catches. I like the smell of sap as it simmers out. If you have only green logs, you will have to keep adding kindling.

There are, of course, a good many mechanical aids to fire-building, but the best, I think, is the Cape Cod fire-lighter, which is an iron or brass pot with a small amount of kerosene in it. A plunger fits into it with a porous stone head (soapstone, I think). To start the fire, you simply lift out the plunger, roll the head in ashes and light it. It burns some time with a steady flame. I had supposed Cape Cod lighters were standard equipment until my friend Lois Holloway came from Woodland, Washington, on a trip with her husband.

"What I've really come for," she said, "is a Cape Cod fire-lighter."

Sometimes Southern friends send me a carton of fat pine kindling, and this is a fire-lighter made by nature. The pine is light gold in color and feels buttery when you pick it up. It lights with one match and blazes immediately. Two or three pieces make a fire.

Finally as to fires. A bed of ashes should always be kept. Often you can start a fire in the morning with no kindling at all, for the embers will be there even if you cannot see them. Housewives who clean the hearth daily make a mistake. If you use your fireplace as a rubbish burner, that is different. Newspaper ashes are black and fly all over the room if you open a window. Advertising catalogs are worse because they leave small black wads as they burn.

A good clean fire makes the heart light. It needs one or two friends sitting by it, not talking too much, just being together. I've noticed firelight seems to make people look less tired or anxious. Usually anyone coming in from outdoors and seeing the fire says, "Oh, how restful."

I once lived in a house with a gas fireplace and it didn't have any magic. Nobody ever sat around that fireplace, or even looked at the regimented blue flames on the imitation logs. I lit it once or twice and instead of the good smell of wood and a whiff of smoke, I smelled the faint perfume of gas. I put Mama's firescreen in front of it after that and let it alone.

The best fire, of course, is one made from wood you have chopped yourself and carried in. It burns better!

This is the hunter's moon and when it is full, it casts a pure brilliance over the countryside. One can almost read by it. The light gives a glow to the trees. When the leaves begin to fall, the moon gilds them. If I walk in the yard. I can see the lights from the neighbor's house. I cannot see them at all from mid-May until autumn for the foliage is so thick all the way up the hill.

I like to see them. And on a clear night, I enjoy riding around the country seeing all the house lights in the valley. Suddenly I see a prick of light halfway up some wooded hill, and it is like finding a treasure. Some farmhouse is tucked away there, and there does not seem to be a road leading to it. Who lives there, folded away on the hill?

Along the road to Woodbury, the lighted houses are like a necklace for the night. In the opposite direction the road is dark much of the way until you come upon Newtown, after you cross the river. Newtown is no longer a village, it is a town. It has a fine shopping center, a library, a beautiful town hall, a bank, and street lights! I hope we never have them, but they do make it easy to walk on the SIDEWALKS.

I have been told that street lighting dates back to the seventeenth century in France and was begun to protect people from robbers and cutthroats. In our country, in 1772, Boston hung four hundred lanterns outdoors at night. Gas lamps suggest the Victorian era.

It was about 1878 when the first open arc electric lamps were used and it was in Cleveland that the era began. At the turn of the century clusters of lights on cast-iron poles were popular. I remember big milk-white lamps which cast a circular glow on the streets of my home town. On Halloween, some of the wilder boys threw rocks at them and shattered the glass globes.

I imagine the day will come when the street lights are underground and cast a shadowless light from some sort of grill. It won't be romantic, but would keep automobiles from crashing into the poles and wrapping around them. The newest I have seen by way of street illuminating is a very high pole with an arm stretched out and the light at the end of the arm. These are, I maintain, perfectly hideous, they resemble scarecrows. They give a good light. But handsome they are not. The lights themselves are fluorescent.

One Christmas the children gave us a yard light, a very pretty hand-wrought iron lantern with a gold eagle on top. It lights the road nicely as I come home from an evening drive. I can see it as I turn the corner by the mailboxes, and it is a familiar star of my own to steer by.

I also have welcoming barks and the cockers and Irish fly to the gate as if they were reporters greeting a famous personage. They are not quite as rude as reporters but they are excited. They all have to be rewarded for their extreme nobility in surviving until my return.

After we are settled down, it is time for our usual walk around the yard. The air from the woods is sharp and yet mellow. This sounds contradictory and that is the way the air is. Some warmth from the day lingers but the thermometer has dropped with sunset. The air just feels good on my face but I do not shiver.

I am particularly fond of the smell of fallen leaves, a rather musty odor. The smell of blue woodsmoke is lovely and the essence of leaf-scent is in it. It is rare now, for most folk use the leaves for mulch or in compost pits or to bank around house foundations before piling pine branches up. I have a small burning of the garden weeds and always stand around sniffing it with pleasure until there is only ash left.

What does the season mean to me? I think about it as I circle back to the house. The one word that expresses it would be splendor. October is the jewel set in the hand of time. I must be certain that I have given my heart humbly to the glory, which is the gift of God. October is nothing to pass carelessly, every bright hour must be cherished.

And may God bless us all and make us glad as the wonder of autumn has once again been given us.

November

NOW in November, the leaves spread cloth of gold and red on the ground. The open fields take on a cinnamon tone and the wild blackberry canes in the swamp are frosted purple. The colors fade slowly to sober hues. The rain falls with a determination in long leaden lines, and when it stops water drips from the eaves.

The voice of the wind changes, for winds are seasonal too. Summer winds blow soft, musical with leaves, except for thunderstorms. Hurricane winds scream. In blizzard time the sleet-sharp gale has a crackling noise. But now the wind has a mournful sound, marking the rhythm of autumn's end. The first beat of winter is not yet here, and country folk tend to spend extra time doing chores or puttering, just to be out of doors.

When Indian summer comes, nothing indoors seems important. I must carry my breakfast tray to the terrace and eat in the wine-bright sun. There is always a haze on the hills, making them dreamlike. Eternal summer shines from a soft sky. Perhaps it is such an enchanted time because it is a promise that another summer will come, after winter goes. Actually there is no set date for Indian summer, it comes when it is ready. Sometimes it seems to come after a cold spell in October but it may even come around Thanksgiving. The later it comes the better, I think, like an extra dividend.

Usually it ends with a swift drop in temperature and grey skies. Frost whitens the lawn and too soon snow-lace drops on the bushes. We proceed with November.

The storm windows, which I hate, are on. The hooks in the back kitchen wear my storm jacket and raincoat instead of light sweaters.

Erma scouts the fence to be sure no holes are there the right size for cockers to squeeze through. Joe rigs up his snowplough, and stacks his woodpile high.

My tendency is to make lists. Most of them are questions.

> Put on snow tires. When?
> Antifreeze in car? Ask Joe.
> Heat on in kennel? Or wait?
> Still time to paint the wellhouse?

I often get up in the night and add to my list. Somehow the main function of a list is to make me feel well organized. Practically speaking, they aren't much use as I invariably mislay them. I make careful grocery lists and leave them behind when I go to the village. But it is nice to know that when I get home, I'll know what I forgot because the list is under the coffeemaker right where I left it when I unplugged the pot. I put it back on the counter by the door and add to it. There is some hope that I may once catch up with just one list for I notice they are smaller than they used to be. They are only one page. This is because I have discovered if I walk slowly down all the aisles at the market, ideas come to me! I look with interest at the soap shelves and I think SOAP, and get it.

I must admit that when Erma does the shopping, my lists are no help because even I cannot always read my handwriting once it cools down. She translates as well as she can and then gets what she knows I need.

I find it hard to shop economically and although I am not an envious woman, I almost envy shoppers who know to a penny what they are going to spend and then COME OUT EVEN! I consider this an art which should not be underestimated. My basic difficulty is in not being able to add. So I never know whether I have spent more than I should or, for that matter, how much I should spend. Jill always did the shopping and knew what the household expenses were and also what we were out of.

I also have a tendency to buy too many things of one kind. I gravitate toward beets one day, another I may think green beans are good (with rosemary), another I succumb to the charm of canned pineapple. The result is the shelves seldom have things that match up to make a dinner. Yesterday I looked hopefully in the freezing compartment of the refrigerator and there was nothing but spinach, spinach, spinach. This has to be consumed before I can put anything else in the freezer. Next week, I admit sadly, it may be full of shrimp.

We used to set up emergency shelves with complete meals on them, in case unexpected company came and I recommend this highly. Jill even made out menus and knew where they were! So now that I am thinking of it, I resolve to organize those shelves, after I have eaten ten cans of boiled onions and six cans of crushed pineapple and so on.

But no matter how thrifty you may be, living is high. It's a long time since Thoreau wrote, "My food alone cost me in money about 27 cents a week." Of course he didn't eat much, he fed on philosophy and beauty in nature, nevertheless—

For a long time, the phrase two can live as cheaply as one has been humorous, but it is my experience that two can live more cheaply than one. For example, a roast is economical, chops and steaks are not. But a roast is formidable for one. An old-fashioned chicken is cheaper than a game hen but lasts forever. Often two heads of lettuce are less than one head at a time. This isn't such an acute problem since Holly will eat one head, but she will not eat the extra bunch of carrots (2 bunches much less).

I am very fond of ham, but even a half ham presents a problem. I usually have ham or roast beef when the children come for a week end and this helps because then I have a very small bit, mostly bone, left over. I can also make a good soup, but not for one. To be good, a soup must almost fill the old iron soup kettle. In winter, the kettle can stay in the woodshed and freeze between times but it has to be real winter. What I call a real soup is too much to fit in the refrigerator.

Our freezer is hotel-size and I turned it off when I realized it would be years before I could work my way through it if it were properly filled. It is a pity for a freezer is a girl's best friend.

Thanksgiving is a welcome interlude for when Jill's children and my Connie and their families come, there are thirteen. A very prosperous turkey vanishes quickly. And everything else that goes with it. Even my granddaughter eats a little minced turkey now.

When I am alone with the cockers and Irish, Stillmeadow seems like a fairly large house. But how it shrinks when cribs and high chairs and playpens appear from the storage house. Four babies have a tidal-wave effect. The two older children, five and seven, remind me of Border collies running sheep.

Since I haven't yet grown used to our own children being grown up and married, it is no wonder I look with amazement at Muffin weaving about on her own. Only yesterday I was looking in through the hospital plate-glass window and trying to see which thimble-sized morsel belonged to me, in a remote sort of way.

And wasn't it only last week that I was putting a blue bunny suit on Connie? Time doesn't march on, it flings itself headlong.

There is a serious pitfall for me, and maybe for other grandmothers. I feel I must have been a very inferior mother, since Connie was raised in the pre-Spock era. I have no idea when the aggressive age begins, when the period of withdrawal, when hostility is correct. Also I gave Connie what seemed to be a balanced diet but it was not full of crushed vitamins, it was merely food. It was just as well for me, for I was a worrying mother. I was the kind of mother who got up four times in the night, first taking off a blanket, then putting it back on, then wanting to be sure she wasn't too hot, taking it off again. I note that Connie and Anne get up as many times but it is because the babies are crying. Muffin, for instance, may rise up in the crib at four in the morning demanding, "Joos, joos." Or Jamie may feel in the mood for a bottle of milk. Left to herself, Connie slept until seven in the morning. She didn't even seem to mind being alternately baked and frozen.

She was a human baby, so presumably she must have had a good deal in common with the babies of today, but her only fault was in always getting measles or mumps around Commencement time when a houseful of visiting alumni were due.

As far as education was concerned, she had no educational toys, since they were not known in our town at that time. She had just plain toys. She taught herself to read at an age I hesitate to mention. Her introduction to music was not via a recorder, she just climbed on the piano stool and picked out funny tunes she made up.

There was a period when she refused to eat unless I told her stories but the family doctor put an end to that. He didn't think eating should be a game, or that she should reward me for stories by swallowing her lunch. I'm afraid he was old-fashioned, but so far as I know, he never lost a baby.

I suppose children grow up more in spite of their parents than because of them. The one vital factor is love, and neither children nor adults flourish without love. Love is to human beings as the sun is to plants.

Love does involve discipline. And discipline is a granite word, not pleasant to contemplate. It is not love to give anyone everything they want just because they want it. It is easier, for instance, to let children look at one Western after another, because it is such fun. This isn't love, it's indulgence. I've watched a few Westerns and conclude they teach a great deal. They teach that the good wins, but only by killing the bad men. Usually they begin with someone already dead and the bad men line up to murder the wrong man who didn't kill the victim at all but was minding his own cattle or horses in Oxbow.

The story gets nicely off with a gun battle in a saloon which is well furnished with ladies that ought to be at home. Then there is a chase (and the horses are lovely). A few slugging matches pick up the action and then the good and bad shoot it out behind rocks. At this point the happy spectators rise and yell, "Get him, Johnny, Kill him." Which Johnny does, shooting from the hip, neat and clean. The finale consists of the hero sliding his gun back in the holster and saying it is too bad. Well, it is too bad, all of it. The message is plain—you are on one side or the other, but you always kill somebody.

Few parents leave six-shooters around the house for casual use, but imaginary ones bang away all day. It would, I think, evidence more love for the children if they were not allowed to sit two or three hours a day watching Westerns. It means the parents have to think up counter-interests, which may be difficult. For it saves a lot of time if the children are settled by the television set while the chores get done!

Like most critics, I cannot suggest a solution for the Westerns themselves. There are a lot of hours to be filled on television.

Westerns are so easy, for there is only one plot, if you can call it that, and you need some horses and some California scenery and you are ready to roll.

I heard of one frustrated father who took the television out for six months. He found it very beneficial but I think it was like burning the house down because there is a leak in the plumbing. Children can get interested in family activities and let the picture tube cool off. In the country, it is easier, for fishing and picnicking and swimming or hunting wildflowers or making bird-counts are available. But in the city, there are museums, the zoo, children's concerts, open-air markets and, in New York, the Staten Island ferry. In any area, life provides many things to do.

If television is a treat instead of a habit, it can be very much worth while. It is unfortunate that the best hours come at a time when children ought to be in bed, but teen-agers who watch documentaries such as David Brinkley's "Our Man in Hong Kong," or "Face the Nation," with men like Henry Cabot Lodge and Lord Boothby from London debating world issues, can learn more about the world than I learned in a year at school. The President's press conferences are living history. And Leonard Bernstein's programs are worth buying a set for. During the winter of 1961, "The Age of Kings" brought Shakespeare into countless homes where the bound volumes of Shakespeare had never been opened.

Love for the children requires discipline in many ways. It is so easy to give children their own way, for children are naturally allergic to the word NO. They are also expert at nagging. And then every parent has a terrible yearning to make the children happy at any cost, and it usually involves a high cost. I think a good many teen-agers get involved in headline auto accidents because it is too easy to say, "Oh, all right, take the car."

With adult relationships, especially marriage, sometimes a wife finds life easier if her husband always has his own way. And there are marriages in which the wife makes all the decisions and the husband is merely useful as a wage-earner. But I doubt whether a marriage is truly happy if it consists of a master-servant proposition.

It takes self-discipline to take a stand on issues that may be important but a one-sided partnership isn't really a partnership at all. A marriage should be two who walk *together* on the *same* path, not with one leading and the other walking docilely behind.

According to statistics, marriage is a shaky proposition today, but on the whole, I think statistics are no more valid than television polls. The backlog of sound marriages that are real partnerships does not get counted. And as far as I know, nobody has invented anything this side of Heaven which can compare with a shared life and the family as a unit.

As I was thinking about various kinds of trouble which most people have at one time or another, a car stopped outside the gate and two men walked up the road. In the country, we always know who everyone is, what they want, why they are going where they are going. In short, strangers are like new planets. Erma was taking the washing out, and went to find out about the men.

"A lost dog," she said, when she came in.

She would not have told me, except she had an idea I saw the car. My windows overlook the picket fence on one side. Besides, Jonquil was barking her stranger bark.

The lost dog was a champion Irish water Spaniel who had escaped from a kennel where he was staying a few days. I started for the gate but Erma said the owner was the woman in the car and she was crying so hard she couldn't speak. By the time I did get to the door, the men got in and the car vanished. Everyone who heard about it went hunting for the dog. So far, he has been seen two or three times, and by now should abandon the delights of freedom with joy.

When we once lost Linda and Little Sister, Jill said they were in better shape than I was when we found them. They were hungry, dirty, but lively. I was practically a hospital case. I think the difficulty is that when your dog is lost you simultaneously have him or her run over, trapped in a fox trap, stolen, killed by a vicious dog, or hung up on barbed wire. It is true that all these cannot happen at once, but they seem to be possible when you begin to think of it.

The gravest danger in our area is that a dog running in the woods may be shot, even out of hunting season. A good many hunters seem to shoot at anything, even at their own companions, or if all else fails they shoot themselves while climbing a fence.

Queer things can happen with dogs. My friends the Tovrovs, on Cape Cod, have a fine pedigreed black Labrador named Smoky. Not long ago, they missed him when it was time for supper. Their house is on a back road, some distance from the town, and the yard is unfenced. So far as I know, nobody fences in anything on Cape Cod. It is not a farming country, so fencing for cattle is not needed. Land boundaries are usually marked by small cement posts over which the bayberries grow and the wild roses.

On this night, the Tovrovs went out and called Smoky, and he did not appear. Orin went down to the beach and he was not there either. He was not visiting his favorite neighbor. Thoroughly alarmed by then, the Tovrovs were rushing to the car when the phone rang.

"I've got your Labrador here at the police station," said Chet Landers, "he just happened by."

So Orin drove down to the station, opened the car door and a happy Labrador jumped in. When they got home, he followed Orin into the house, greeted Midge, ate supper, and curled up on the sofa.

About an hour later, Midge went to let the cats in, and following them was a black Labrador, who looked with disfavor at the empty feeding dish. The phone was ringing, so she answered it in a hurry.

"Listen," said the voice of Chet Landers, "I'm calling about that Labrador."

"We've got two," said Midge, "as of now."

"Both perfectly at home," added Orin, who was sorting them out. The first one was NOT Smoky, but they not only looked as alike as two black peas but, as Orin said, they acted alike. And how did the stranger know where the food dish was kept and which was his spot on the sofa?

It turned out that after Orin had gone happily home, a frantic owner called Chet to report his prize Labrador missing—they had looked everywhere—

"Think I know where he is," said Chet.

So the police department chalked up another successful rescue, and the Tovrovs are still wondering why the lost dog acted as if he had always lived with them. It is a little strange, the more you think of it.

At least our dogs would not get in a strange car, not even Holly, who has a passion for riding. And they would do a lot of prowling about in any strange house, quartering the field, as it were. And after a brief friendly visit, they would be crying at the door to be let out to go home. Once or twice I left Holly with a friend while I went on a trip, such as to the dentist, but she sobbed so that I gave it up. She'd rather be shut in her own house.

As Thanksgiving time comes again, it seems to me it is very sudden. After Thanksgiving it will be winter, and I don't feel I had enough sweet corn or garden-ripe tomatoes, or enough summer, or for that matter enough of October's bright blue weather. I am reminded that I never did order those Christmas cards last August and now it is probably too late.

It snowed yesterday, in a careless sort of way, afterward the yard looked like a Christmas card sprinkled with bits of sparkle. This may be what brought Christmas cards to my mind. Today the sun came out and the air warmed, and Christmas did not seem so imminent. But it was windy, almost like March, and I had the illusion that there might be snowdrops in the border if I looked. Instead, I looked for bittersweet and found a few berries overlooked by birds and travelers. Bittersweet should be picked earlier when it is orange and just opening. It darkens to a Chinese red as it stays on the vine. It should be hung upside down to dry or it just lies down when you make a bouquet of it.

One year, before our vines had been ruined, I used bittersweet with hemlock for the mantel for the holidays and it was lovely. It is a pity that so many of nature's special children get killed, for if you pick carefully and pay attention to the vine or bush or tree, it does no harm. People tear off branches of apple blossoms, for instance, leaving a ragged end as a good place for rot. They dig up shrubs too and in return leave eggshells, beer cans and other picnic debris. A kind of madness comes over some Americans when they are away from home.

The strange thing is that country people will give travelers almost anything, provided the taking does not destroy. It is common for gardeners to pick an armload of zinnias and present them to anyone who stops to admire them. Or to cut apple blossoms where it will not damage the tree, or give away lilacs or roses.

"Ask and it shall be given you," is a good motto, better than "Take what you can pilfer."

Gardeners love to share. We planted some special lilacs some years ago and Jill used to dig up shoots annually to give away. The Borlands never come without a carton of their special treasures. We put in Mr. Clark's iris and Miss Blinn's daffodils and eventually gave some of them away to other gardeners. This sharing makes a garden a friendship affair.

Perhaps the givingest gardener I know is Helen Beals. She is so generous that she will give away her choicest blooms, even if it leaves her garden ragged.

"Come and dig up whatever you want," she says.

The first time she came to call, she brought a bucketful of rare dark Persian lilacs such as we had never seen. In season, she not only brings flowers to her friends but arranges them in a container. She also brings gaiety and warmth and comfort, if you need it.

It is hard to describe one's dearest friends, but I have, on occasion tried to describe Helen to people who do not know her. She has great courage, for her personal life has been heavy with sorrow. Since her husband's death, she lives alone in a much-too-big house and without, as she says cheerfully, any money. In season, she gives book reviews which are the best I've ever heard, and out of season she spends every minute helping somebody who needs help. She candidly admits she is seventy but adds she can still do push-ups. She is always persuading me to reduce and then serving me a most elegant dinner because there is no fun reducing when you are with someone. She herself is always reducing or about to, but I think she is a satisfying size.

Her enthusiasm bubbles over everything from politics (about which she is very firm) to education, and she is the only friend I have except Faith Baldwin who can talk about literature a whole afternoon and listen to me talk about it. Her mind is quick and lively, full of sudden turns.

"Come over," she will say, "and I'll put forty-four beans in your cup."

She is one of those rare women who are completely selfless, in which she resembles Jill. Somehow I have a theory that women who are self-centered feel the march of years, hence years make a sorry impact on them. If this be true, Helen will be forever young.

Finally, she has absolutely none of that corroding trait, self-pity. When she is ill, she says it is a nuisance, but she never mentions it unless you happen to drop in and find her laid up. She never bothers because it is sometimes hard to make ends meet, she says you avoid many worries if you haven't a lot of money. If she did have a lot of money, she would not have it long, she would give it away to people in trouble.

I wish there were more people with such zest for life.

The winter birds come as the weather turns grey and cold. I call the juncoes my weather forecast for they appear suddenly when it will be bitter. When it turns warm, they vanish. They are called snowbirds, which may be a better name for them. They are slightly over six inches in size and are slate-colored, except for a white abdomen and tail feathers. Their bills are almost pink. They live in the thickets by the swamp all winter, coming out on snowy days to eat at the ground feeder. Only in a case of dire emergency will they feed from a window or tree feeder.

The chickadees prefer my window feeder and when they crack sunflower seeds by knocking them on the sill, it sounds almost as loud as my typewriter. Often they come and peer in to see what I am up to, for they are not only friendly, but curious. They are also demanding, and if the seed shelf is empty they sharply and incessantly tell me so, until I give in and leave my work and feed them.

The bluejays are as colorful as tropical birds but they are not very welcome, as they chase all the small birds away and gobble all the seeds and tear chunks of suet off, usually screaming. They have their place, however, as they warn other birds when danger approaches.

Of the woodpeckers, the downy is my favorite. This is a small friendly bird, the male with a scarlet patch on his head. The con-

stant tapping sound the downies make is pleasant to hear, for they are after grubs under the bark of the trees. They have a special note for spring, a high "peek—peek—"

Most of the birds pay no attention to the dogs, but I do not have cardinals or bluebirds in the yard, for they are shy birds and obviously do not care for being barked at. Steve and Olive, having neither dog nor cat, have bluebirds and cardinals and occasionally I see them along the edge of the meadow. Sometimes I hear the cardinal whistling clearly in the swamp, a lovely heartening sound.

Many people who come to the country after living in the city do not, at first, notice the birds. Then at a party, the old residents launch into discussions of birds they have seen and what is the best all-round food. It isn't long before the newcomers appear with a bird book and binoculars. They usually see a rare bird right away, which gives them stature. The next week end, they begin nailing up feeders and melting suet for bird cakes. They are, to put it mildly, hooked.

From there, it is just a step to deciding they cannot go to Florida for the winter because it isn't fair to the birds. All of us share this point of view. Everyone supplies a tale of frozen birds around an empty feeder.

Of course, some people do not like birds. I have one friend who is afraid of them, but she buys peanut butter by the GALLON all winter and fares forth in the worst blizzards to feed the birds. She says she just feels she ought to!

Birds are necessary, for they lead the battle against pests. Without the birds, man would have a rough time getting along. But this is beside the point really. They fill the air with music and make the darkest day bright with color. Watching their flight patterns, the loneliest heart is lifted. And they are a mystery, a lovely mystery.

It is strange how small things spark memory. I was cutting the string from a package today when I suddenly laid down the scissors and worked at the triple knots. For I thought what Father would say at my wasting all that string. Father considered buying string a foolish extravagance. We had a drawer in the kitchen where bits of string were put away, although Mama felt we wasted more time trying to tie them together than necessary. I was often enlisted as a string-tier, but I was not very reliable for often my string knots came untied just as Father was wrapping a mineral to send away.

Father was the queerest economizer I have ever known. If Mama sent him uptown to buy two cans of asparagus and a steak (twenty-five cents) he would come home with a case of asparagus, one of tomatoes, two roasts, and several cases of canned corn (he loved corn). He said it saved money. But when the fruit cellar was stocked with enough for a hotel, he would get in a shopping mood again and come home with another carload.

"May as well have things on hand," he said happily, "and it's cheaper to buy by the case."

It might have been, except three of us could not consume forty-eight cans of asparagus in one season. And it presented a problem to Mama. She solved it partly by giving away a lot and this was a difficult proposition for Father did not believe in giving things away unless he felt in the mood. Mama had a number of friends who were in financial straits from time to time, and she used to carry baskets of what she said were "tinned things for tea" and always gracefully accept a gift from them such as turnips or squash. Mama's philosophy was simple, you shared whatever you had with whoever might need it.

Father was completely erratic in his economy, as he was in most things. Once, after a spell of being economical, he went to Chicago on business and bought oriental rugs for almost all of the house. They were good ones too, and I am still using some of them, although they do not suit an early American house at all. They just do not wear out. Another time he came home with a bolt of turquoise silk for dresses for Mama and me, because it was such fine silk and a lovely color and he liked it. A bolt was, of course, more economical than a few yards.

Privately, Mama thought we would look like an institution, but since Father had no idea how much material it took to make a dress, she just made two, and put the rest away. We did not wear them at the same time for the mother-daughter costumes had not been introduced.

I've mentioned before the time he bought a whole bunch of bananas. It wasn't his fault they all ripened at once. I took bananas to school every day until my schoolmates said they didn't want any bananas ever again. At home we had banana cake, banana ice cream, fried bananas, banana salad and banana gelatin dessert. Even Father got tired of bananas.

I really should not criticize Father, for I take after him. I never fail to buy six cans of something when I need one. And I do not save string. No, I save paper clips.

Thanksgiving is a very special holiday for it is national, religious and nonsectarian. It has, so far, escaped most of the commercialism that surrounds Christmas. And it is peculiarly a family holiday, a time for homecoming. I have always loved the exciting, wonderful Christmas celebration, although more and more I hear people saying they wish it were over because they are so tired.

But Thanksgiving does mean the giving of thanks to God, and it is a holiday belonging only to our country, reminding us of the Pilgrims who found a day in the midst of their battle for survival, to praise God and ask for his blessing.

The traditional turkey has lost its grandeur since turkey is available any time of year. There isn't anything special about vegetables out of season either for they are always in season along with fruit and mincemeat for pies. But the gathering of families around the table has the beauty of tradition on this day.

Will Durant says, "Religion is the last subject the intellect begins to understand." I notice people seldom talk about it when they get together, except in church groups. What they now talk about is how soon a man will go into space, the danger of war, the amount of fallout and how it will affect the future. They talk about modern art and whether it will go down in history or into the scrap heap. They talk about the foreign policy of the government, about desegregation, about education, in fact about many subjects, important and trivial. Sometimes I am tempted to say in the midst of the conversation, "I know all of this is interesting and we should discuss all of these matters, but what do you believe about God?"

I do not see how man can live without belief in some eternal power. A cosmos cannot be accidental, there must be a cause and there must be a meaning. From the beginning of man, there has been a striving toward some supernatural power. Primitive peoples found spirits in nature, in trees and in the ocean, for even then man realized there had to be something beyond accident. The concept of one God, or one law, or one power, grew slowly as mankind developed more power over his world.

And a good many bloody and futile battles have been fought by men trying to make other men believe their image of God was the right one. In this century the wonders of science have often superseded religion. But science is limited. Science can figure ways to encourage seeds to grow, but science cannot put the secret life into it. Science has made incredible strides in studying illnesses of the mind, but science cannot explain why we have minds at all. Science cannot explain good and evil, or love or death.

Science can dissect a body and understand the intricate working of its structure, but science cannot tell where the spirit goes when the body dies. No one can see a loved one die and not know instantly that although nothing physical has gone, the individual, the mysterious self is no longer there.

Has that been snuffed out? If not, where has it gone? Is the spirit absorbed into some vague master consciousness? Or may we believe personality itself is imperishable?

I suppose our beliefs do not greatly matter as long as we believe in something. For no matter how we ignore it, we all face that moment of truth when we simply have to do something about death. For birth and death are our heritage. We can't ignore either of them.

Most of us have moments of crying out, "Why was I born?"

Well, why were we? I think there was a purpose, and that there is a meaning to life. Perhaps I believe this because it is very helpful in time of trouble or sorrow to so believe. Possibly I believe in immortality because it appears to me to make sense.

This may be why when I am with Faith Baldwin, we tend to sit up most of the night talking about life and death and God and Heaven and the purpose of existence, in short, what is it all about? Such discussion, between two who are closely attuned, is both stimulating and comforting. Everyone needs one friend with whom to talk with no self-consciousness.

Thanksgiving wouldn't mean much without a God to be thankful to. I did not, of course, look forward to the first Thanksgiving without Jill. Solitude I have never minded, it can be enriching, but loneliness is different. But I think it is wrong to cross off holidays on the calendar.

I went out for a walk to think about it. Lovely late light slanted across the leaf-deep yard. The sky was a tender blue and cloudless. Blue haze hung over the hills, soon to turn to violet. The cockers and Irish for once were not leaping about, they moved idly around the house, not really in a tally-ho mood.

The pond was somber and still. Two wild asters lifted pale stars at the edge. How had they escaped the frost? I sat down on the damp bench and listened to the quiet. And I reflected on how much I had to be thankful for. I was thankful that love is imperishable, and for the loving-kindness of friends, the warmth of children, the velvet touch of a faithful paw. Thankful for the tasks to be done, and willingness to work at them, thankful for the beauty of the world, for the changing seasons in my valley.

In fact, I had to give up listing what I am thankful for because it was almost moonrise, and a bevy of dogs were making hungry barks. This was entirely unnecessary because they all had been fed earlier, but they enjoy helping me get supper. By the time they finish helping, I have a nice reducing meal left. Then they like to help load the dishwasher and clean up any scraps. I have to be careful not to step on Jonquil, but Holly usually lands a paw on me.

The kitchen is small. It began life as a milk room and the electrical equipment leaves only a narrow traffic lane. It is a lovely place for memories and there is enough room for all of them, however. I can take out the memory of the time when the children were small and Don and Connie flattered me with sparkling conversation while they quietly lifted the doughnuts or cookies from the cooling board as I put in the next batch. I remember the excitement of Dorothy's first cake, which was lopsided.

I remember sitting up most of the night in the kitchen with Jill while we put up chicken in quart jars. Anyone who ever has tried this will know the battle that went on as we tried to fit the cut-up chicken in those recalcitrant jars. We had a cold-pack canner and

more courage than sense. Toward the end we played records while we timed the canner. We thought it was the most delicious chicken we ever had tasted, although some jars had nothing but breasts and a few seemed to be full of necks and backs.

Then I remember the kitchen the day of Connie's wedding. After that day I could understand how a submarine galley works. Val had to carve the turkey in the back kitchen and this would have been easy except for Holly. The cockers were put aside in the kennel but the kennel doesn't keep Holly in. So she stayed in the back kitchen with Val and the turkey. She enjoyed it very much.

I am told more accidents take place in the kitchen than anywhere else in the house. Ours have been minor such as setting the wall on fire when the stove was on, and shouldn't have been. Or sticking a trayful of dishes in the oven when there was no counter space left and then turning the broiler on later. And occasionally the dishwasher is carried away by enthusiasm and floods the floor.

After the cockers and the Irish and I have put the kitchen to bed, we go outdoors again to be sure the moon is where she should be and the rabbits where they should be. The night is cold, but it is not yet the cold that chills the bones. The stars seem very close, some of them seem to be blossoming in the bare branches of the sugar maples. I walk on fallen leaves (which must be raked tomorrow).

Night is a vast dark sea with the moon a distant light in a mysterious harbor. Stillmeadow seems a small ship to be in such a limitless ocean, but how steadfast it looks under the tall spars of the giant maples! Light shines through the small-paned windows, and I am extravagant enough to keep the house lighted all over just because it looks, to my eyes, so beautiful glowing in the dark.

So as I go in, I have a grateful heart. And as Thanksgiving Day nears, I feel a sense of hope—a hope that the world may find peace, perhaps in our time.

THE CALENDAR TURNS

December

THE ground is hard with frost so the gardeners begin to mulch the roses and put up burlap wind shields on the windy side of delicate plants. Salt hay is harder to get than straw so straw mulches are more common in our valley. Some people use wood chips, and for acid-loving plants oak leaves are good. Snow is nature's own protection, which is why farmers shake their heads over an open winter.

The first real snow comes usually the first week in December, a prelude to winter (which officially begins the twenty-first). A few feathers drift down, so casually that I wonder whether it is really snow or a bit of white ash from the incinerator. I check the sky and see they are definitely coming down. It won't amount to anything, says everyone at the market. But I notice we all stock up with extra supplies, in case it should amount to something!

There is an excitement about this first snow and I've wondered why. I think it is because we face up to winter, after a lot of useless trying to put it off. Here it is, the challenge, as it has always been. I think if we suddenly had a bit of Florida now, we should be upset.

"Guess we're in for a hard one," says Joe.

"Yup, that's what the woolly bears say," comments George.

"Hope you all have plenty of wood," says Louis.

"Days are getting mighty short," remarks Steve.

"I made it thirteen above this morning," says Mr. Bennett.

Ski-jumpers must have some of the same sensation as they poise at the top of the dangerous run. This is it, here we go!

The time we get fretful is in mid-March when it ought to be

spring and another blizzard whoops down. Then the year-rounders say they have had enough, they are certainly going to Florida next year. Next year they will say the same thing. But there is never a mass migration to Florida, only a few people go for a brief time. Most of the valley residents stay put.

"It's good enough for me right here," says my neighbor Willie. "Cold don't bother me."

Since Willie drives eighty miles daily in the course of his work, I was surprised.

"There's no place like Connecticut," says he firmly.

He spent some time describing the wonders of Connecticut to me. He and Wilma had picked me up on the coldest night we had had, with a biting wind blowing and the thermometer about eight above. We were going to Savin Rock for a sea-food dinner and while the car was warm, Wilma and I were quite stiff with cold just getting in and getting out.

"Little cold does you good," said Willie.

The dinner was delicious, the coffee restored some warmth to me.

"May as well drive to the ocean," said Willie afterward.

The ocean was black and the wind was like a sheet of ice. The strip of amusement places was a ghostly, shabby sight. We were the only living beings in sight.

"It's not like this in summer," Willie said.

By the time we got home, the wind had died and it was at least less painful to breathe. Some people, I reflected, would stay at home by the fire on such a night, but they would miss a lot. It is the people who give in to winter that have a dull time!

The first snow intoxicates the cockers and Holly. They reel around the yard, snapping at snowflakes. When they come in the house they are frosted with stars. The house will be damp from now on, so will the sofa covers, but I tell myself moisture is good for a house. The dogs are good humidifiers.

The big snow generally comes toward Christmas although occasionally we have a green Christmas which disappoints the children. I look for a big storm around Christmas and another over New Year's. This may be just an idea due to the years when the children came home from school for the holidays and it ALWAYS seemed

almost impossible to meet their trains or get to them at the end of vacation. When the snow is falling so thickly that one cannot see the front of the car, it can take an hour and a half for the ten-minute trip to the nearest town with a railroad station.

One year, I remember, Don had to get out and walk ahead of the car so we could see which was road and which wasn't. The children thought it was a wonderful adventure, but Jill and I were glad to get them safely to the train, not to mention going back on that road to reach home.

There is a persistent illusion most of us have in the country that as winter sets in, we shall have long winter evenings. And when it gets dark in what seems like mid-afternoon, there is no reason not to have them, but I have decided evenings are no longer in December than in August. I have a stack of books saved for them, old favorites that I want to reread such as Keats's Letters and Shakespeare's early plays and Byron's poems and all of Katherine Mansfield and some of the new books like John Graves's *Goodbye to a River* and Neill Cameron's *Shelley and His Circle* (two volumes).

Actually I know that by March, I shall put some of them aside for summer reading. Eventually they all get read, but not just on the long winter evenings. Most of the evenings, I work at my own writing because when I am walled in by winter, there is no temptation to go outdoors and do something else! Besides, I work better at night.

I envy those people who spring up in the morning, brisk and vibrant. But I can't even think until I have time to relate myself to day. It takes all my energy to get up and I wonder whether it is worth it. Jill used to be banging around just as I groggily lifted my head and she had a terrible habit of coming in with coffee and saying energetically, "Now we've got to decide about giving a buffet this week end." Or, worse, "Where is your last bill from the oil company? I think there may be a mistake in the accounts." Or, still worse, "You know it is time for you to go to the dentist."

My answer was always to groan and turn my back. She could NOT help it, because she had all night to think things up and always was awake part of the night. She would go to bed at a reasonable hour and then get up and prowl. If I got up too and we had a snack, I would be dished half the next day. I notice Erma has the same way of being organized early in the day. By the time she comes, she has already hung out her own wash, cleaned her house, done a few errands. She brings me a tray with breakfast on it (not just coffee and grapefruit) and has a cup of coffee with me. She looks incredibly fresh and shining, like a newly picked peach.

"There's something we have to talk over," she begins.

I seldom follow what it is and presently she says, "I know when you keep saying yes you aren't listening. I'll ask you again at lunch."

I've always felt guilty about this inability of mine to leap full steam ahead the minute I wake up, or to wake up at a decent hour, for that matter. Then I read a most comforting article which said that some people are day people and some people are night people and they are just made that way. Every person has, the article said, his own rhythm. I felt fine, until I went on reading and found out there were ways a night person could become a day person, with training. The training sounded rugged.

I finally asked my doctor about it.

"I just can't get started in the morning," I said miserably.

"Well, what do you do the rest of the day?"

"Well, I work."

"What do you do at night?"

"I usually work," I said.

"Then if you put in that much time working," he said, "why does it matter when it is? I wouldn't worry about it."

Nevertheless, I cannot help feeling it is somehow not moral to waste the golden morning hours. It just does not seem right. And I believe most people afflicted with "night person" rhythm feel the same way. I have two dear friends who rise at six and by ten they have accomplished the day's work. Sometimes they drop in around ten-thirty and find me weakly drinking coffee and not dressed.

"Oh, aren't you up YET?" they say, "I thought you'd be up by NOW."

"I worked until eleven last night," I remarked doubtfully.

I can just see them thinking this is peculiar. Why didn't I go to bed early and get up early?

But I remember the days when I had to rise with those misguided birds to get Connie off to school. And when we used to leave at six-thirty for a dog show. I managed it, but I had a headache and felt thoroughly dispirited. By afternoon, I was operating satisfactorily and by the time the sun set, I was ready for anything.

Last summer I had a long discussion with my dear friend Wes Gardner about how sunrise looked. He bounds up and out at day-break. I got up and watched sunrise a number of times and agreed nothing could compare with it. But I didn't admit to him that I went right back to bed after I had the sun on its way and started my own day some hours later.

Now that I've learned about day people and night people, I begin to think the rhythm is inherited. My mother hated to get up early and was always pretty quiet until mid-morning. Father got up around five-thirty and managed to be patient until six but then he got lonely. In summer, he arranged things by mowing the lawn under the bedroom window. In winter, he ran the car out in the driveway (under the bedroom window) and gunned the motor, slammed the car doors, banged the hood up and down.

When Mama gave in and got up and came downstairs, he would say, "Oh, there you are. About time you got up. It's seven o'clock. Where's Gladys?"

Mama didn't dare say I had been out late at a football dance, because he would instantly say, "I don't want her ramming around at all hours. She ought to stay home and get to bed."

Mama got me up, if he was in the mood to make an issue of it. If not, she distracted him by making waffles for breakfast. With her iron wafflemaker, three people could not eat waffles all at once anyway, so this was a successful maneuver.

"No use wasting the day," he would grumble as he poured half a cup of maple syrup on his waffles. "Not healthy to lie around."

He went full-tilt all day, in fact he was known on campus as the professor who never walked, but always ran. Then around nine o'clock at night his terrific vitality suddenly ebbed.

"We better get to bed," he would say, "or we'll never get up in the morning."

And when he went to bed, so did we.

I used to shut my door and douse all but one small light and read and write poetry (I called it poetry). Mama used to tiptoe to the sewing room and shut that door and Father never heard her pedaling away for once he fell asleep, the trump of doom would not bother him.

I was always able to rise at six to go to the lake or play tennis but this was a triumph of love over self. I would also have walked through fire with equal determination if my dearly beloved had been on the other side. But when I got to college, I tried to take courses that did not have eight o'clocks. One reason I almost lost the battle of Advanced Algebra was that I had to take the eight o'clock for that. But I loved the night seminars, how I loved them!

It was exciting to walk out of the dormitory and savor the night and to leave early enough to be able to go by way of the lake and see the moon coming up. And the corridors in the building were empty, for there were then very few seminars. The classroom had a magic it never had in daytime, glowing with light and smelling of chalk. I sat near the window so I could see the stars. And I always got A on an evening exam. The world seemed full of promise, unless I happened to remember that eight o'clock would come the next morning.

Years later, when I was teaching, I took the afternoon or night classes and found them a delight. One way or another, I have managed to avoid too much of this early-morning business and I am so sorry for people who have to get to work early every day—until I reflect some of them must be day people and would purely hate to begin work at four in the afternoon.

Lately the coffee party has come to my valley. My neighbor Wilma recently gave one and when she told me about it, I asked just what time it would be.

"Ten o'clock," she said.

"Don't ask me, Wilma," I begged.

So she didn't. She said everyone had a wonderful time, and I am sure they did. They had hot muffins and fresh-baked sugar cookies and a gallon of coffee.

And this reminded me that I might have managed the coffee but that would be all. And my contribution to the gaiety would have been to sit and stare into space.

For I am out of step on this hearty breakfast too. I know one should have a third of the day's calories at breakfast, to work up energy for the work of the day. Lunch can then be negligible and dinner a few ounces of lean meat, half a cup of two green vegetables, a green salad and fresh fruit. But the time I am really hungry is around eleven at night. Then I begin to dream up recipes and think happily of lobster thermidor or fried chicken. I am very fond of eggs, except in the morning. I like crisp bacon, but not until lunchtime.

So I think appetite has a rhythm too and everyone does not have the same pattern. If I have to eat breakfast, I would prefer something like baked beans or macaroni and cheese and who would recommend that?

Father's breakfast was a special one. He had shredded wheat or oatmeal with cream and crumbled bacon and syrup or honey on it. Then he tossed off a couple of eggs or a few slices of French toast, with syrup. And four cups of coffee. He said it kept his strength up!

Father never heard of a calorie. I thought of this when I heard the charming English actor Robert Morley say in an interview, "I don't believe in calories. I never saw one and I never tasted one, so I simply don't believe they exist."

Father was raised in a pre-calorie era and the eight children in the family ate fried fish or chicken, fried potatoes, and apple pie for breakfast. Father died at seventy-seven of a heart attack due to climbing a mountain a bit too rapidly. Some of the others were carried off at early ages such as seventy or even sixty-nine. Grandfather died in his mid-seventies from trying to lift a corner of the barn to put some timbers under it.

So either the heritage couldn't be licked or the diet was fairly satisfactory, right up to the three teaspoons of coffee to every cup and a pot of coffee always on the stove. All of them, especially Father, felt they liked light meals, such as roast beef, mashed potatoes and plenty of good rich gravy, steamed, buttered cabbage or a side dish of baked beans topped off with apple pie (their favorite).

Now that eating has gone out of fashion, I mean real eating, I sometimes think of the suppers at Grandmother's. I forgot to say there was always hot bread too and clover honey or strawberry jam for spreading. As I tick off a thousand calories a day, I wonder— But nowadays one must keep the bean pole in mind at all times. That's the goal to aim for.

There is one thing we are not noted for in this country, and that is moderation. Countless numbers of people have now given up eating entirely and subsist on four glasses a day of a formula. It's full of vitamins, so the next step will be to put the glasses away and take four pills daily.

What then will become of the cookbooks? And what will the magazines use to replace the food pages with the delectable dishes pictured in color? Where oh where will be the sauces of yesteryear? It's bad enough now when the magazines run two pages of a nine-hundred-calorie diet and pictures of a two-hundred pounder who now, after this diet, wears a size twelve. They follow this with twenty recipes using sour cream, butter, rice, parfaits, hollandaise (½ cup butter, 4 egg yolks, etc.). Plus a four-color spread of hot breads, coffee cakes, muffins, all using nuts and brown-sugar glaze and with lovely pots of jam or honey on the side.

If they believe in the reducing part, why do they do this? Magazines are many things, but consistent they are not. Or maybe they think reading the reducing diet will drive the reader right out to the kitchen to knock out a strawberry shortcake (serve with heavy cream).

I submit, wistfully, that anyone can find out how to reduce. A calorie chart tells you all you need to know, or you can assume that whatever tastes wonderful is OUT. Or you can get a list from your doctor. I think that Mrs. Zilch out there in Oregon did a fine job losing 140 pounds and I'm glad her husband now loves her again. And it's nice that the girl they all laughed at is now the belle of the ball as she steps out in her size nine frock (designed by the fashion staff). But I'd rather have a thoughtful article on the world situation and plug away at my diet by myself.

And while I'm at it, I must say I am sorry we now face at least four years, possibly eight, of every woman trying to look and dress like Jacqueline Kennedy. I don't believe she wants to be a model for the country, for she seems to be an individual who wouldn't care to be a pattern. Her hair-do is a disaster for most women and her hats give the average woman a look as of rummaging in the attic and clapping an old reticule on.

A little thought would make it evident that even her kind of beauty is not copyable. Of course if one must copy someone glamorous, Mrs. Kennedy is preferable to Marilyn Monroe or Diana Dors. But why do American women have this dreadful herd instinct anyway? No two women are ever alike, not even twins, although they can come close to it. It is discouraging to see a group of women all wearing skirts to the knees just because this is the year for it. The length of a skirt should suit the height and shape of the wearer and also the type of legs she walks around on. Some women look very well with their waist line at their hips and some with the waist creeping up toward their necks. Most look better with the waist line where nature put their own waist.

The new hats, at this moment (maybe not next week) look as if someone had mistakenly turned a rowboat upside down on the wearer. Hats that permit only one eye to peer out or hats so big the wearer can't get through a revolving door without a jam really add little to feminine charm.

But I am certainly a small voice suggesting it would be nice if women made their own fashions just for themselves, individually.

As I turn to the last leaf on this year's calendar, I realize we are near the end of another cycle. There are many signs of it for the thermometer leaves the pleasant fifties and sixties and begins to mark the thirties and twenties on its course to the below zeros. Days grow shorter until the solstice when they begin lengthening again. The sky is a cold blue and the stars glitter like ice chips. I suppose this is because the atmosphere has no haze in it as in late summer.

In the house, the sun only gets around to my desk in late afternoon, and the rest of the day my room is rather shadowy. If I had fewer piles of papers to move, I would be tempted to carry my typewriter to Jill's room which is full of sun now. Instead, I turn the light on after lunch and pretend it is twilight anyway.

I notice I am more restless. I keep going to the kitchen to heat up the coffee or I decide to water the African violets, for the kitchen and the violet shelf are sunny. I believe most people are drawn to the sun although I know a few who love grey days and dark rainy ones. The dogs follow the sun, ending by the back terrace which catches the very last rays of sunlight. They no longer like to be let out at my door which is north, so I have to traverse the whole length of the house every time to get to the back door, which is preferable. It suits me better in a storm too for the snow sweeps in if I open my door and the back door is protected by the wellhouse.

Now Erma brings out the oil lamps and cleans and fills them and sends me to the village for extra candles. If we have a sleet storm, the current may go off, in which case there is no heat, no electric appliances working, no water being pumped.

"We may as well get ready," says Erma, "just in case."

And in case—extra wood is stacked by the fireplace along with two lumps of cannel coal (which last all night). The chafing dish is clean and filled with alcohol. The canned-heat is brought up from the cellar with the lamps and I get new batteries for the portable radio which no house in the country should be without. I tried to get one last summer for Millie and Ed and was told they just were out of fashion now, I'd have to get a transistor. So my battery radio is a collector's item.

I don't know why I cherish it, for a storm goes on until it ends and just hearing a news announcer say how deep the snow is in Iowa isn't much help. Nor that it is eighty in Miami. But I like to have it by my bed anyway.

I can cook over the open fire, and I happen to like boiled coffee, or over the canned heat, although I have never been able to put together the stove that came with it. I prop a pan under the folding part that won't unfold. I can read, barely, by an oil lamp but cannot see how Abraham Lincoln read by firelight. And I can just pray the pipes won't freeze before the furnace goes on.

Time is a problem unless I remember to get out my watch and wind it because all the electric clocks go to sleep. And if the phone goes out, I can't call Erma to see what time it is!

Jill had an electric blanket and occasionally the current went off in the night and she quietly froze wondering what was the matter. I gave up mine when it appeared electric blankets cannot stand an Irish setter and a blond cocker playing games on one. I don't miss it because I never felt I should be warm without half a ton of blankets weighing me down. And I once tried Faith's electric typewriter and found I couldn't bang away on it, so I have an un-electric machine.

The deep freeze used to be a worry, especially when we had a historic sleet storm. Jill piled auto blankets, fifty *New York Times* and *Herald Tribunes* on top, plus an old rug. This kept it in good shape for seventy-two hours but the catch was we couldn't open it to get anything out to eat. We had everything in it, bread, butter, meat, chicken, vegetables, fruits, soups, stews, even corn on the cob and lobster. But we ate canned soup until the current went on. The house can chill down fast even with two fireplaces going.

I can manage very well, but I do miss a good light to read by. The oil lamps cast a lovely glow, so do the candles, but they do not make reading easy. And the other nuisance, aside from the pipes, is washing dishes with hoarded water from a pail. There is no doubt but that civilization has softened me!

In December of 1960, snow came early, with snow flurries on the eighth. On the eleventh the thermometer dropped to zero and the big blizzard struck, leaving seventeen inches of snow. On the twelfth, it snowed again. On the eighteenth came more snow and sleet. The pipes froze. On the twenty-eighth and twenty-ninth we had snow and sleet, and the worst winter on record in our valley was well launched.

When Joe shoveled the paths, the banks on either side were so high the cockers could not negotiate them. Jonquil had to be rescued a few times until she learned to stay in the tunnel. The snow was a dry tight snow so that on the worst day, it took Joe four and a half hours to shovel his place out and mine. It was incredibly beautiful, but far from comfortable.

My car, which was by the front gate, became a mountain, and some hapless owners spent several days digging cars out where the snow had drifted ten feet high. It snowed inside my storm windows, which had never happened in thirty years, so that I looked right out at snow and had to kick a door open to see what was happening outside.

I must admit there is a majesty about such an exhibition of the power of nature. When the sun came out, the drifts stretched away like sand dunes sculptured by the wind. Icicles glittered from the wellhouse. The sky was such an intense blue it did not seem real. The chickadees were flying to the feeders, chattering away. "Dee-dee-dee," they said anxiously and then "dee-dee-dee" in a definitely grateful song.

Now along the valley come the Christmas trees piled high in trucks. They used to come in wagons pulled by big farm horses. Now they travel faster but less romantically. Most of them come down from Maine, for Christmas trees are a special business nowadays. The roads are spicy with pine fragrance and the roadside stands have piles of trees beside them. Most of the trucks, however, are bound for the city and do not stop long. We still get some of our trees from our own wooded hills, and some of us cut our own on our land.

Jill planted a whole slope above the swamp with Christmas trees a number of years ago but we bought our trees just the same. This is a curious fact—if you plant a tree, you are not going to cut it down. You argue that it had better grow another year or two. Then it is doing so well—and is such a fine tree—why not leave it longer?

We used to cut trees in the woods above the pasture but we cut only where they needed thinning and this meant our Christmas tree was always lopsided. We backed it against the wall on the scant side. But after the children were not at home to help drag the tree in, we gave it up and bought trees someone else had cut and lugged.

I hate to think of the forests that have been laid waste down the years by ruthless cutting. It takes years to grow a tall lovely tree and not long to chop it down. It is better to buy a living tree which can be set out after the holidays but in the city this isn't possible. And children need Christmas trees, and not artificial ones either. The artificial ones are decorative and some of them play tunes which is dreadful to think of.

For a tree is a symbol of life and a gift of nature. It should come proudly into the house, smelling of the woods and sap. And after the holidays are over, it should leave pine needles to be swept up for days afterward. It should be decorated with ornaments saved from year to year which are traditional. It should glitter with blue and silver balls and tinsel and candy canes and have sparkling snow around the base. There are now sprays which add the sparkle.

Christmas tree lights, I feel, should be used outdoors and NOT on tinder-dry inside branches. It is asking for trouble to use lights on the tree. It is easy to plug a light in near the tree, not near enough so heat from the bulb can reach the needles. Anyone who has a fireplace and burns the branches in it has a good idea of how inflammable pine is. In fact I once nearly set the roof on fire doing just that.

Early in December we all begin to consider the outside decorations. In many of the villages, the garden clubs or civic groups give prizes for the best decorations and this sometimes results in some unfortunate attempts to have bigger and better decorations. I like doorways framed in fresh green pine and wreaths or swags of pine and cones and dried grasses and bright berries (not dyed). In short, I like the natural bounty of nature used simply.

Inside the house, I use greens and bittersweet and cones (not painted) and I would never win a prize for something different and strange.

My problem is the front door decoration. It has to go on the storm door, for if it is on the main door, nobody can see it. The storm door has the same small panes as the windows. So the wreath or swag has to go on the storm door and when the door is opened, it swings out like a sail and hits people. Some of it falls off too. One year I ignored the door and decorated the house itself near the door.

"Surely does look queer," said Jill.

For one thing, the house trim is dark green and to make the decorations show, pieces of a torn sheet had to be tacked underneath. And, this being a 1690 house, the two sides of the door trim are not the same, one is fatter than the other.

I tried stringing outdoor lights on the pine at the left of the door, but they had to be plugged in on the inside, so the door never could be closed. Also the dogs kept tripping over the light cords. Now I settle for the wreath and try to nail it down so it won't fly off when someone comes in in a hurry.

We tried to grow our own holly but it died even though we put tents of burlap around it. There are some wonderful holly farms this side of Philadelphia but I think it is not so cold there in winter. A few people manage it but we failed utterly. My dear friend Lois Holloway sends me a box of holly from the state of Washington and this is lustrous, deeply green and thick with scarlet berries. And my friend Lilith Lidseen from the South sends a carton of Southern greens which are beautiful, many of them strange to me.

In the village, a giant pine stands at the crossroads and this is lighted for Christmas. It is so tall, it seems to have a star on top and you can see the colored lights as soon as you turn off Jeremy Swamp Road onto the highway. Now that there are so many superhighways being put through the state, I tremble when I look at the pine for there is always a chance it will be cut down and the road widened, so people can drive faster and have more accidents.

Sometimes I think the time will come when roads will take over the country and the only scenery will be more clover-leaf intersections. It is heartbreaking to see how these throughways gobble up peaceful farmlands, slice off gentle hills, and demolish woodlands. Our nearest river town, Seymour, used to be a casual settlement along the riverbank. When we came to Stillmeadow, a covered wooden bridge crossed the river. In summer it was cool and damp and still echoed to the clop clop of farm horses now and then. Now a flat cement span has replaced it and on the far side great bastions rear up where the new highway is being built. The town will be down under the cement fortress, what's left of it, that is. There will be, I suppose, an exit and maybe an entrance somewhere, and as I walk along Main street, I can look up and see thousands of cars whipping along overhead. I don't like the prospect. The town itself will seem like a subterranean settlement.

I can foresee, in my worst moments, a time when there will be nothing but highways and superhighways and throughways and there won't be any land left. Possibly there will be parking places and people will live in their cars, driving around all day, and pulling in at night.

Something is wrong, I think, with our sense of values. Why must we speed up? Why do we hurry faster and faster? What do we gain? Do we accomplish more by the hours we presumably save by hurrying? In my own life, I find that if I have what I call a "nervous day" and dash frantically from a hasty breakfast to a quick supper, I haven't, in the end, accomplished a single thing worth while. Not a single thing. All I have done is get keyed up and tired out.

What I haven't done is savor the delight of the day, for every day has delight if we take time to look for it. And when I think it over, I feel I have wasted a day, and no day will ever come again. Fortunately, country living doesn't encourage mad rushing. A countryman works as hard or harder than most city men, but in a more deliberate and easy tempo. The only time I see country folk running is when there is a fire or when somebody's cows have gotten out of the pasture. When Joe shovels the snow, he pauses every few minutes, and looks up at the sky, or observes the print of pheasants on the snow, or watches the flight of the bluejays or listens to the rap-rapping of the pileated woodpecker from the swamp.

At the store, everyone pauses to visit, nobody charges on and rushes out trying to get there faster. After church, families do not run to their cars and speed away, they linger and visit. The cars that speed through the village generally have out-of-state licenses, and the drivers never even notice the beautiful pre-Revolutionary church or the lovely ancient brick Bullet Hill schoolhouse.

I wonder whether slowing down wouldn't be valuable.

I am sure a good many people will point out to me the importance of being able to get quickly from one part of the country to another, and often it is. But getting there quickly becomes a habit. And many homemakers and rising young executives may say they have to make every minute count. We have a number of these in the valley, who commute to nearby cities. Some of the young marrieds never have a spare hour, much less a spare evening. I notice the speed-up because when we came to Stillmeadow, it was quite common for young neighbors to drop in for a cup of tea or call up and say casually, "We're just starting supper. Come on up."

Except with Steve and Olive this no longer happens. Plans must be set two weeks ahead and the calendar marked because there are so many activities every day that there is not any time free any more. There are dozens of parties and dinners but no informal visiting, which is a pity. It makes me wish we could go back to the time when everyone had an AT HOME day and visitors came and went as they felt like it.

Possibly I am just feeling nostalgia for a bygone time. But when I was in high school, there never was an afternoon when I didn't expect to have a cup of tea and some cookies with my mother when I got home. I cherish the memory of those hours. Mama was a busy faculty wife, which means very busy indeed, and had a full schedule with church activities and Clio club and Dickens club. But she never seemed to be rushing and always had time when neighbors dropped in to settle down over tea. And there were many evenings when the family stayed home.

Perhaps leisure will again be fashionable and we may enjoy living with some tranquillity to balance the speed!

The momentum of Christmas itself can be frightening. The giving of gifts has become a mammoth operation and almost immediately after Thanksgiving, we are advised to hurry—hurry for there are only so many shopping days left. Unless you do your shopping in August, you join the nerve-racking race in jammed stores. The towns put up the Christmas lights and decorations and in one town I know Christmas carols were broadcast ALL DAY long in the streets beginning early in December.

By the week before Christmas, fatigue sets in but then there are cards to mail, and this is another big business. And you must shop again for gifts for those people that you do care for but forgot, what with one thing and another, and for those who send you expensive gifts so you feel you must send them something expensive to even things up.

There isn't much time to think about the religious significance of Christmas because you are madly wrapping presents. And there is no time to walk in the snow and rejoice in the wonder of winter colors. The year is drawing to an end and it would be wise to reflect on the past year and strengthen the spirit for a new one so soon to begin.

Somehow we need to find the meaning of Christmas once more, the deep miracle of the birth we celebrate. And to measure its worth not in dollars but in the spirit.

At Stillmeadow, we have always tried to have to have a tranquil Christmas Eve with the children gathered around the open fire, with Christmas Carols and with corn to pop and marshmallows to toast. But of late years, Stillmeadow has been about as quiet as Grand Central Station at rush hour.

I find it hard to collect myself enough to answer Jill's grandson when he asks, "Does water ever get sour?" And this requires time. One difficulty is that the children seldom arrive before the day before Christmas, and all at different times. They bring cartons of gifts all of which are carried up those ladder-steep stairs, wrapped, and carried back down (I do not understand this either). At times, the traffic is so thick I go outside the house and around it to get to the kitchen.

But after the babies are settled down "snug in their beds" and the five- and seven-year-olds have pinched all the packages and reluctantly, step by step, gone upstairs, some quiet reigns. The house smells of pine and spice and bayberry candles. The huge candle we first lit years ago still burns in the window, although it is much shorter. We used to warn Don not to tip it over, now I warn him not to knock his head on a beam, for he is over six feet tall now. He used to be able to get inside the great fireplace and stand up, now he has to bend way down to put a log on the fire.

As I look around the circle, I can hardly believe the children are grown up enough to be married and a new bevy of babies is coming along. I am thankful that the girls' husbands and Don's wife have only come into the family, not separated it. I think this is rare, and it is wonderful. They are all very verbal and they argue a lot, but it is a close warm unit, this family.

As always, the girls find out that they are giving me duplicate gifts, and this is our favorite family joke. One year was known as my Piaf year, another the casserole year, one was the pajama year. For weeks they consult and encourage me to say what I want, but since I like almost anything, it isn't much help.

I did make a mistake once as to duplicate gifts. I received three copies of the same book from three different friends. I laid two copies away in the Christmas chest and the following Christmas inadvertently gave back one of them to the friend who had given it to me. I was filled with remorse until the next Christmas when I got the same copy back from the same friend! I put it away this time with a note: "Under NO circumstances give this book to Ruth."

Anyway, it showed we all liked the same book.

We no longer all go to the church service, the reasons not to are bedded down upstairs. Our babies, if they wake up, want their own mother or father to bring the milk or rock them. Muffin, my own granddaughter, will go so far as to lean against me and look up with a most enchanting smile but she would raise the roof if I picked her up when she had a nightmare (I understand they have nightmares). Connie never had this kind of monopoly for I was often at college directing a play or talking to the Y.W.C.A. She was the only faculty baby at one time and the girls all begged me PLEASE to let them baby-sit. We didn't call it that, we called it "staying with her."

So they took turns, rationing the privilege and any one of a number would be the one to pick Connie up if she cried. I sometimes thought they picked her up if she didn't. What they all liked best was to play with her when she was awake and she was probably thoroughly spoiled by a lot of people.

I do not think I ever would have been willing to have a hired baby-sitter. For the time I visited Connie and we went on to Dorothy's for dinner, I was nervous all during dinner and insisted on going back immediately after. I didn't like the idea of a strange person in charge of Muffin. I thought Connie and Curt were unnaturally calm. But of course everyone cannot have a college student body as baby-sitters.

Babies are raised more scientifically nowadays. Young parents have Dr. Spock, who is consulted faithfully and often. I think his main value is in making the parents feel secure. At least they seem calmer and more casual because they have an authority right beside them. I think they have more fun with the babies. It is hard to be gay and carefree if you are terrified most of the time.

On the other hand, babies have been growing up for a long time, most of them reaching adulthood without too much damage. Except those destroyed in the path of war. I pray long and earnestly that the babies of today may grow up to find a world released from war. I am told there has never been a time in all of history without war, but early wars were not like war today. The Revolution, for instance, was a bitter and devastating struggle but it did not consist in blowing up the earth.

Now the science of war has reached the point of no return. The world could be demolished just by mistake when some bomb went off. Nations are all pretty jumpy because of spending most of their resources preparing for an inevitable war, and this is an easy way to have one.

But in this season it is well to reassert that the hope of mankind rests in faith. As a man thinketh, so he is. Nothing much happens unless you believe in it and believing there is hope for the world is a way to move toward it.

"And suddenly there was with the angels a multitude of the heavenly host praising God, and saying, Glory to God in the highest, and on earth peace, good will toward men."

As we light the candles on Christmas Eve, these are staunch words to hold by. I must say the latest "New English Bible" puts it in a sorry way: "All at once there was with the angel a great company of the heavenly host, singing the praises of God: Glory to God in highest heaven, and on earth his peace for men on whom his favour rests."

It sounds very pedestrian. But at least the word peace is left and isn't "nonaggression pact." And how many heavens are there if we specify the highest one instead of just Heaven?

And I believe God's blessing is for all men, not qualified as to men on whom his favor rests.

In any case, the substance is generally the same although I begin to wonder what the next new Bible will have to say! However, I have two copies of the King James Bible which I can hand down to Connie, in case it goes out of print under the impact of modernization. Meanwhile I can enjoy the majesty and poetry of the Bible I find perfectly easy to live by.

Winter has its own beauty for us who live with it. It is not recommended in travel guides unless for ski addicts and there are no ski runs hereabouts that are famous, such as there are in Vermont and New Hampshire. Ski fanatics go right on north. In May, the lilacs and apple blossoms attract tourists and in summer the rich green countryside seems wonderful to those who come from desert land. The roses are a special attraction. In autumn the blazing glory of the trees is perhaps the greatest wonder for travelers. All during October cars are drawn up along the roads while tourists wrestle with color cameras.

But the winter beauty belongs to us who battle the blizzards, get dug out of snowdrifts, undergo the misery of frozen pipes, the numb hands on the snow shovel. It is for us who buckle on the galoshes, wear two sweaters under storm jackets and watch our breath freeze as we go to the gate.

And we see the bare branches lovely with fallen snow or cased in ice which glitters when the sun comes out reluctantly. We see the meadows with blue shadows across the snow and we hear the brook water running softly under a sheath of ice. We know the beauty of a world dipped in pearl and we listen for the owl, melancholy in a black night. We know the delicate prints of pheasant and rabbit and the rare shape of a deer's hooves on new snow.

We see the delicate beauty of a winter sunset with pale green and lemon in the sky after the sun begins to sink. And we experience the splendor of moonlight on snow. Even on moonless nights the snow itself gives light, delicate and silvery.

There are other joys too which involve meeting the challenge which winter always brings. One of the sweetest sounds in the world is the song of the snowplough as it booms down the road at midnight. Then there is the breathing of the furnace as it goes on again. This is delightful music. There is the sound of snowy boots stamping in the back kitchen as a neighbor makes it down the road to see if I am all right and do I need anything.

There is the quietness when snow falls, I think nothing is so quiet as a windless fall of snow. There is the smell of snow which nobody has ever made perfume of. There is the pattern of firelight on an old oak floor, an image of the fire on the hearth translated into shadow.

I do not enjoy being chilled to my bone marrow, and I often look at the dazzling pictures of the beaches at Hawaii after I take off three layers of woolens. I think a person would have a fine life in Hawaii or Florida or California or any place where there is no winter. Everyone has dreams and I sometimes dream of never wearing wraps, of living in eternal summer. And always on a day of the worst sleet storm I have letters from friends who tell me the roses are blooming where they are and it is so hot they read what I write of winter so they can COOL OFF.

At this point I feel silly putting on my boots and storm jacket just to go out to fill the bird feeders.

I can only conclude that those of us who are New Englanders do not transplant well. It wouldn't seem natural not to have the great storms of winter, the knife-sharp cold, the snow piling against the picket fence. A house would not seem as snug unless winter walked around outside. And there would never be the excitement of finally being able to get the car out and drive to the village. If you could hop in any minute and whisk away there would be nothing special about being able to get two miles to the village.

And nothing can compare in any land in any climate with the way we feel when the snow melts, the brooks run free and the peepers make their chilly sweet song in the swamp. Without winter, we should not have the special miracle of spring.

In December, we look toward spring but on the way, we get a great deal of joy out of such things as a warm house, a good wood-pile, and a world of silver outside. We feel triumph when we get the car motor to catch and a great satisfaction when we negotiate the snow-deep roads. We love winter parties when everyone turns up saying they had to dig out three times. It means they really did want to come!

I sometimes wonder whether New Englanders are just born peculiar, but then I look at the purity of snow and the pattern of dark branches against the sky, and I decide we are not queer at all. We just like four seasons a year.

The Yule log burns to ash and becomes a thing remembered. The Twelfth-night greens crackle on the hearth and then they too are gone. The Christmas tree ornaments are packed away and put in the attic. The old house settles with a sigh. It is time to put the thermostat down, get a storm jacket on and step into boots.

The cockers and Holly are already at the door and rush out ahead of me. They all stop to munch snow and then roll in it. After that, they dash across the yard barking at nothing. I take a few steps feeling the snow crunch pleasantly. When the dogs quiet down, there is no sound at all. Stillmeadow is an island in the winter night but I can see three lights up the hill across Jeremy Swamp Road.

The moon seems to stand still and the stars are like daffodils in the meadows of the sky. If I breathe softly, I might hear the music of the spheres, or so it seems. I am in a moment out of time. I hold the universe in my hand and understand the meaning of all things.

And then I hear the neighbor's beagle baying in the old orchard and my dogs answer. I am in the familiar world again, in my valley, in winter. But I know the season moves on, the pulsing life of spring will spread a green veil over meadows and hills, the warm tide of summer will brim the hollows and autumn will blaze against the sky.

As I go in to the fire, the words of faith come once more: "And on earth peace, good will toward men."

CHRISTIAN HERALD ASSOCIATION AND ITS MINISTRIES

CHRISTIAN HERALD ASSOCIATION, founded in 1878, publishes The Christian Herald Magazine, one of the leading interdenominational religious monthlies in America. Through its wide circulation, it brings inspiring articles and the latest news of religious developments to many families. From the magazine's pages came the initiative for CHRISTIAN HERALD CHILDREN and THE BOWERY MISSION, two individually supported not-for-profit corporations.

CHRISTIAN HERALD CHILDREN, established in 1894, is the name for a unique and dynamic ministry to disadvantaged children, offering hope and opportunities which would not otherwise be available for reasons of poverty and neglect. The goal is to develop each child's potential and to demonstrate Christian compassion and understanding to children in need.

Mont Lawn is a permanent camp located in Bushkill, Pennsylvania. It is the focal point of a ministry which provides a healthful "vacation with a purpose" to children who without it would be confined to the streets of the city. Up to 1000 children between the age of 7 and 11 come to Mont Lawn each year.

Christian Herald Children maintains year-round contact with children by means of a *City Youth Ministry.* Central to its philosophy is the belief that only through sustained relationships and demonstrated concern can individual lives be truly enriched. Special emphasis is on individual guidance, spiritual and family counseling and tutoring. This follow-up ministry to inner-city children culminates for many in financial assistance toward higher education and career counseling.

THE BOWERY MISSION, located at 227 Bowery, New York City, has since 1879 been reaching out to the lost men on the Bowery, offering them what could be their last chance to rebuild their lives. Every man is fed, clothed and ministered to. Countless numbers have entered the 90-day residential rehabilitation program at the Bowery Mission. A concentrated ministry of counseling, medical care, nutrition therapy, Bible study and Gospel services awakens a man to spiritual renewal within himself.

These ministries are supported solely by the voluntary contributions of individuals and by legacies and bequests. Contributions are tax deductible. Checks should be made out either to CHRISTIAN HERALD CHILDREN or to THE BOWERY MISSION.

Administrative Office: 40 Overlook Drive, Chappaqua, New York 10514
Telephone: (914) 769-9000